Eating Disorders
A Multiprofessional Approach

Eating Disorders
A Multiprofessional Approach

Edited by

DOROTHEA HINDMARCH, DipCOT, SROT, MBA
Croydon and Surrey Downs Community NHS Trust

W
WHURR PUBLISHERS
LONDON AND PHILADELPHIA

© 2000 Whurr Publishers
First published 2000 by
Whurr Publishers Ltd
19b Compton Terrace, London N1 2UN, England and
325 Chestnut Street, Philadelphia PA 1906, USA

British Library Cataloguing in Publication Data
A catalogue record for this book is available from the British
Library.

ISBN 1 86156 168 7

Printed and bound in the UK by Athenaeum Press Ltd,
Gateshead, Tyne & Wear

Contents

Contributors

Lorna Atkins currently works as a family therapist both at St George's Eating Disorders Service, South West London and St George's Mental Health NHS Trust, and at the Ridgewood Centre, Surrey Hampshire Borders NHS Trust. She worked for many years as a counsellor in GP practices where she also ran stress management, bereavement and support groups for patients. She is at present in the final stages of a two-year advanced training programme in the supervision of family and systemic psychotherapy. She has a diploma in counselling, a diploma in family therapy and is UKCP registered.

Adriana Cuff BA, BSc (Hons), SRD is a nutritionist and a State Registered Dietitian currently working at The Peter Dally Clinic, an eating disorders unit in Pimlico, London. She previously worked at University College Hospital and The Middlesex Hospital specialising in Paediatrics and working with food intollerances and allergies and at St. Mary's Hospital, Paddington working in a hypertension and cardio-vascular prevention clinic. Adriana has also worked as a freelance nutritionist contributing to part series publications and books on healthy eating.

Ben Davidson BA(Hons), RMN, MInstGA is a psychiatric nurse, group analyst, university lecturer and Buddhist. His special interests are ideology and clinical practice in the field of mental health, with a particular focus on interpersonal power, ethics and spiritual growth. He co-ordinated until recently the Pathfinder User Employment Programme at South West London and St George's Mental Health NHS Trust, supporting the paid employment of people with a history of serious mental health problems in clinical posts within a large London Mental Health NHS Trust, in connection with which he won the 1999 *Nursing Times* National Nursing Award. He has recently taken up the position of senior lecturer at Southbank University, teaching and supervising student nurses. He also sees patients for individual and group psychotherapy at the Maudsley Hospital.

Lucy Elkins is a freelance journalist and writer. Most recently, she has been working as a producer at the BBC for the *Breakfast with Frost* programme, having moved from Sky News where she worked as a journalist in the political department.

Bonnie Gold MA, member IGA, is a group analyst working in both the private and the public sector. She is a former director of training at the Institute of Group Analysis (London). She is currently on the teaching staff of the Institute's London and Glasgow qualifying courses, course tutor for the Institute on the MSc in group analysis at Birkbeck College, University of London, and clinical supervisor on the MA in group psychotherapy at the Tavistock Clinic. She is a member of the Institute of Group Analysis and the British Association of Group Psychotherapists and an associate member of the Association for Psychoanalytic Psychotherapy in the NHS. Her areas of professional interest are eating disorders and gender issues in group analysis and she conducts patient groups and supervises staff groups in these areas.

Dorothea Hindmarch DipCOT, SROT, MBA, member IGA has worked in the field of mental health in the UK for 20 years. Her professional interests are staff groups and organizational management. Her clinical work has been with adults in hospital and the community in the field of mental health.

Daphne Horder SRD, Dip Advanced Psychodynamic Counselling (WPS), is a community dietitian who has worked in London for many years, promoting good health through healthy eating. She works with people of all ages as well as advising and training other professionals whose work involves some aspect of giving nutrition advice. She is particularly interested in the feeding of young children and the development of eating habits. Since she trained as a counsellor she has brought together the psychological and nutritional aspects of eating. She worked for ten years as a therapist at the Peter Dally Eating Disorders Clinic, and has a small private practice.

Jinnie Jefferies BEd, MSc, Adv Dip Psychodrama, UKCP psychodrama psychotherapist, is director of the London Centre of Psychodrama and Group Psychotherapy and the Filyra Institute of Psychodrama, Greece. She is also senior psychodramatist at HMP Grendon, and a programme maker for the BBC and Channel 4 on the use of psychodrama with different client groups.

Laura Lock DipCOT, SROT has been head occupational therapist for the St George's Eating Disorders Service since 1994. The service accommodates severe or 'hard to treat' sufferers, providing an intensive multidisciplinary programme that spans eight months. The service is led by Professor J. H. Lacey, who heads the St George's Eating Disorders Service. This is part of the South West London and St George's Mental Health Trust.

Paul H Robinson BSc, MB, BS, MRCP, FRCPsych, MD, Associate Member of the Institute of Family Therapy, is a consultant psychiatrist at the Royal Free Hospital in north London, and an honorary senior lecturer at the Royal Free and University College School of Medicine.

Mary-Jayne Rust is a Jungian analyst and art psychotherapist in private practice in North London. She has many years' experience of working at the London Women's Therapy Centre, where she has run groups and workshops for women with eating problems.

Barbara Warner CQSW, Adv Dip Family Therapy (IFT Lond), UKCP registered, systemic psychotherapist, is head of family therapy and course director at the Prudence Skynner Family Therapy Clinic, South West London and St George's Mental Health NHS Trust. She is also chair of the professional affairs board at the Association for Family Therapy.

Michele J. M. Wood BA (Hons), Dip ATRATH SRAst (Art), is a senior art therapist at Charing Cross Hospital. She is also a lecturer in art therapy at the University of Hertfordshire and a visiting lecturer at Goldsmiths' College, University of London. She is a founder member of the Creative Response Art Therapists, a group which works in the fields of AIDS, cancer, palliative care and loss.

Foreword

There are many books on eating disorders which are written for the individual clinician and even more for the sufferers themselves. Many describe a particular psychotherapeutic orientation or give a learned – or sometimes not so learned – account of the biochemical and socio-cultural underpinnings of these ubiquitous disorders. This book therefore is overdue. It attempts what none have managed successfully before, to say 'a plague on all your houses: there is another way'.

There is no standard treatment approach for anorectics and bulimics which is equally successful for all. Indeed, despite decades of clinical research, we do not have a clear idea of what is successful and even less what is likely to be successful for any individual patient. There are few treatment facts. Behavioural techniques can temporarily relieve binge-eating; but we do not know how to prevent its return, save only that some patients benefit from cognitive therapy and others from focal, brief psychodynamic treatments. What works for one individual does not work for another. The treatment of anorexia nervosa is even less sure. We know that family therapy and family counselling are essential components of the treatment of children. Possibly too, SSRI antidepressants might assist adult anorectics. Outside these facts, we know little. Indeed, all we definitely know is that we don't know.

This book is refreshing because it doesn't claim to have the answer. It doesn't fruitlessly argue over orientation or quizzical outcome-results – not that these are not important, but rather it emphasises that it is the way treatment is delivered, and the structure and ethos of treatment which are important.

The principles of the multi-disciplinary approach are firmly based on democracy and equality of decision-making, which includes the view of the patient. It recognises and nullifies the danger of an individual clinician working in therapeutic isolation. It emphasises that there is a role for the charismatic prima donna (of either sex!), but recognises the need for his/her enthusiasm to be tempered by others. It allows the formation of an exciting team and one that provides a thrilling environment for professional practice.

To work effectively, the multi-disciplinary approach must be based on planning and structure, concepts which are vital for our eating-disordered patients to internalise during their treatment. Because the group is of all the talents, complex problems can be thrashed out. There is self-audit, mutual tuition and education. Patients have long recognised that there is no one answer to their problems, thus the multi-professional approach allows treatments to be customised and creative whilst being orchestrated in a safe, controlled structure.

The multi-professional approach to eating-disorders demands a particular style of working with patients. First, the relationship can only be based on an alliance. By working together, in equality, the patient and her professional advisers can focus on the resolution of behaviour and distress, together with the psychopathology from which both stem. When disciplines work together, openness and the sharing of clinical material is essential. This mirrors well that second core element of treatment; that is, that there should be no duplicity: that treatment must be honest.

At St George's the multi-disciplinary team meeting is the key event of the week. All professions are represented; each has an equal voice. Equality of professional opinion is essential, but equality of individual staff not so. The team meeting must always put greater weight on the view of key players: the patient's individual therapist, her individual occupational therapist or key nurse.

When creative, effective clinicians come together, there will be differences of opinion. How to deal with these? Two principles are essential. First, that all professionals at the meeting accept 'Chatham House Rules': that is, that there'll be no tittle-tattle or reporting of the discussion outside the room; no saying to the patient that X said this, Y that, but I felt the other. The second is that there be 'cabinet responsibility'. This means that although there can be disagreement, once a consensus (unanimous or by a majority) is reached, everyone – even those who disagree – sign up to the decision.

The chapters in this book have been written by a family therapist, group analyst, psychotherapist, art therapist, drama therapist, dietician, psychiatrist, occupational therapist and nurses. Here is a collective century of clinical experience, here is practical wisdom. Whatever your orientation or professional background, this is the way to provide a district service for eating disorders. Indeed for the severely ill anorectic, it is the only way. I commend the book to you.

J Hubert Lacey
Professor of Psychiatry
St George's Eating Disorders Service
The Medical School, London
June 2000

Chapter 1
Introduction

DOROTHEA HINDMARCH

Robert Graves wrote that myths have two functions: to answer difficult questions and to provide a social function by justifying existing social systems, which account for traditional rites and customs (Graves, 1959: 176). I remembered Graves when I began thinking of the Greek myths while musing on the chapters for this book. The myth that came to mind was that of Theseus and the Minotaur. Ariadne gave Theseus a ball of string or clew,[1] which he could use to guide himself through the labyrinth. I hope that this chapter will act as a guide to the reader in making your way through the book. The tale also conjured up the image of the role of the team in helping an individual suffering from an eating disorder to negotiate their way through the labyrinth formed by the disorder, allowing monsters to be safely slain and then guiding the way back through the labyrinth to health. Eating disorders form a set of conditions which mainly affect women, and the thought of the young maidens sacrificed to the Minotaur to assuage the gods triggered connections with some of the material in the chapters dealing with the sociopolitical aspects of a disease process embedded in our social order. The myth symbolizes many of the features of these conditions and is worth reading in conjunction with the book if you don't already know it.

The chapters are set out to offer the reader a range of perspectives across the various treatment approaches. The book contains descriptions of reality-orientated models of treatment, such as occupational therapy and dietetics, to multifaceted approaches, which reflect individual, familial, social and political aspects of these conditions. Most chapters make reference to the context in which the treatment is being provided, whether this is institutional, social or environmental.

The 11 other chapters that make up the book have been placed in order of their level of resolution. For example, the first of these deals

1

with the role of the psychiatrist, who has traditionally in the UK acted as the clinical leader. This is primarily an institutionally based role although the services may operate in the community. The clinical focus of the medical model has evolved from a biological reductionist model of diagnostics, treatment and cure. This puts the individual at the centre of the field of vision whereas the final chapter deals with the eating disorder in the sociopolitical domain. The chapters fit along a continuum from the psychobiological to the sociopolitical, and from the individual to the large group.

Psychiatrists and eating disorders

The reference to the myth of the Minotaur reminds us that although myths have their uses, they are often barriers to understanding, and the chapter on psychiatrists and eating disorders dispels a number of common myths about psychiatrists. The psychiatrist is often felt to have magical powers, the ability to read minds. We confer omnipotent qualities on to the doctor that affect our powers of thought and reason. This chapter describes the arduous nature of the medical training and the breadth of experience and knowledge of the doctor by the time he or she has become a consultant psychiatrist. In my introduction I have classified the medical role as reductionist, focusing on the individual biological system. However, the psychiatrist is an expert in the fields of biology, anatomy, psychology and the sociological aspect of disorders. This breadth and depth of knowledge places the psychiatrist in a prime position to act as the clinical team leader, a position not always to be envied.

The author has divided the chapter into five sections:

1. What is a psychiatrist?
2. The medical approach: referral
3. The medical approach: diagnosis
4. Understanding and treating eating disorders
5. Developing good services for patients with eating disorders.

The progress of a patient through the services illustrates the role of the psychiatrist in completing a differential diagnosis, eliminating physical and psychiatric causes of the disease and determining the appropriate treatment plan. In Chapter 3, written by Lucy Elkins, it is clear that if the general practitioner had been able to consult the specialist services then she would have been treated for her eating problems a lot earlier. The subsequent disruptions to her life might have been prevented. The physician uses diagnostic tests to detect imbalances in the body's biological system in order to treat and prevent the secondary effects of starvation and vomiting on the body. The importance of the role of the physician is unquestionable, as death from eating disorders is uncommon but a possible outcome of these conditions.

Section five of Chapter 2 is essential reading for anyone managing this specialty because it sets out a 'step approach' to the provision of services. The underlying principles are early detection, minimizing the disruption to the person's life and safety. The services must be local and responsive. There are seven steps from minimum intervention where the patient is monitored for any deterioration, given advice and information, to inpatient treatment with 24-hour care.

The chapter acknowledges the costs of these conditions to the National Health Service and the patient. A significant consequence can be the loss of potential in young women who, if not helped early enough, will be subjected to lifelong suffering. This is an informative text covering all aspects of the role of psychiatry in the management of these conditions.

A personal perspective

This is a particularly important chapter which should be read by everyone connected with the provision of eating disorders services. It is a personal account of suffering from an eating disorder and traces its development from early teenage years into adulthood. The illness creeps up on the person by stealth, gradually eroding or developing in place of normal patterns of behaviour. The result is a preoccupation with weight and food. This insider perspective of an eating disorder describes the desperate desire for help and the attempts to get it which fail. These are important lessons for everyone concerned with the individual sufferer. In this case the person describes intense feelings of self-loathing and prefers to dismiss the implication that the cause is simply a response to a fashion statement or media persuasion. To see it in simplistic terms denies the profound nature of the suffering involved. Although it is the view of one individual, and stresses the need to see each person in his or her own right, it does give the reader an insight into the experience of the sufferer.

The chapter makes important suggestions about the type and range of services that should be available, with the one overriding principle that the services should be easily accessible and responsive. It is clear from this account that had they been so, perhaps the disorder would have been spotted earlier and the most appropriate treatment begun sooner.

Another important principle that emerges is the importance of providing 'bespoke' services, which can be shaped to meet the needs of the individual. For this person certain treatment approaches felt too threatening and the focus on weight gain without consideration of the psychological aspects of the disorder led to non-conformity and avoid-ance. Sound practical advice similar to the work described in the chapters on occupational therapy and dietetics and nutrition helped to provide information and develop coping mechanisms.

An important if not crucial player in the management and early detec-tion of eating disorders is the general practitioner. If, as some of the liter-ature suggests, these disorders are becoming increasingly more widespread in the population in the West, then the education and training of general practitioners everywhere should include the detec-tion of these disorders in the population, especially in young women who are the majority of sufferers. Young women are the mothers of the next generation and their approach to their mental health needs will impact on us all in years to come. Investment now will help prevent future suffering.

Psychiatric nursing

This is an account written by a nurse reflecting on a period during his training when he spent six months working on a psychiatric ward which specialized in treating eating disorders and adult mental health patients. It is a stark and honest account of the relationship between the staff group and the patient, the nurse and the patient and the patients with one another. It illustrates how the beliefs of the staff group and what they are trying to achieve can get lost in the daily routine of work on a busy psychiatric ward. It conveys the tension between the philosophy of the treatment approach and its implementation, describing how the former can get lost in translation. The description of the ward, the 'shit' and the 'vomit', elicits feelings of revulsion in the reader and a desire to turn away. The chapter moves on to recall the histories of the patients to illustrate the psychological debris of confusing and often uncontaining early experiences. This chapter has a profound impact on the reader in that it deals with the stark realities of the disorder, culminating in the death of a young man, Nigel. Ironically, the subject is male whereas the rest of the book tends to deal with female sufferers, who are the majority of people affected. Most importantly, this chapter promotes writing as a tool for reflection on clinical practice. It suggests that a process of mental reflection is necessary to understand what is happening in the relationship between the nurse and the patient, and the nurse and the staff group in general. This is a principle to be taken into any area of clinical practice for all staff. It goes beyond the need to give thought to the clinical work and the setting to suggest the written word as a means of distancing oneself from events and reflecting on the dynamics and purpose of the clinical intervention. This message should be acknowl-edged by managers and professionals as essential to avoid complacency and to encourage 'authentic and honest' relationships in the treatment of patients and clients.

Occupational therapy

From the earthiness of the ward we come to the chapter on occupational therapy. It was almost with relief that I read of the importance of engaging the patient in looking at how they manage their daily lives. The title 'Reoccupying the preoccupied' neatly illustrates the aims of the treatment programme, which is to enable a person to resume a normal, healthy lifestyle which puts food, and thoughts and behaviours related to food, in perspective. This very practical and focused approach is unique in the book. It offers sensible and helpful suggestions to the sufferer on how to deal with life in general. It works on developing a more appropriate set of habits and behaviours, which by their very existence reduce the amount of time to carry out the obsessional behaviour. With time the individual can learn to substitute a range of skills and interests which preclude the distorted habitual behaviour concerning food and weight.

Dietetics and nutrition

Dietitians remind the reader of the simple fact that our own survival was dependent on our mothers feeding and nurturing us from the day of our conception. Feeding and its impact on our lives are inextricably linked to our relationships, initially with our mothers and families, and later to other social roles. As society has changed so have our patterns of eating and our eating behaviours. Ironically, we are better nourished and taller than our predecessors; however, the practice of dieting is now an accepted norm. This chapter alludes to the mind–body duality where the mind has lost touch with its bodily needs; sufferers of eating disorders no longer respond to the body's signals regarding hunger and satiation. Dietitians have a wide and varied role in the treatment and prevention of eating disorders, and this is described in the chapter. There is repeated reference to the importance of working in a multidisciplinary team in order to be able to meet the depth and range of needs of the patient group. The references to the work with eating-disordered patients who were pregnant during their treatment are particularly interesting. Pregnancy provided the team and the dietitian with particular problems, but also provided the women themselves with the opportunity to think about their own maternal experiences as infants themselves. The impact of distressingly low body weight and the need for legal action to prevent death is dealt with in a compassionate and understanding way. The effect on the body's chemical balance is described, together with its need for replenishment if death is to be avoided. There is a call for an economic evaluation of treatment where psychological and social factors can be taken into consideration as part of successful treatment outcomes along-side weight gain which currently tends to be the main factor included in criteria for success. It is impressive how a highly scientific and poten-tially biological approach manages to incorporate dynamic aspects of the disorder.

Family therapy

Families cannot help but be affected by the presence of a sufferer of an eating disorder. How much they are willing or able to contribute to the understanding, resolution or management of the problem will vary. However, few people who work with sufferers, or are sufferers themselves, can deny the influence of the family on the individual as a container of social values and taboos. The political emphasis on the family as the unit of social organization and social cohesion acknowledges the potential power for good but minimizes the difficulties often encountered. The two authors of this chapter have brought together most of the combinations of family members to engage in the therapeutic work. The method of work described is based primarily on family systems theory, although the chapter describes other models in less detail. The perspective of the family therapist is unique, he or she occupies a place between the family and the team, holding the knowledge of the patient in all their complexity, within a matrix of interactions. The vigilance required to negotiate the network of commu-nications is characteristic of the role of the family therapist. The family therapist acts as a guide to help the family and the team through the corri-dors of the past, present and future, challenging the hidden monsters, which seem unfathomable and unspeakable to the patient and the family. The consequences of not confronting or slaying the monsters is literally death, for the patient with an eating disorder may choose death rather than confront the pain of living. The monsters manifest themselves in the issues of sexual abuse, parental neglect and violence. These are profound matters, which may involve the courts and the police. This chapter is very grounded in its honesty. There is academic consideration of the theory and clinical research, but the chapter never loses sight of the work's purpose to bring about change in the system to free the individual through the devel-opment of insight, understanding and, potentially, resolution, however painful.

Group-analytic psychotherapy

In this chapter the author describes the group-analytic approach and its application to eating disorders. There is a section at the beginning, which outlines the clinical setting and briefly discusses the work of S.H. Foulkes, the founder of the Institute of Group Analysis and a pluralistic theoretical approach to the individual. Group analysis offers the possibility of viewing the eating disorders in an individual, familial, social and cultural context. The work in the group aims at developing the ego functions in the personality whereby the autistic symptoms are replaced by thought, understanding and a change in relationship to the self. The group acts as a forum for 'ego training', which facilitates socialization and a revision of personal boundaries. Germaine Greer (1999) describes how women find it difficult to resolve the conflict between the nurturing role and the need for aggression and competition demanded in the world of work. At puberty, when females are at risk of developing eating disorders, it is just these issues of identity that are impacting on the emerging personality. The issues raised in the clinical illustrations in this chapter and the commentary that accompanies them focus on identity and the state of identity confusion often experienced by the person with an eating disorder.

A woman's relationship to her mother will be the keystone to her feelings towards herself: whether she can nurture herself or whether she will sublimate her own needs in meeting the needs and desires of others. The author indicates that certain family characteristics occur in bulimic families – the false self presented to the outside world, the need to 'keep it in the family' or where bad or negative feelings are taboo. The resulting repression and denial will lead to self-hatred and to attacking themselves. The women in the group have to learn to differentiate their feelings; the overwhelming anxieties and the need for control have to be translated into knowledge of emotional matters and the learning of a language of expression rather than resorting to acting out feelings through obsessional behaviour and rituals. A group will offer the person the opportunity to develop trust and feel held; the sometimes intolerable nature of the dyadic relationship can be made safe and manageable. The often punishing nature of the relationship between the patient with eating disorders and the therapist mirrors the nature of the transference.

The boundaries offered by the therapeutic group setting will provide a place for exploration of relationships to other members of the group and to the therapist. However, the group is not divorced from the cultural values and norms of the society in which it is set and these will be reflected in the group. The analyst will need to be aware of his or her own prejudgements and the forces operating on the group to conform to the norms of the culture at large.

The writer challenges the value of working in a homogeneous group where there is limited access to the views of others not suffering from eating disorders and which are often female-dominated groups. Issues of gender cannot be fully examined in a single-sex group.

The prevalence of women's distorted relationship to food is a persistent theme throughout the book, dieting, thinness and eating control being acceptable preoccupations. Women are being given greater freedom without sufficient support and help in dealing with the responsibilities that freedom confers. Women's sexual freedom has resulted in the loss of a protector in the form of father or brother without enough preparation for adult life. The comedy series *Absolutely Fabulous* illustrates the breakdown in generational role models: the daughter is more responsible and paternal than the wayward and irresponsible mother; the father is absent and equally frivolous. The social and cultural conflict lies in the difference between what is considered socially acceptable for a woman, which is usually a myth, and the reality of being a woman and all the feelings and messiness that involves.

In the final section of the chapter the author deals with the negative effect of the group, where the potential for destructive forces to be unleashed while working through the ambivalence in a struggle for identity has to be recognized and worked with. The problem for women – and eating disorders primarily affect women – is to find a place in society where maternal and paternal values can be expressed. The group can be a place where the person can learn how to translate adequately feelings into thought and understanding and where a sense of a true self as capable and adaptive can emerge.

Eating disorders: A psychodynamic approach

Psychodrama is another group approach to the treatment of eating disorders. It differs from the group-analytic approach in that it employs action techniques as a prompt to recall and change. The concept of ego training or the development of a greater sense of self is the primary object of the therapeutic intervention.

The working through of repression and role conflicts occurs in the context of the 'here and now', where dramatization acts as a bridge between past anxieties and fears of abandonment and the present.

The therapeutic process and the theoretical concepts behind the model of psychodrama are described in detail. The work is illustrated in vignettes. Central to the work is the concept of roles and role clusters, which are conferred on us through families and social pressures operating on us throughout our development. The drama begins with the protagonist self selecting to work on a problem. The beginning of the drama may involve inanimate objects; in one example the person swaps roles with the food in the fridge where she finds the confrontation with food a trigger to feelings of fear and anxiety. As the drama unfolds, the feelings and emotions associated with this are traced back through time until the origin of the feelings is recalled. Others who take up roles and join in the drama as it unfolds will support the protagonist in the group. At the end of the session the group will share their experiences and in this way all the group members are able to recognize aspects of the drama that reflect personal material.

All of the chapters have included a definition of the two conditions of anorexia and bulimia nervosa and this chapter is no different. It raises the issue, frequently discussed in the book by different authors, of whether they are two distinct disorders or variations of a single but complex process.

Art therapy

The author describes the dynamic relationship between the individual and the work of art in art therapy. In this process the therapeutic intention is to bridge the gap between the self and the body, which is described as an inherent split in patients with eating disorders. The chapter begins by describing the setting where the art therapy group took place and how the relationship between the art therapist and the client differs from that of other psychotherapeutic approaches. Art therapists are now required to achieve state registration before they can practise in the UK: this was instituted in 1997 and reflects the establishment of art therapy as an independent profession.

As the chapter progresses it deals with the theoretical background to the work in the clinical sections on the art therapy group. The main feature of the chapter is the description of an art therapy group from its inception to its ending. However, what makes this chapter particularly interesting is the way in which the author parallels events in her own life, that is her pregnancy and the establishment of the art therapy services. It has to be acknowledged here that the group the writer refers to was set up several years ago when art therapy was gaining ground and becoming accepted by the establishment.

The writer raises the reader's awareness of the relationship between the work produced and the person's internal world. The process itself is important, the end product having significance in relation to the individual and the group. The images produced during the sessions reflect both individual and group dynamics. As creativity is activated during the treatment process, the group members are able to tolerate increasingly difficult emotional issues without the need to act out or avoid painful feelings. The art work acts as a buffer between the therapist and the client containing overwhelming fears and destructive impulses. The transitional space created by the art work is central to the work with eating-disordered clients because of their fear of loss of control. The art work separates the self from feared internalized bad objects and the external object – that is, the therapist. The chapter ends with the women in the group able to express their feelings about the therapist's pregnancy and the ending of the group. The therapist's pregnancy demonstrates the power of female creativity and maturity, which the female eating-disordered person is afraid of.

Consumerism and being consumed

This is the penultimate chapter in the book. The author is a Jungian psychoanalyst, and the chapter covers the widest angle of vision. The chapter begins recalling a young child's desire for, and ownership of, a Barbie doll. The doll is a vehicle for influencing and persuading the young child what is desirable in women – one of her first role models. It is of ridiculous proportions – if life-size it would be deformed. It is a male image of what it is to be a woman. It is a symbol of femaleness that is devoid of maternal or female characteristics.

The chapter uses the metaphor of the camera lens and its level of resolution to put the experience in context for the person who is suffering from an eating disorder. The author feels that to understand what is happening to the patient, the person has to be helped to see how her behaviour is linked to society. She is acting out a process that is beyond her own control – hence, the paradox of the illness is that if the sufferer can control food and weight she will somehow be in control of her life. And this is despite the fact that what is going on around her is beyond her control and has to be understood and not turned inward to self-hatred and self-loathing.

How the political and economic forces in society operate on the individual is illustrated in the vignettes, which describe the individuals in an environment which is predetermined by social and cultural expectations and fragmentation. The destruction of the environment through overuse of resources and the loss of connections between people in a highly mobile and complex system have the potential to result in chaos as the individual strives for a personal sense of self and identity. This is an enjoyable, readable chapter, which asks many questions of the reader.

The multidisciplinary team

At the beginning of this chapter reference was made to the myth of Theseus and the Minotaur in the labyrinth. In the concluding chapter, the author has brought together all the members of the multiprofessional team. Eating disorders and the people who treat them form a complex labyrinth, which has to be negotiated by the person who is ill, and/or their relatives. They are generally very distressed at the time. A team which has at its fingertips access to a wide range of different treatment approaches is the best method of getting the most effective treatment in the shortest period of time and most efficiently. The final chapter represents the way out of the labyrinth. The monster has been slain and the maidens released from the threat of death in the sacrificial slaughter. Each chapter has presented the reader with a solution to the problem of eating disorders. In the final chapter we have all the stakeholders, including the patient: the problem now is how to deal with the complexity of the whole. It requires vigilance and good management. It may be that several elements are missing from this book. There is no economist, physicist or politician to give account of their perspectives. The problem is keeping the boundaries around an ever-widening perspective of a complex pattern of behaviours. Eating disorders are a modern monster in our midst.

Note

[1] Clew is a ball of string and is the derivation of the word 'clue' meaning to provide information towards solving a problem or a puzzle.

Chapter 2
Psychiatrists and eating disorders

PAUL H. ROBINSON

What is a psychiatrist?

Psychiatrist comes second only to tax inspector as a communication stopper in a casual conversation. Police officer comes a short way behind. However, contrary to common images, a psychiatrist is not a psychoanalyst, mind reader or psychologist but a person who has studied medicine, worked as a hospital doctor in medicine and surgery for at least a year, and then sooner or later gone on to specialize in psychiatry. During the forced feeding of information that occurs during pre-clinical medical training, the student is given a diet rich in anatomy, physiology, biochemistry and pharmacology, with sociology and psychology sprinkled on like pepper or parmesan. In the final three years of medical training, the main menu changes to medicine and surgery, and the side dishes and condiments now consist of psychiatry, general practice, paediatrics and public health. Eyes, ears, skin and bone can be missed by a dose of flu or a hockey tour and, by the end of training, the medical student is a bloated airship of equations, receptors, anatomical loci and drug actions and interactions like a million-piece jigsaw that has yet to be solved.

Gradually, as some of these puzzle pieces join together, the doctor begins to recognize some fragments, and to realize that medical problems are not all soluble in anatomical or biochemical terms. People's various problems organize themselves into those with a chemical or anatomical basis, such as diabetes or cancer, and the remainder, which sometimes seem to be the majority.

The chemical and the anatomical, indeed, are recognized as two levels of a series of systems of explanation that include, in addition, psychological, family and cultural systems, with one system nestling

inside the other like a set of Russian dolls. This approach can accommo-
date two or more systems being used to describe the same clinical
problem. Thus, depression can be seen as a molecular disease, partly
genetically determined, a crisis in personal development related to early
experiences and life events, a behaviour pattern which mirrors the
behaviour of other family members, and a culturally determined
response to a phase in the life cycle.

A doctor studying disease will soon realize that some situations
demand mainly organic assessment and response, whereas others
require a more psychological or family/social approach. When the
doctor's interest is excited more by the latter than the former, the
chances of that person ending up in psychiatry are that much higher. It is
ironic that the psychiatrist is, by non-medical colleagues, often granted
the role of champion of the medical model of illness, whereas non-
psychiatric doctors may openly or secretly regard the psychiatrist as non-
scientific, not properly medical, or even (to quote) 'a waste of a medical
training'.

The study of eating disorders is a good area for the physician who is
interested in psychological and social approaches to troubles of the
mind, but who retains a deep interest in physical diseases and their treatment. On the biological–social continuum, theories of causation and
approaches to treatment of eating disorders lie quite far to the psychosocial end, while they cause physical problems that are so severe that they
can end with the death of the patient. The role of the consultant psychiatrist in this area is both unidimensional and integrative: the first in
providing medical and psychiatric diagnosis and treatment, the second
in facilitating psychological and systemic approaches to the solution of
the problems presented by patients with eating disorders. The strad-
dling of this fence requires a good sense of balance, an ability to resist
being categorized and a tolerance to the inherent discomfort of such a
position.

The medical approach: referral

Referral of people with eating disorders to specialist centres comes
primarily from general practitioners. The changes in the UK National
Health Service have placed the GP at the helm of medical treatment, and
the government promises to extend the role of the GP in acting as
gatekeeper to expensive specialist services. For people with eating disorders who do not mind visiting the doctor, this presents only the problem
that some GPs do not make referrals of patients with eating disorders
when it is appropriate, sometimes because the conditions are not recognized. For the rest of the population with eating disorders, about 1% of

young women, services are unavailable because most of these women do not find it possible to approach their GP. This leads to the situation in which most sufferers from eating disorders (mainly bulimia nervosa) are not receiving help. It is incumbent on health services to find ways in which girls and women (as well as men) with eating disorders can seek help before the problem has become established and, perhaps, irreversible.

The filter dividing the sufferer from the GP is, therefore, of fine mesh. The few that get through it, assuming that they are correctly diagnosed, are then either treated in primary care or referred to specialist services. An important role of the psychiatrist is to provide a link between primary care and the specialist team. The process of referral is accompanied by a sharing of medical responsibility for a patient. This is a very important step, because a patient who is behaving in a self-destructive way may cause extreme concern to the GP. Sharing the problem with a consultant can help to alleviate some of the anxiety caused by the patient's behaviour, while a management plan is developed.

A case description follows, which will be used to illustrate some of the issues to be raised.

> Karen, a young woman of 18, is being seen individually by a psychotherapist for treatment of anorexia nervosa and bulimia nervosa. She continues to lose weight, and is monitored weekly by her GP. The psychotherapist calls the GP to express concern about the continued weight loss. She has reached 42 kg (6 st 8 lb). The GP sees her and finds that she has a significant fall in blood pressure when she stands up, causing faintness. Blood tests show that she is mildly anaemic, and that her blood potassium is dangerously low (1.9 mmol per litre, lower limit of normal 3.5). The GP immediately calls an ambulance and the patient is admitted to a medical bed, where she is given potassium in a drip. Unfortunately, this results in a raised serum potassium; her heart stops, but she is resuscitated by the 'crash team'. She survives and leaves hospital the following week, when she resumes starving, overeating, vomiting and abusing laxatives.

In this case, the medical team at the hospital has been involved, but it is unlikely to continue to treat the patient long term. The GP makes a referral to the consultant in the local eating disorders service. Because of the pressing nature of the situation, the GP calls the consultant and requests an urgent appointment. The two doctors discuss the physical state of the patient, and the consultant asks for the patient's height in order to calculate the Body Mass Index (BMI: weight in kg/(height in m)^2). The practice nurse recorded this the last time the patient was weighed. She is 5 ft 5 in (1.67 m). BMI is therefore $42/(1.67 \times 1.67) = 15.1$ kg/m^2. The normal range for BMI is 19 to 25, the threshold for anorexia nervosa is 17.5 and below 13 major medical complications are likely to ensue.

Both doctors are here using training in physical risk assessment, but, more importantly, the GP knows that he or she is speaking to someone with experience in dealing with gravely physically ill patients. This role of the psychiatrist, involving knowledge of the functioning and malfunctioning of the human body, as well as of the mind, is important for other doctors, but is also important for non-medical therapists, as will be seen later.

The medical approach: diagnosis

Doctors love making diagnoses. A tricky medical case presents a challenge similar to that enjoyed by Sherlock Holmes. A particularly rare case might be dubbed a 'fascinoma', and be presented to an admiring audience of physicians at a clinical meeting. The diagnostic approach is revered because medicine has a history of discovering single, sometimes treatable causes for seemingly disparate groups of symptoms. Thus, a bloody cough, a fever, a red rash on the legs and loss of weight were found to be associated with a certain type of bacterium, the tuberculosis bacillus, once the scourge of opera's leading female characters, now usually curable with medication. In the field of eating disorders, some diagnoses of anorexia nervosa have been made in young women, concerned about feeling too fat, who have been found, on investigation, to have a disease of the bowel such as Crohn's disease, or even cancer. The patient may therefore have a serious medical illness, with the addition of intense concern about weight, and may welcome the weight loss that accompanies the physical illness. The relationship between the physical wasting disease and anorexic self-starvation in an individual can be very difficult to disentangle. Indeed, in some cases, weight loss due to the physical illness can trigger off a full-blown episode of anorexia nervosa.

Constructing a list of possible causes of a symptom such as weight loss is termed differential diagnosis, and is a vital step, as physical disease, for example thyrotoxicosis or diabetes, missed at this stage may not be identified for a considerable time, as symptoms are successively attributed to the eating disorder.

Differential diagnosis in the area of psychiatric evaluation takes two forms. First, psychiatric conditions can cause weight loss and vomiting, and exclusion of these is analogous to the exclusion of physical disease. Examples include:

1. Depression with loss of appetite (the original meaning of the word anorexia).
2. Paranoid schizophrenia with delusions that the food is poisoned.
3. Psychotic depression with delusions that inhibit eating (for example, 'My mouth has disappeared', 'I am too evil to deserve food').

4. Inability to swallow due to spasm of the muscles of the throat ('globus').
5. 'Psychogenic' vomiting (vomiting without an identified physical cause and no other eating disorder symptoms such as body weight and shape concerns).

Patients with eating disorders may also suffer from other conditions that are considered within the rubric of psychiatry. Diagnosis can be very difficult, because many symptoms of eating disorders are shared with other conditions. Illnesses that commonly co-exist with eating disorders are depression, obsessive-compulsive disorders and personality disorder, and psychosis can occur, but is rarer. The ways in which different symptom clusters overlap is striking.

> Karen, after referral to a specialist eating disorders service, is found to be depressed, have sleep disturbance with early wakening, and to have frequent thoughts of self-harm. She is constantly plagued by thoughts of food, and has compulsive rituals which including counting her food and clothes in groups of four. She washes her hands compulsively after bingeing, and feels very disturbed if disturbed while carrying out her ritual behaviour. She cuts her arms and legs regularly and burns them with cigarette ends.

Karen almost certainly fulfils criteria for anorexia nervosa, bulimic subtype, major depression, obsessive-compulsive disorder and borderline personality disorder. However, some of her symptoms, including depressed mood, sleep disturbance and obsessions and compulsions may well be significantly related to body weight, and be part of the starvation syndrome, well described by Keys et al. (1950) in studies performed on underfed volunteers during the Second World War. Thus, while psychiatric diagnosis remains important, the connections between different diagnoses should be acknowledged, so that treatment can be rational and integrated rather than piecemeal. A guide to the diagnosis of two major eating disorders, based on accepted criteria, is given in Table 2.1.

Understanding and treating eating disorders

The role of the psychiatrist in a multisystemic approach

As a doctor, the psychiatrist is a plant rooted in the soil of biochemistry and anatomy. During psychiatric training, other explanatory views of human behaviour and experience present themselves, and different doctors find themselves more or less receptive to these different models. One of the most influential views is the psychoanalytic model, and a proportion of trainees themselves enter analysis and train as psychoanalytic psychotherapists. Another school espouses the systemic approach,

Table 2.1. Definitions of anorexia and bulimia nervosa according to the tenth revision of the International Classification of Diseases (ICD-10)

F50.0 Anorexia nervosa

Diagnostic guidelines

For a definite diagnosis, all the following are required:

(a) Body weight is maintained at least 15% below that expected (either lost or never achieved), or Quetelet's body-mass index (Weight (kg)/[height (m)]^2) is 17.5 or less. Prepubertal patients may show failure to make the expected weight gain during the period of growth.

(b) The weight loss is self-induced by avoidance of 'fattening foods'. One or more of the following may also be present: self-induced vomiting; self-induced purging; excessive exercise; use of appetite suppressants and/or diuretics.

(c) There is a body image distortion in the form of a specific psychopathology whereby a dread of fatness persists as an intrusive, overvalued idea and the patient imposes a low weight threshold on himself or herself.

(d) A widespread endocrine disorder involving the hypothalamic-pituitary-gonadal axis is manifest in women as amenorrhoea and in men as a loss of sexual interest and potency. There may also be elevated levels of growth hormone, raised levels of cortisol, changes in the peripheral metabolism of thyroid hormone, and abnormalities of insulin secretion.

(e) If onset is prepubertal, the sequence of pubertal events is delayed or even arrested (growth ceases; in girls the breasts do not develop and there is primary amenorrhoea; in boys the genitals remain juvenile). With recovery, puberty is often completed normally, but the menarche is late.

F50.2 Bulimia nervosa

Diagnostic guidelines

For a definite diagnosis, all the following are required:

(a) There is a persistent preoccupation with eating, and an irresistible craving for food; the patient succumbs to episodes of overeating in which large amounts of food are consumed in short periods of time.

(b) The patient attempts to counteract the 'fattening' effects of food by one or more of the following: self-induced vomiting; purgative abuse; alternating periods of starvation; use of drugs such as appetite suppressants, thyroid preparations or diuretics. When bulimia occurs in diabetic patients they may choose to neglect their insulin treatment.

(c) The psychopathology consists of a morbid dread of fatness and the patient sets herself or himself a sharply defined weight threshold, well below the premorbid weight that constitutes the optimum or healthy weight in the opinion of the physician. There is often, but not always, a history of an earlier episode of anorexia nervosa, the interval between the two disorders ranging from a few months to several years.

---

and some psychiatrists find the integrative method attractive as it promises to combine the biological, the psychological and the social contributions to behaviour. Some psychiatrists are strongly influenced by cognitive and behavioural theory, and a few train to apply it to clinical problems.

The role of the psychiatrist in the multiprofessional team, whether it is dealing with schizophrenia or anorexia nervosa, can be a narrowly medical or an integrative one. In treatment of eating disorders, the doctor can provide medical and psychiatric assessment and diagnosis, and offer medical means of approaching the problems. Most psychiatrists would, however, see themselves as having a wider brief, and aim to know enough about the various models to be able to refer patients to appropriate therapists who are specialists in their own approach. This places the psychiatrist in relation to the multiprofessional team in a position analogous to the general practitioner in relation to the various specialist services. The frequency with which a psychiatrist refers to each element of the service depends on a number of factors, including his/her own view of the important causes of the patient's problems, the confidence in which the particular therapist is held and the relationship between the psychiatrist and the therapist.

Returning to our case history:

> Karen comes from a family in which an aunt suffered from anorexia nervosa and the mother from depression when Karen was 12, at which time there were serious marital problems for her parents, during which Karen was her mother's confidante. Karen's eating problems began when she first developed breasts at 14, by which time the parents had divorced and she was living with her mother and sister.

The approach to understanding this case depends on the life experience, including education, of the observer. Psychiatrists are trained to consider biological, psychological and social aspects of a case, including all these levels in an explanation of aetiology ('why has this person come to behave and feel in this way at this particular time?') and treatment ('what changes in my behaviour would help solve the problems that the patient (or society) is posing?'). Psychiatrists and schools vary according to the degree to which thinking is influenced by the three realms, but few are unremittingly of one persuasion, although individual psychiatrists are often labelled as *biological* or *social*, sometimes by themselves.

Thinking about Karen in a number of different ways illustrates the differing approaches. The biologist might point to her family history, and posit a genetic contribution to her development. How a genetically controlled process could lead to anorectic behaviour is not at all clear. An inherited personality characteristic, such as low self-esteem, or perfectionism, could predispose an individual to anorexia nervosa, as could a genetically overactive satiety system, making it easier for certain individuals to starve. The psychologist, on being asked the cause of this patient's problems, might point to her mother's depression, her father's absence, the break-up of her parents, and pubertal changes and their impact on self-esteem, body image and self-perception as a young adult.

Lastly, the family therapist could point out past and present systems, including Karen's closeness to her mother, an increasingly distant father and a disengaged sister. The eating disorder currently maintains her mother close, keeps the sister disengaged, and the father at a distance but still engaged. Wider systems of relevance might be the school she has attended, with an emphasis on excellence and competitiveness, and the norms of Western culture, espousing thinness as representing success.

The approach to therapy can be classified in a similar way. The biologist would seize on starvation, with its secondary effects (depression, abdominal bloating, obsessiveness, preoccupation with food), and say that unless the biological effects of starvation are dealt with, no progress can be made. The logical treatment is, therefore, nutritional and might involve dietetic advice, supervised meals, peer group pressure, tube feeding and even forced feeding. On shakier ground, the biologist might have a theory about a biochemical cause of anorexia nervosa, which suggests a certain type of treatment. One example is the addiction theory, which suggests that the anorexic is addicted to starvation, and produces excessive endogenous opioids (morphine-like chemicals produced in the body) which perpetuate the addiction. The treatment is to block the action of the opioids with a drug antagonist such as naloxone, which should remove the addictive power of starvation. It is an elegant theory, but there is no practical evidence that it is valid. This has not stopped some doctors from giving naloxone, or a similar drug, to patients with anorexia nervosa for long periods, at some risk, vast expense and with no useful therapeutic effect. Another example is the use in anorexia nervosa of chlorpromazine (a major tranquillizer which stimulates hunger) or insulin, which stimulates hunger by reducing the blood sugar level. Since there is no evidence that raising hunger levels improves eating in anorexia nervosa, these potentially dangerous treatments are useless. These practices point to the need for all treatment (bio-, psycho- or social-) to be evidence-based, where evidence exists.

The psychologist, considering the developmental interpersonal and intrapsychic problems of the patient, might recommend dynamic psychotherapy, in order to address present and past conflicts, or cognitive behavioural therapy, to challenge ways of thinking and behaving that may initiate and perpetuate the eating disorder.

The family therapist might suggest that the family meet together with him/her to discuss ways in which interactions could be altered so as to encourage the patient towards a more healthy lifestyle; could visit the patient's home; might involve her place of work, or schooling, to try to alter pressures towards thinness; or even book him- or herself a place on a popular and influential TV show in an attempt to influence cultural norms in the direction of accepting fatness as a normal constituent of the healthy body.

Physical treatments in patients with eating disorders

Treatment of starvation

Early observers drew attention to the pitiful state of the patient with advanced anorexia nervosa 'like a skeleton clad only in skin'. It seems incomprehensible that a young woman or man would court death in the pursuit of thinness. No theory, whether biologically, psychologically or systemically couched, can really explain how this is possible. The first task of any attendant, whether parent, sibling, doctor or nurse, is to overcome the horror at what the young person is inflicting on herself. This can quickly turn to anger when, in a desperate defence of her starvation, the patient resorts to lies and subterfuge, which can easily alienate those trying to help. Families, nurses and others who take it upon themselves to nourish the patient require intense support and guidance in what is one of the most frustrating experiences that can be endured.

In the monitoring of a patient who is severely underweight, namely below a BMI of 13, there are a number of pieces of information that should be sought regularly. They are as follows:

1. Body weight and BMI.
2. Does the patient have muscle weakness?
    Any history of difficulty walking, climbing stairs.
    On examination, difficulty rising from squatting.
    On examination, difficulty sitting up from lying flat.
3. Is there evidence of low blood pressure?
    Any postural dizziness?
    If so, does the BP drop on standing?
4. Are there any changes in the blood count?
    Anaemia is common but usually not significant.
    White blood cell count can fall.
    Platelet count can fall, giving rise to tiny haemorrhages under the skin.
5. Is there any evidence of liver damage?
    Microsomal enzymes can rise markedly, presumably due to fatty degeneration of the liver.
6. In patients who vomit or abuse laxatives, measure urea and electrolytes.

The frequency with which these data should be recorded varies with the rate of weight loss and the frequency of vomiting or laxative abuse. Patients losing weight should be monitored at least weekly. Patients at a low but stable weight do not need such regular evaluation. However, all the tests should be carried out when the patient is first seen, so that a baseline for future evaluation exists. Patients who vomit or take laxatives can die at any weight as a result of abnormalities of heart rhythm caused by low serum potassium, although low-weight patients seem to be more likely to develop low potassium.

When a patient begins to eat after a long period of poor intake, the food provided should be increased gradually over a few days. Prolonged starvation leads to delayed gastric emptying, and rapid refeeding can cause gastric dilatation and even perforation, which can be fatal. A further danger is low phosphate during refeeding, which should therefore be monitored. Lastly, rapid refeeding has been associated with delirium and a psychotic state, which usually clears up within a few days, sometimes requiring antipsychotic medication.

In advising a patient about diet, it is worth knowing that, in order to gain 1 lb (0.5 kg) a week, an extra 500 kcal per day need to be eaten over and above the food required to maintain weight.

How can the patient's healthy weight be determined? This important question has a number of answers. If it can be established that the patient was, say, 54 kg before the onset of dieting, and that menstruation was lost around that level, then that weight is likely to represent the patient's healthy, menstrual weight. In practice, it is rarely possible to be so confident. The patient's weight may have fluctuated significantly, or she may have been premorbidly obese, and under these circumstances, premorbid weight may be unreliable. BMI can be used, but the range (19–25 kg/m^2) is large, and it is not possible to establish where in the range menstruation is likely to begin. The same can be said for population-based weight tables.

A more scientific approach is to use ovarian ultrasound to determine ovarian maturity when the patient has reached the lower limit of the normal range, say at BMI 19, and to repeat the scan at intervals in order to determine the weight at which the ovaries reach a mature appearance, after which menstruation can be expected. The ovarian scan shows three patterns:

1. Immature, in which there is little structure visible within the ovaries;
2. Intermediate, in which there are multiple small follicles visible;
3. Mature, in which there is a large dominant follicle which represents the developing ovum.

Treatment of electrolyte disturbance

Patients who vomit or misuse laxatives have an increased risk of electrolyte disturbance, dehydration and renal failure. A potassium level below 2.0 mmol/l is a medical emergency. Between 2.0 and 3.5 the level is low and the measurement should be repeated in a few days. The treatment of low potassium in these patients is to stop vomiting or misusing laxatives. Oral potassium supplements (for example, Slow K) are sometimes used, but they can cause intestinal ulcers, and should be used only if treatment of the bulimia fails. Treatment of severe potassium deficiency of rapid onset is cessation of potassium-losing activities and, sometimes, oral potassium supplements. Cardiac monitoring may be required and intravenous potassium, which can lead to a raised potassium level, is usually unnecessary.

These patients are losing both potassium and sodium in the vomitus, urine and stools, and, if they stop vomiting or laxatives suddenly, can develop sodium overload and oedema. This is particularly likely to happen during inpatient refeeding, when sodium intake is high. Oedema can be massive, and should be suspected if weight gain is unexpectedly high. Eventually, the kidneys re-establish equilibrium, and excrete the excess sodium. However, by then the patient may have restarted laxatives in an attempt to accelerate the process. Normalization of kidney function may take several months.

Treatment of osteoporosis

In the past few years it has become clear that patients with anorexia nervosa are at risk for bone loss which occurs during amenorrhoeic intervals. It is thought that amenorrhoea of as little as one year can cause significant bone loss, and contribute to fractures later. It is detected using a bone mineral density (BMD) scan which uses low-level X-rays to determine density in lumbar spine and femoral neck. A BMD scan should be performed on any patient who has been amenorrhoeic for a year or more, and the scans repeated annually.

The treatment of post-menopausal osteoporosis involves oestrogen replacement, calcium, vitamin D and drugs to increase bone formation such as biphosphonates. In anorexia nervosa, only weight gain has been shown to improve bone density, with hormone and other treatments as yet inadequately evaluated. At present, concern about osteoporosis should encourage patients to gain weight so that menstruation returns as quickly as possible.

Treatment of depression

Depressed mood is a common feature of eating disorders and has many roots. There may be an inherited element, as first-degree relatives are often depressed. There is, in patients with anorexia nervosa, an organic element. Starvation leads to depression, and some of the depression lifts when patients gain weight. Bulimia, when it is present, is extremely disruptive and can lead to depressed mood which improves as soon as the eating pattern gets back to normal. This leaves a group of patients whose depression seems unrelated to weight or bulimia, in whom it may be appropriate to make a diagnosis of depressive illness. Treatment with antidepressant medication may improve mood, and in view of the cardiac problems and potential for deliberate self-harm found in patients with anorexia nervosa and bulimia nervosa, it would seem sensible to use a drug less cardiotoxic than the tricyclic antidepressants. The SSRIs have an alerting and, perhaps, an appetite suppressant action in some patients, and should be used cautiously in patients with anorexia nervosa. Drugs such as lofepramine and nefazodone could be used in this group. In patients with bulimia nervosa at normal weight, fluoxetine has been shown to have an anti-bulimic effect, and would seem to be the drug treatment of choice in a patient with bulimia nervosa who is depressed and requires an antidepressant. Its use as a first-line treatment for bulimia nervosa should be discouraged, as psychological treatments, described below, are more effective and their action lasts well beyond the end of therapy, which may not be the case for fluoxetine.

Psychological treatment of eating disorders

Various approaches have been used in the treatment of eating disorders, and a few have been subjected to controlled evaluation. Thus, in the treatment of bulimia nervosa, cognitive behaviour therapy has been found to be effective, as has interpersonal therapy (Fairburn et al., 1993). In anorexia nervosa, two types of individual therapy have been compared, supportive and focal psychoanalytic therapy. Both can be helpful in some groups of patients. The supportive approach is the method most likely to be available to primary and secondary generic services outside specialist units. The patient is seen regularly, generally weekly, for an hour, by someone with basic training in a mental health field (for example, psychiatric nurse, occupational therapist and others). The sessions cover weight, eating, mood, social and occupational life, and the aim is to help the patient overcome the symptoms and make desired changes in other areas. Supervision is essential, as the therapist does not generally have a psychotherapy training, and can be from a trained analytic psychotherapy supervisor, or another suitably trained mental health professional.

Hunger strikers from Mahatma Gandhi to Bobby Sands have been among the most powerful of political protesters. How much more potent, therefore, for the hunger striker to be your own child. Although experts argue about the causes of anorexia nervosa, parents are usually convinced that their daughter's behaviour is the result of a lack on their part. The combination of fear, anger and sorrow, together with mutual recriminations that often occur, can only be imagined by those, including most therapists, without a personal experience. The child who is refusing her mother's food, refusing her breast, engages her mother in an intense struggle to counter that refusal. Little wonder, therefore, that mother and daughter become increasingly preoccupied with one another, or that the father, on being excluded from this mother–daughter couple, spends longer at work and becomes peripheral and uninvolved. A sibling, particularly in the face of a long-standing eating disorder, may also distance him- or herself from the mother–daughter dyad, and increasingly seek activities outside the home. This pattern (over-close mother and daughter, uninvolved father and sibling) is commonly seen in the families of patients with anorexia nervosa and may arise by a complex interaction of action and reaction over time that eventually produces the observed structure.

The practical problems and intense emotional distress experienced by families with an anorexic member make family treatment for the disorder of primary importance. It can also be helpful in the case of patients who have left home, although the content of the therapy is naturally different.

Two types of family intervention have been well described in anorexia nervosa. One is whole or cojoint family therapy in which parents are generally encouraged to take control of their daughter's eating, and ensure as far as possible that she returns to a normal weight. This form of therapy tends to provoke confrontation between parents and patient and sessions can be very distressing. However, in many cases such therapy can be effective treatment. The other form of family intervention has been termed separated family therapy, and involves the parents being seen regularly and the patient seen by the same therapist at other times. The message to the parents is similar to that given in cojoint family therapy. They need to work together in order to ensure that their daughter puts on weight. Recently, family therapy has been provided to groups of four or more families with a member suffering from anorexia nervosa (Multi-Family Group Therapy) and this approach is likely to prove of increasing interest.

Family interventions can be given either in a clinic or at home. Family sessions at home can be used effectively, particularly in families who find it difficult to cooperate fully with hospital treatment. A session at home can help correct the power balance. The therapist is no longer a monarch in his or her castle, but a guest in a family's home who can be ejected at any time. Family work at home can take the form of a therapy session, but could also be practically grounded, with help around food preparation and other aspects of home life, which may have been discussed in a more formal family therapy setting. This sort of work may best be performed by a nurse who has been trained in eating disorder assessment and management, and who can bring that expertise to the family in a non-judgemental and helpful way. Such a community eating disorders nurse could be based in an eating disorders service, or in primary care, and have a liaison role with GPs, hospital services and occupational and educational medical services.

Developing good services for patients with eating disorders

Stepped care for eating disorders

It is generally accepted that treatment for eating disorders, as well as for any other psychiatric or medical disorder, should involve the minimum of disruption in the patient's daily life. Accordingly, if a patient can recover as an outpatient, or simply by following a self-help manual, this should be the treatment offered. Nevertheless, there is a great difference between the rates of hospital admission for anorexia nervosa for different units. In some, many patients are admitted, in others almost no one is admitted, with little evidence that one or other treatment is superior. The financial costs are enormous. Outpatient treatment would amount to between £3000 and £7000 for a year's intensive treatment, whereas inpatient treatment for three months followed by nine months of outpatient treatment usually costs between £20,000 and £30,000. Day care falls somewhere between the two. The cost is not only financial. Anorexia nervosa is an illness in which, paradoxically, the patient's search for autonomy leads her to behave in a way that encourages others to be intrusive and protective. The less she eats, the more she feels in control, but the more others will wish to act to make sure that she puts on weight. It is true that the patient can become so defiant that her life is at risk, in which case authorities have no choice but to act, sometimes against the patient's will, in order to save her life. This occurs fairly rarely, however, and it is possible that many patients are being admitted to hospital who could be treated as outpatients. These patients are being given treatments that are more intrusive than necessary, and that may cause harm in the long term. As no adequate research exists to back up these statements, how are we to plan services for patients with eating disorders?

One approach is to adopt a set of principles of care, and to follow its implications in each case.

Such a set of principles might include the following:

- All patients will be offered care that is based on outcome research evidence where it exists.
- All patients will be offered care that represents the minimum interference in their daily lives, consistent with clinical recovery.
- Care will be offered to patients that fits the patient's needs, rather than patients being given treatment that meets the needs of the institution.

Many clinicians, patients and families would regard these three principles as given, and might be horrified to learn that their care might be varied depending on institutional needs.

The implications of these principles for care are that interventions would be weighted towards autonomy and home-based treatment, and that hospital admission would be a last resort. This is a reasonable approach, although it must be repeated that no controlled evidence exists that it is superior to inpatient treatment. It is to be hoped fervently that such a study can be funded. The principles would be consistent with a community weighted stepped care approach. Figure 2.1 illustrates a stepped care approach.

Treatment is always weighted towards the left of the diagram, to provide every opportunity for the patient to recover by means of her own will rather than that of others. The existence of more elaborate services recognizes the fact that patients with eating disorders are often ambivalent about treatment, and some will require more intensive and persuasive forms of therapy.

The services associated with each of the steps are as follows:

1. Self-help manual: This includes self-help manuals and books (for example, Crisp, 1980; Palmer, 1989; Cooper, 1995; Fairburn, 1995; Schmidt and Treasure, 1993; Treasure, 1997).

2. Services provided by self-help organizations such as the Eating Disorders Association in Norwich (Tel: 01603 619090).

3. In primary care, the general practitioner can monitor physical and mental state (weight, electrolytes, depression and so on) with help from the practice nurse while the patient is seen regularly by a trained counsellor, preferably with access to supervision from a person experienced in the treatment of eating disorders. A useful way to work can be to provide the patient with a self-help manual and for the doctor or counsellor to follow up its use in the surgery.

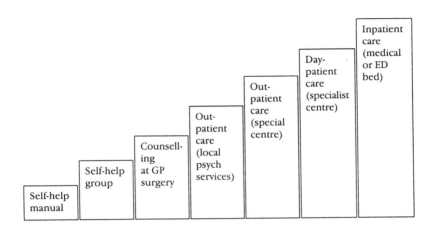

Figure 2.1. Stepped care for eating disorders.

4. In the local psychiatric service, much depends on the extent to which the personnel have had experience of eating disorders. Several types of patient can usefully be managed in the local service. First, the patient with relatively uncomplicated bulimia nervosa could be treated by a doctor or psychologist using cognitive behavioural techniques, and utilizing a self-help manual to guide treatment, as in primary care. Second, a patient with severe anorexia nervosa who has had a number of admissions to specialist units may come to be the responsibility of a local service, in which case the patient may require admission, if very low in weight, to a psychiatric bed and treatment by the generic team, perhaps with consultation and advice from a specialist service. Last, a patient in the chronic phase of anorexia nervosa may present problems analogous to those of any long-term disorder in the realms of housing, occupation, secondary depression and chronic physical ill health. Such a patient might best be managed using a rehabilitation model, and be subject to the care programme approach or case management, as would a patient with chronic schizophrenia or depression.

5. Specialist outpatient services: A specialist service for eating disorders should offer the following:
   • Assessment by a psychiatrist with special expertise in the field.
   • Telephone advice to workers in primary care on risk assessment and management.

- Access to services for more severely ill patients, including inpatient psychiatric care, inpatient medical care and day care.
- Outpatient treatment of eating disorders with availability of individual treatment (supportive, dietetic and cognitive-behavioural (CBT)), group CBT, family therapy and family support.
- Supportive therapy can be provided by psychiatric nurses with appropriate training and team support. Other forms of therapy are usually provided either by professionals trained in the particular method, or by trainees under close supervision.
- Willingness to work with the patient and family wherever it is most helpful, including at home and in primary care.
- Initial assessment using recognized instruments with regular follow-up at intervals to generate information on outcome.

6. Specialist day care: The day hospital or centre provides intensive treatment for patients with eating disorders who can make use of a structured programme. Although outpatient care generally offers a maximum of once- or twice-weekly sessions, day care can be provided up to seven days a week. In addition to the various forms of therapy given in outpatients, day patients will have regular sessions with a key worker who coordinates care, meals on the unit (sometimes supervised by staff), and group work. The last can take a variety of forms. Some, such as community meetings, are aimed at enhancing group cohesion and identity whereas others, such as drama, art, nutrition, assertion and body image, can tackle some of the core symptoms of the eating disorder. Engagement of the patient in the day service can be greatly enhanced by a home visit by one or, preferably, two team members near the beginning of treatment. This provides a great deal of information to the staff, introduces the team to the family, and shows the family that the team are willing to leave the security of their institution.

The organization of such a centre requires considerable thought. Staffing needs to be adequate to avoid high case loads among workers who will usually also be carrying a case load of outpatients. Support to the staff is essential, and this includes the following:

- good line management
- professional development, including appropriate external training
- case supervision by a skilled professional, to include supervision of both individual sessions with patients or groups, and case-load management
- regular team planning or 'away' days to consider developments in the service.

Some day units have a 'staff day' during the week, in which patients either do not attend or are unsupervised, so that some of these essential activities can be pursued.

Team meetings on such a unit can be organized in a number of ways. The team will be carrying a large case load, including outpatients, day patients and those waiting for assessment or treatment. A weekly team meeting is essential in order to process new referrals and to handle concerns about patients referred, waiting for treatment or in treatment. It is useful to have a list of patients causing current concern, so that anxiety is shared by the team, and a plan of action developed. For example, each week a nurse may be seeing a patient with anorexia nervosa. The patient's weight drops significantly, and she begins to complain of fainting. The nurse asks the doctor to review the patient, who is found to have low blood pressure due to vomiting and weight loss. Blood tests are taken and brief hospitalization is considered. The case is discussed at the following team meeting and the patient kept under frequent review.

Keeping track of all patients under the care of a service is a major task, and the help of a well-designed database will be much appreciated. Such a database can identify patients currently at risk ('current concern'), those undergoing different sorts of treatment and those requiring follow-up at specific times. In addition, patients at particular risk, such as those with osteoporosis or chronic illness, can be listed, as can those who have children in whom there may be concerns about physical and psychological development.

7. Inpatient care: What about the patient who fails to respond to day care, whose weight continues to drop or who does not gain weight in spite of structured meals and individual, group and family therapy? First, the patient may not be attending the agreed day programme. Second, she may not be eating enough either in the unit or at home, and third, she may be vomiting or over-exercising. Here the general management of the service becomes extremely important. The budget must include provision for additional nursing in order to support patients who are going through this very difficult phase of illness. These resources can be used in a number of ways. An extra nurse can be used at home to help the patient through breakfast and get her to the day hospital. Should this, combined with evening and even weekend nursing, fail to help the patient achieve weight gain, then the case must be reviewed with the team, the patient and the family. If weight is low but not immediately dangerous, the patient can be given a week to reconsider her place in the programme, perhaps with a view to restarting it or being discharged. If the patient

is in a dangerous condition, either very low weight, or physical decompensation, then admission is probably unavoidable. The choice is to admit to a medical or psychiatric bed under the care of a general team, but with help and support from the eating disorders team, or to admit the patient to an inpatient eating disorders service. The decision will depend on what is available locally. Some eating disorders services rely heavily on day care and hardly use inpatient care, whereas others have large units for residential treatment of anorexia nervosa. Admission, if resisted when the patient's life is seriously at risk, may have to be under Section 3 of the Mental Health Act, 1983, which has been used lawfully to admit patients with anorexia nervosa. Once in hospital, the patient may still resist weight gain, and may require close observation to prevent vomiting (although it must be appreciated that this means that she may have to use a bed pan and not be allowed in a bathroom alone) and intensive help to eat. The situation in which this still fails to achieve weight gain is the one in which more intrusive treatments, such as tube feeding, may be considered. Under such circumstances, as well as to effect admission, the Mental Health Act may be required to enforce treatment. Section 3 allows for treatment, such as medication, to be given against the patient's will, and provision of nutrition has been considered by the courts in England to constitute treatment under the Act, and can therefore be given without the patient's consent. In practice this would mean insertion of a naso-gastric tube, and might require the use of sedation. The latter needs to be given with utmost caution in a very underweight patient, because of the danger of hypotension, and the presence of an anaesthetist should be considered in a severely compromised patient.

Cases have been reported in which a patient has been left to die rather than receive treatment against his or her will. Most psychiatrists regard this as indefensible in the majority of cases, and current opinion is that no patient can ethically be denied life-saving treatment, even when this has to be given against his or her will, under the Mental Health Act. This is an area for debate, with issues of personal choice, freedom and dignity on one side, and the right to life-saving treatment for a potentially fatal psychiatric disorder on the other.

Tube feeding may be necessary in an exhausted patient who is simply too weak to take in enough nourishment to gain weight. At levels of BMI under 10, muscular weakness can be profound, and continuous expert nursing is mandatory. Nutrition is given through a fine-bore naso-gastric tube with the help of a pump delivering liquid food at 50 ml/hour, building up to 100 ml/hour or more, depending on the tolerance of the patient. Various preparations are available, and a popular example is Ensure (1 kcal/ml) and Ensure Plus (1.5 kcal/ml). Calorie intake should be built up to about 3000 kcal per day, and electrolytes and physical assessment performed daily.

Inpatient treatment varies in different units, and in some, inpatient care would continue only until the patient was out of danger, after which day care would recommence, whereas in others the patient would be kept in hospital until weight is at a healthy level.

The role of the general medical services in the care of a patient with severe, acute anorexia nervosa varies with the interests of the particular physician. Some, with a special interest in eating disorders, may be happy to keep the patient in a medical bed and provide psychiatric treatment. In most cases, however, the role of the physician is to supervise resuscitation in a patient whose cardiovascular or some other important system, has decompensated. Once the patient is stable, she can be moved to a psychiatric bed until it is regarded as safe for her to be discharged.

Making the case for specialist services

You are working in an area in which there is no specialist service for people with eating disorders. How can funds be justified to establish such a service, and how do you start? The impetus for the establishment of specialist services in the NHS over the past six years has been the demand for such services. The NHS reforms of the early 1990s separated purchasing and providing care, so that services not available locally could be purchased from outside the area of the particular authority. Fundholding GPs had similar power to purchase a variety of services from whoever was willing to provide them. The result has been that many patients referred to NHS clinics for eating disorders, particularly severe anorexia nervosa, were referred to the few specialist units around and paid for on a case-by-case basis, by means of what is termed an extra-contractual referral (ECR) and is now referred to as an Out of Area Treatment (OAT). A patient with anorexia nervosa might need to gain 20 kg or more in order to return to a healthy weight, and at a rate of 1 kg a week (a not unreasonable rate) this would take five months. A unit charging £250 a day would send a bill to the health authority for £35,000 for this patient, and it is not, therefore, surprising that an average ECR annual budget for eating disorders for each health authority was about £130,000. Multiplying by 124 (the number of health authorities in the UK) gives a total of £16.1m a year (1997 figures). Little in the NHS concentrates the mind like money, especially when lack of funds for services causes closure of wards, cancellation of operations and inadequate community care. A great deal of money is being spent, and the task of someone wishing to set up a local service is to convince the purchaser (whether health authority or Primary Care Group or Trust) that alternative services will be efficient, professional and effective. In order to address this, a number of questions can be asked:

1. Why have specialist services at all?
2. What sort of services should there be?
3. What sort of treatment needs to be offered?

1. Why have specialist services at all?

The evidence in favour of specialist services comes not from controlled studies but from clinical experience. Although patients with uncomplicated bulimia nervosa can be treated effectively by a lone psychologist using published techniques, patients with severe bulimia, with self-harm and alcohol misuse, and those with severe anorexia nervosa, do not fit in well to generic services. Admission to a medical ward is usually appropriate for a patient who is collapsing from low potassium or low weight, but as soon as the acute medical problem subsides, and the patient starts to refuse food, or behave in other ways characteristic of her eating disorder, management becomes the realm of the psychiatric team who are cordially invited to take over the patient. The staff on a general psychiatric ward are used to dealing with severely ill people with schizophrenia, mania, psychotic and substance misuse, and find the management of patients with anorexia nervosa and severe bulimia difficult and frustrating. Many nurses feel that to deal with someone with acute schizophrenia and another with anorexia nervosa in the same environment stretches their skills and resources dangerously far.

There is, therefore, a powerful demand for specialist services from generic services in which patients with eating disorders rest uncomfortably. The sufferers themselves have also indicated (through a survey of members of the Eating Disorders Association) that they would like more professionals available who have specialist skills in treating eating disorders.

2. What sort of services should there be?

The following discussion applies to services for patients over the age of 18. Younger patients are currently not usually treated in specialist services, although a case could be made for combining services at commissioning and management levels, while maintaining important distinctions in the treatment of patients of different ages.

Reference to Figure 2.1 above will show that specialist services include outpatient, day patient and inpatient care, and all three should be available locally. The balance of these services depends largely on the model of care, and needs careful thought. Provision of the elements will also depend on the likely need for them from a particular community. A community eating disorders service with facilities for medical and psychiatric assessment, home visiting, outpatient treatment and liaison with primary and secondary care (including medical, surgical and psychiatric services) requires the following as a minimum: (WTE = whole time equivalent).

- 1 consultant psychiatrist with special training in eating disorders (0.4 WTE).
- 1 trainee psychiatrist (0.4 WTE)
- 1 clinical psychologist with experience and training in eating disorders (0.4 WTE)
- 1 family therapist (0.4 WTE)
- 2 nurses with experience and training in eating disorders (2.0 WTE)
- 1 secretary/receptionist (1.0 WTE)
- Supervision from an appropriately trained therapist (0.1 WTE).

Depending on the rate of referral, such a team should be able to cope with referrals from a population base of 250,000–300,000. The team will require access to a nearby specialist centre with resources for day care and inpatient treatment. This centre would also provide services to two other such community eating disorders services, and have its own outpatient catchment area, giving a total population served by the specialist centre of 1–1.2 million.

Such a centre could also take responsibility for organizing overall management of the service, training and research. The staff group would be approximately as follows:

- 1 consultant psychiatrist with special training in eating disorders (0.6–1.0 WTE)
- 1 trainee psychiatrist (0.5 WTE)
- 1 clinical psychologist with experience and training in eating disorders (0.6 WTE)
- 1 family therapist (0.4 WTE)
- 1 service manager (1.0 WTE)
- 6 nurses with experience and training in eating disorders (6.0 WTE)
- 1 experienced occupational therapist (1.0 WTE)
- Creative therapists (1.0 WTE)
- Dietitian (0.4 WTE)
- 1.5 secretary/receptionist (1.5 WTE)
- Supervision from an appropriately trained therapist (0.1 WTE)
- Welfare rights/social worker (0.2 WTE).

These staff numbers are rough estimates, and the staff need depends largely on the demands of the population and its primary care teams. The day hospital team should be able to provide a five-day-a-week service, and sufficient budget needs to be set aside to pay for treatment of severely unwell patients who may need 24-hour nursing, either at home or in a hospital bed. The organization of such a service implies that for every million or so population, there would be a central coordinating unit with an intensive day service and access to inpatient care and other forms of more intensive care, and a number of surrounding community eating disorders services providing outpatient and home care (Figure 2.2).

Figure 2.2. The diagram represents a central specialist eating disorders service with access to intensive treatments, management and academic functions, with three satellite services in surrounding communities. The whole service would provide assessment and treatment for a population of about 1 million.

3. What sort of treatment needs to be offered?

The community teams described are able to provide a range of specialist therapies. The doctors provide medical and psychiatric assessment and monitoring. The psychologist offers CBT group therapy for patients with bulimia nervosa and binge eating disorder. The nurses offer individual supportive therapy and domiciliary treatment for anorexia nervosa, and for patients with bulimia nervosa who prefer not to attend a group, and the family therapist sees families of patients, mainly with anorexia nervosa. A variable amount of assessment and treatment would take place outside the centre, in the patient's home, or in primary care, the school medical service or other locations. The sorts of approach used would vary with the patient.

The intensive services, day and inpatient, provide dietetic advice, assistance with eating and group therapy, as well as the other therapeutic services available to outpatients. Close observation by skilled nurses will be required for a minority of severely ill patients.

A common role of the consultant psychiatrist is to reconcile seemingly disparate views of the same problem by different members of the team. In practice, all approaches – nutritional, pharmacological, cognitive-behavioural, psychodynamic and family – may be appropriate for an individual. Facilitating discussion between doctors, nurses, psychologists, dietitians, occupational therapists, psychotherapists, patients and family members is an important task. It often (although not invariably) falls to the psychiatrist.

Chapter 3
To be or not to be – The patient's viewpoint

Lucy Elkins

Introduction

I am an anorexic. Like most sufferers, I find it hard to pinpoint exactly how long I've had anorexia: it's not like you wake up one day and think, 'Right, I'll develop an eating disorder today'. Rather, it sneaks up on you and slowly advances its hold over your life, until, if left unchecked, it becomes all-consuming.

According to the doctors, this is my second bout of anorexia. The first occurred in my teens, when I was almost unaware of it and from which I fully recovered. This second bout has exerted an increasing force over three or four years, reaching a crunch point in 1998 when I reached a weight that was classed as appropriate for treatment by hospitalization.

To say I have absolutely no memory of the first instance is not strictly true. According to my medical notes, my GP diagnosed me as anorexic when I was 12, following a lengthy bout of glandular fever. At the time I remember it merely as a suggestion, vehemently denied as nonsense by myself and my mother: 'she's not anorexic, she's just not well', was the general theme.

In retrospect, I do have vague memories of feeling a thrill if, on a visit to see the consultant, I received the news that I had lost weight. With the benefit of hindsight I also remember being tremendously depressed, actually making a half-hearted attempt at suicide during this period. I also remember thinking that 'glandular fever', as I thought it was, was probably to blame for many adolescent suicides, if everyone suffered as badly as I did with it. How I recovered I don't recal,l but obviously this was anorexia.

I'm five foot three and my weight peaked when I was 20 at around 10 stone 4.

Problems arose in my private life in my early twenties and possibly this was the trigger to kickstarting my eating disorder.

In 1998, aged 29, I hit rock bottom, with my weight under 5 stone 8 lb. I had been dropping weight with increased speed during the previous two years and by the start of 1998 I was around 6 stone 10. I rapidly deteriorated. The irony was that to outside observers this came at a time when everything else seemed to be picking up. I became engaged to an old flame and gained a new job in a senior position on the widely respected *Breakfast with Frost* programme. However, inside, something was going very wrong.

I like to think that I am a recovering anorexic: I am 7^1/$_2$ stone, have a renewed career, a boyfriend with whom I enjoy a normal relationship, but I don't pretend to have put this behind me yet. But I hope that, as a relatively lucid and eloquent sufferer of an eating disorder, my experiences may help give a little insight into this illness and our approach to it.

What it feels like to have an eating disorder

Anorexia Nervosa: The Wish to Change (Crisp et al., 1996), *Anorexia Nervosa: A Guide for Sufferers and Their Parents* (Palmer, 1989), *The Secret Language of Eating Disorders* (Claude-Pierre, 1998), *Autumn Dawn: Triumph Over Eating Disorders* (Cox, 1995): this literary collection has amassed on my bookshelves over the past three years. I have turned to the pages of these collected works in between doctors' appointments, starvation, exercise and bouts of despair: turned to them for hope.

To me it seemed that every voice that tried to help was repeating the well-worn 'eat more and you'll feel better' mantra. I couldn't cope with that. I was looking for some magic phrase, a marvel medicine, a magical potion to stop me. But there is none, of course, and that is probably one of the hardest issues ahead for someone, like myself, trying to conquer an eating disorder. You're faced with having to alter behaviour and attitudes that in some circumstances have been present for years in exchange for a belief in others, a belief that what they are telling you is true, that by doing as they say your life will change. It's like asking a committed atheist to suddenly believe in the word of the Gospel and become a regular church-goer. Except that the trauma is not so great, the extent of change is not quite so monumental.

I can't remember the exact moment when I knew that I needed help, other than a vague recollection that my actions and behaviour were taking the form of a kind of self-imposed misery. Yes, there had been rumblings of concern about my demeanour and diet from relatives and friends. However well intentioned this initial voicing of concern, for me and others can easily backfire.

In my own case, having being slightly overweight in the past, I would glow under the praise I received for returning my figure to more manageable proportions. So, when people started telling me I was getting a little thin, I interpreted it as jealousy. Others, I concluded, were envious of my figure and trying to get me fat again. Therefore, I would avoid any advice they might give me and make sure I stuck to my guns.

I'm not alone. A friend and former anorexic who went through a brief period of the illness in her early twenties recalls: 'Everywhere I went people were offering me food because I was thin. I began to think it was some kind of conspiracy and that everyone was trying to fatten me up. I stopped trusting everyone.'

Anorexia is often summed up as a fear of being fat. It isn't like that to the sufferer. It is fear, full stop: and against that background the notion of becoming overweight is not usually the trigger that inspires or guides anorexic behaviour. It is an inability to cope with various situations, and the only way out is to impose control.

Fear is one part, self-hatred another. Only as I recover do I notice how the illness makes you deprive yourself of all pleasure and comfort. It involves doing everything you 'ought', not 'want', to do. I could never let myself sit down and relax with a paper or a book unless I was absolutely exhausted. I would never allow myself to stay in bed beyond 6.30am. Feeling unwell, constantly tired and down is a welcome sensation, because it gives you something to hide behind and is the standard of existence you feel you deserve as such a hateful person. Confusion rules and you are rarely aware that it is the eating disorder that is making you do these things.

Eating disorders are sadistic: a patient will be taking pleasure from the pain and that must be understood when offering them the hand out of that pit. Former anorexic and bulimic Ann Cox conveyed very eloquently in her book, *Autumn Dawn*, how people in our position almost welcome pain. This is how she describes feeling after a period of purging:

> I felt so ill and weak – and it was wonderful. The pain in my head, any feelings or emotions, were all taken away and no matter the acute shortage of breath, the distorted hearing, the inability to stand upright to walk and the devastating weakness, I was safe for a while. Everything was on hold (Cox, 1995: 23).

Along with that goes a feeling of helplessness. I used to say that trying to beat anorexia was like standing at a door with a key in your hand. You know there must be a way to get through the barrier, but something that seemed so simple for some, that is, non-anorexic behaviour or putting the key in the lock and turning it, took on the mantle of an impossible conundrum. The denial of pleasure became so acute in my case that I would actually video highbrow programmes that I had no desire or interest in seeing and make myself watch them.

Has the incidence of eating disorders increased?

Reading reports about eating disorders in newspapers and magazines leaves the impression that they have struck society like some modern-day plague, almost as if the stick-thin images of models such as Kate Moss parading down catwalks or pouting from magazines gave birth to anorexia and its kind. But this is a myth.

I also believe that it is a dangerous myth: somehow it links the problem of an eating disorder to vanity, that sufferers starve themselves because they want to be as beautiful as these women. This is misguided and untrue. It is simplifying a complex disorder into a kind of female jealousy. I would agree that it is wrong that the so-called supermodels' figures came to be portrayed as 'typical' or 'the norm'. My counsellor told me that a recent study had discovered that nearly all supermodels' BMI falls within a unhealthy range of 17–17.5. I hope that fashion designers will, in the fullness of time, be able to put their own personal vanity to one side to try to remedy this distorted message to the majority of women who are more likely to be a happy and healthy size 14 plus.

Social pressure is one of a number of factors that can bring on an eating disorder. There may be biological reasons or it can even be the result of misguided peer pressure. These, or any number of things, can contribute or tip the scales to developing an eating disorder. Vanity is rarely, if ever, involved: quite the reverse, if anything.

Once you have reached a certain level (for example, aged 28, 5 ft 3 in and 5 stone 8 lb at my lowest adult weight) I think that in the main you know you are no longer attractive. It ceases to be connected to the way you look. All sexual urges have vanished as a rule anyway, so what does that matter? It is common practice for us to avoid mirrors and windows for fear of seeing our own reflection and inevitably not liking what we see.

We have to be honest; research into the reasons for the onset of eating disorders is still in its infancy. But I think it is of paramount importance that we dispel this link between 'celebrity slimness' and eating disorders, as it is harmful: it gives the wrong message to the sufferers and to the general public about the very raison d'être for this dreadful illness.

If there has been an increase in the incidence, one has to question what is bringing this on. My experience is that there aren't quite as many common denominators to eating disorders as are suggested: we don't all lie, we don't all hate food, we weren't all sexually abused and so on, but, in the main, we are not as able as others to deal with stress and all suffer from a pitiful lack of self-esteem.

Stress is a much-maligned word: in this sense I'm talking about the difficulties one may encounter through life. For example, my own admittedly unscientific research has found that to anorexics or bulimics a few harsh words spoken to them during a heated moment can have a devastating impact on them: it compounds their negative attitudes to themselves and therefore induces periods of bingeing or starvation. It may be a B minus for an essay, an inability to meet a tight deadline at work, even a throwaway comment from a friend: any of these situations can penetrate the often flimsy shield patients have for 'dealing with life'.

Therefore, I think the increase is more likely to be down to the increasing expectations of society on individuals. Never before has there been so much emphasis on 'success'. Never before has there been so much pressure, especially on young women, to 'get on'. Spurred on by their mothers, who 'never had such opportunities', it is easy to see why bright girls especially fall victim to an eating disorder as they perceive their ambitions as not enough. They feel they are failing if they don't want to follow the bright lights, or have difficulty keeping up. The world becomes confusing and undisciplined: and so the patient finds one area of achievement – food control.

Finally, here is something that expresses the self-hatred and worthlessness that they feel and, often, in the beginning, if the eating disorder comes with weight loss it can bring praise from others. So, the patient feels she has achieved: she has sentenced herself to the misery she feels she deserves and at the same time is pleasing those around her – look at her successful body. That is, until it goes wrong.

Pure existence is complicated enough for someone with an eating disorder. For example, many of us anorexics have a tendency towards perfectionism and because of the lack of spontaneity the illness allows, mentally or physically, our days tend to be regimentally planned: a delayed train is not reason to sigh, it's a big deal; being asked to stay for half an hour after work is a catastrophe – when will you fit in that 45-minute exercise video?

Modern life is terribly stressful because we are so reliant on other people and other things working: and invariably they don't. It is useful to keep this in perspective. Again, I reiterate, this is *not* a modern-day plague. The word anorexia derives from the Greek 'orexis', meaning appetite. It means literally 'for want of an appetite', which means the word is misused in this context: we anorexics have an appetite all right. It is just that our appetite for self-hate is greater than that for food.

The term was relatively common in Elizabethan times, and it was then that there was the well-documented 'French Fasting Girl of Conflens' in

1599, a young girl who starved herself for three years following a minor illness: she was emaciated and cold but constantly on the go.

The term anorexia nervosa was coined by a Frenchman and an Englishman, Sir William Gull and Professor Lasegue in Paris, who came up with the phrase in the 1870s and helped put the disorder in the medical mainstream.

The idea of starvation or deprivation is not a new one: the ancient Chinese used starvation to try to embarrass people who owed them money into paying up. And many religions have a form of starvation as part of their philosophy.

In modern times we have refined the idea of slimness and purity. Slimness has become not only the epitome of attractive appeal but the epitome of success. It is a frightening fact that many studies have proven that slim, attractive people find it easier to get jobs, partners and many other perks in life. This will not change until society feels prepared to embrace role models who do not fall within these parameters. But don't blame the media: we have to blame ourselves.

There is also an entire industry that generates billions of pounds through feeding on the insecurities each individual has about his or her body shape. Studies have shown that girls who diet at a young age significantly heighten their chance of developing an eating disorder: this must be of concern to us all.

While researching this chapter I was struck, each time I visited a bookshop or a library, by the whole sections of works available on the 'diet and fitness' theme, while I struggled to find a single reference to eating disorders on the shelves.

Eating disorders are a statement without words: binge eaters are afraid of success, they do not feel worthy of it. Anorexics don't feel worthy of anything and become frightened by the responsibilities that the world puts on to them – these slim, attractive, often successful individuals.

This background has helped link slimness into our subconscious as worthy and good. Bulimics feel a similar pain and express it in a different way: the common thread for all is self-hatred.

Seeking help

As I have said, for about the three years prior to 1998 I had been aware of a problem, and for two of these I had been actively seeking help to a greater or lesser degree. It's hard enough accepting that you have an eating disorder, let alone trying to get help. This is to do both with the condition and society's attitude to it. First, eating disorders by their very nature lead sufferers to be secretive about their problem. So, discussing any form of behaviour of which you feel so ashamed that you hide it from others is bound to be difficult.

One girl described it to me as being like an alcoholic: half of her wanted to get help, but the other half didn't know how she would cope without the eating disorder.

Second, despite high-profile cases, there is still a stigma attached to eating disorders, as nearly all those people I know who have one would confirm. Many people don't tell their closest friends or colleagues, let alone relatives, so, understandably, baring all to a health professional is bound to be a traumatic process. This is why it is vital that it must be as simple as possible for someone to reach out for help when they need it.

In this country the first port of call is either the GP or, if you have the funds, a private clinic. I felt embarrassed when I went to the doctor. At that point I didn't resemble the emaciated frames one sees sporadically in the newspapers: I was about 7 stone at this point. I felt like the original fat fraud. The first couple of times I bottled it: in retrospect I wanted the doctor to say it first.

I was trying to convey anorexia in code. I complained of exhaustion and permanent virus-type symptoms (true enough) and confessed in a slightly smaller voice that perhaps I didn't eat an awful lot and maybe I did do quite a lot of exercise. My GP's reaction was 'if only I had that problem with all my patients' and gave me the verbal equivalent of a pat on my head and sent me on my way.

This farcical situation continued: I was sane enough to realize that I was on a rollercoaster which was moving further and further into diet Cloud-cuckoo-land and I didn't know what to do. I couldn't find the brakes within me.

One evening I collapsed in tears. I had got through my 11-hour working day to return to the charade of preparing myself supper: nuggets of vegetables cooked up with tomatoes. Then I had forced myself to do a fairly energetic fitness video even though I really didn't want to and was on the brink of exhaustion. I decided to call the Eating Disorders Association the next day. Although it was utterly sympathetic to my plight, it confirmed that the only way to get free help was by recommendation from my GP. It was time to bite the bullet.

Finally, when my own GP was off sick, his locum listened and looked and decided to refer me to a special NHS clinic.

We expect a lot from GPs, and the idea that they can be specialists able to tune into encyclopaedias full of disorders is both unfair and unrealistic: like a Peugeot mechanic trying to fix a Rolls-Royce.

But surely this is a ludicrous situation. I was an intelligent, educated, eloquent 27 year old. If it took me more than a year to get help through my doctor, which I was asking for, how much harder must it be for the many who will scamper away, who wouldn't have the courage to go back again and again, for the young girls and boys whose self-confidence is so lacking that they are using starvation or bingeing as a form of communication anyway?

Surely it is vital for there to be some alternative route to gain access to professional help, for those unable or unwilling to discuss an intensely personal subject with their GP and for the others who can't afford the private route.

NHS outpatient treatment

Having run for the post every day, waiting for my appointment card, a few months later my time finally came. I felt relief: I was going to be in treatment and everything would be fine.

The first visit lasted just under an hour: my newly appointed specialist weighed me and talked to me before dispatching me with a questionnaire. I sat in the café next door and filled it in, wondering how many other people in my position had done just that.

I was amazed by the questionnaire. It consisted of themes such as 'would you like to be thinner?' (have they never heard of the Duchess of Windsor?), 'do you feel happy with your self/your weight?'. I dutifully filled it all in and dropped off the form.

An hour later I was called back in and the specialist broke the news to me that I was anorexic. He told me that he expected the news had come as a shock, which I thought very strange, and he said that I might need to think about that. He also said that he would be monitoring me and I would be seeing a nutritionist and that there might be some other options, and so on.

I left feeling reassured: OK, nothing had changed but it sounded like a start. That was back in April. My next visit was a month later. My original doctor was off sick and I had half an hour with another who didn't ingratiate herself to me by kicking off with the old 'your sexual experience'.

In the following six months I had three subsequent visits. Each lasted half an hour and had a weigh in and a token 'how are you doing' question. Before you say I should have said 'not very good', I did several times. Each time he would tell me to put on half a kilo a week; on one occasion I had put on 6 pounds (I'm still not sure how ... maybe it was excessive wind, or maybe it was because I had just returned from four days off in the country with my fiancé – enforced because I had been breaking down at work). I was shocked. I left the clinic feeling too fat to throw myself under a bus (surely I couldn't fit): an anorexic who has just been told she has swelled by almost half a stone in a month is not what one would call a happy person.

Each visit to the clinic would be preceded by an extra cautious watch on my weight. I felt it humiliating to go: there, the resident patients would wander around looking like little ghosts to me. (I may or may not have looked as thin as them, I don't know.) Hence, each time I went there I would feel fat and unworthy of any help. I also think now that subconsciously I was keeping my weight down, because I had convinced myself that their only apparent interest was in fattening me up and I wasn't prepared to let this happen until I knew why this monster illness was raging a battle of wits with my sane self.

It was frustrating: I did have the will to get better, but I didn't know how to stop the demons. I was used to succeeding; surely I could beat this. It was a classic case of my head in the sand, of not appreciating how ill I was nor realizing it was too tough to beat on my own. Does the average cancer patient decide it is time to administer his or her own chemotherapy?

My story is not an isolated one and I think it helps to underline the need for greater access to outpatient treatment: a visit now and again is not going to change anything. More regular visits, especially at the start of seeking help, could be a really positive step. I also think it would be cost-effective. Outpatient treatment is much cheaper than inpatient treatment, and from what I hear from those who have been through it, the provision of more adequate outpatient treatment from the start could prevent them from ever needing inpatient help.

Crisis point

One of the greatest causes for sadness for me is that unless a sufferer's illness reaches a crisis point in terms of either weight or a failed organ, for example, then they often never seek help at all, or alternatively pay lip-service to a type of recovery that suspends them in limbo between here and the eating disorder.

This can take a terrible toll on the person. They limp through life but don't live it. Since I have 'come out' I have been truly amazed at how many people tell me they have had or still have anorexia. So much so that I now doubt that there is any such thing as a naturally slim adult in the Western world.

People with eating disorders are all too aware of the concern they have caused, and feel guilt because of it. Therefore, they are only too happy to tell people that they are 'getting there' when they aren't. It is easy to delude yourself. Any small concession in altered behaviour is a big deal to the sufferer: if they do not feel any different then it reinforces what they suspected, that life is not pleasant.

An oft-repeated phrase I hear is 'as long as I stay over such and such a weight then the doctor says I'm OK and don't need to go back in'. Far too many eating disorder sufferers learn to mask the illness with a presentation of borderline healthy weight, but their attitudes are anything but healthy: think of it as a devil occupying an angel's body. These people are still controlled by their eating disorder and live lives of abject misery. The eating disorder has become so strong that it pushes the sufferer to continue with anorexic/bulimic behaviour, which they become so addicted to that they hide it by weight gain, for example, rather than give it up completely.

Quite often it takes a jolt to end this chain of self-abuse. Certainly I know this to be true in my own case. I changed jobs in the spring of 1998, thinking a change of routine would help. But I couldn't be kind to myself and downgrade the stress factor in my job: oh no, I started as a senior journalist on one of the most high-profile political programmes on BBC1.

In retrospect, when I look at photographs of myself taken at the time, I am genuinely concerned and amazed that anyone should have employed me at all. I was soon struggling to cope. I often felt the need to cry and frequently did during the day. I had long ago toughened myself to cope with the stares as I went through my lunch routine: chopping and slicing my salad at my desk: smothering my plate with sauces to kid colleagues (and myself) that I was having a huge plate of food. Physically, my stamina was so bad that I would either have to just pick up my bags and run or lie down on the floor at the end of a long day.

I was now about 6 stone and the prospect of not eating became as frightening as the idea of a five-course lunch, as I knew I would faint without pathetic attempts at nourishment. I would shake and become irrational; tears verging on hysteria would well up inside me.

On one occasion, when a meeting between myself, my editor and one of the country's best-known comedians overran my appointed lunch hour, I became so distressed that the tears spilled down my cheeks: I just hoped that the comic would think I was overcome by his wit.

None of this was helped by my sleeping patterns. I was surviving on around 4 hours a night. I put this down to stress. I didn't realize that rumbling stomachs do not lead to a restful night's sleep – the penny has only just dropped on this one. Hence, I had spent large amounts of my not insubstantial income on relaxing essential oils and so on, never linking my insomnia to my eating disorder. I wish one of my doctors had spelt it out for me.

I was on a rollercoaster of despair. My wedding had been postponed, partly because my work meant my fiancé and I had seen very little of one another and also because anorexia played a part in the non-wedding: who wants to pledge 'till death do us part' to someone who resembles a ghost already?

My fiancé, Guy, and I decided to have a holiday: it was in place of our honeymoon and would provide the perfect opportunity for us to spend some time together and for me to work out what to do with regard to work and my illness.

It did not go as planned: our dream of two weeks in Turkey quickly turned sour. By day two we received news from England that Guy's father had died suddenly, and so had to start making arrangements to get Guy back home. By day three Guy had developed Turkish tummy and was confined to bed. I was left alone in Turkey for a week. Showing classic anorexic 'feeling shutdown', I pretended, even to myself, that it was life as normal and nothing was amiss. Actually it was nearly the beginning of the end.

Importantly, during this time I had a flash of clarity about why I had been inflicting this starvation on myself. As I had progressed at great speed up the career ladder I had lost sight of what I had achieved. I had been given more and more responsibility that I had no desire to have, and instead of saying 'enough' I had gone through this silent scream in the hope that someone would notice and say 'stop, you don't have to do this any more'.

It seemed crystal clear and simple on the beach: the only thing preventing my recovery was my job, and there were no rules that said I had to do that. I resolved to quit and go freelance. I felt drunk on the discovery and that day I ate a mouthful of garlic bread with the oil still visible on the top (progress, believe me).

However, the instant I landed back in Britain the rollercoaster crisis returned: first, my stepbrother who I had last seen two or three months before didn't recognize his waif-like sister. And then came the broccoli moment....We stopped on the way back to my flat for a nice light Chinese meal and a glass of wine. I chewed on a stalk of broccoli and the bulk felt huge and unmanageable: the plate of stir-fried greens just looked insurmountable. I realized my 'flash' was only part of the answer: in fact the problem was more complex.

Suddenly I knew I could no longer cope, and without help I thought I might well die. Trying to negotiate the stairs to my top-floor flat was well nigh impossible, and when I weighed myself the following morning I realized I was in serious trouble: when the scales finally say 5 stone something, there is a jolt – half of you wants to cheer, the other half is frightened.

I phoned the NHS clinic, desperate. I begged to see my doctor or even talk to him. I was told that the best they could do was the appointment I had for 10 days' time that had been booked a month previously.

I did not have the strength to get to work and seeing as I was still a relatively new recruit to a senior position on a high-profile programme at the BBC, this was crisis enough. I barely had the strength to walk to the toilet. I felt all out of fight and desperate to get some help.

The clinic suggested my GP. I was so weak I could scarcely make it. As a concession I ate a couple of grapes to power me there. Somehow I made it the few steps it takes to get to the surgery: one of the doctors agreed to see me. She too tried phoning the clinic, but was given the same response as me. Importantly, though, she took the time to listen for a few minutes (naturally, I felt endless guilt at taking so much of her time).

Can this be right? Surely this illustrates a vital gap in the treatment and care of people in my position. An emergency facility must be part of any specialist unit.

When I did eventually get to see my doctor at the clinic he acknowledged that he had got the telephone messages I had left for him but had not done anything about it. 'I was worried when I heard what you weighed, you dipped well into hospitalization weight area,' he said.

I was lucky, I had family and friends to act on my behalf: God help a less fortunate soul. I am not accusing my specialist of negligence. His workload is, or was at the time, simply too big. But I hope this highlights to others the inadequacies of the system.

Private treatment

My GP suggested going to a private clinic. I was frightened. I knew I had sunk, and yet the simplest thing, feeding myself, did not seem possible. I was in a daze. I couldn't make it to work: I called and lied and said I had a stomach disorder.

I still couldn't make the decision to call a clinic myself. It gets back to feeling worthy: I still had that recurrent fat fraud feeling. A relative intervened and made an appointment on my behalf. I was relieved.

That afternoon I saw a nurse who was so concerned that she made the consultant psychiatrist come to see me at 8am the following morning. He had found a suitable counsellor for me by 4.30pm. This was different: for the first time, I was asked about my feelings about the illness: and I wasn't weighed. I came further along the road to recovery in one hour than I had in six months. This counsellor didn't fob me off with 'a tablespoon of mashed potato each day'; he tried to trace my problems. He treated food as an aside, while emphasizing the need to put on weight: to be emotionally and physically healthy.

He also asked me what foods I liked so we could work out a meal plan that would fit in with me. Basically, I left feeling as if you get what you pay for.

That night I made myself pasta for the first time in about four years and ate about six pieces of it. It was such a triumph, I called my mother to tell her the news even though she was on holiday in Turkey.

To feed or not to feed?

As I have mentioned, when I first sought treatment there was almost a determination on my part not to put on weight. I felt scared of doing so when I felt that nothing was changing inside my head. No one was talking to me about it: or offering what I could see as constructive help. I would visit the NHS clinic once a month and be weighed and told to put on more weight.

I was still so ill and messed up that there was no way I was going to try to swell on some doctor's say-so. I didn't feel equipped, at that point, to deal with the consequences.

It also gets back to how it feels to have an eating disorder: as I said earlier, you are not conscious of the fear of fat being the overwhelming problem in your life. More likely it is the abject misery that someone in that position suffers which is of primary concern to them. Many sufferers feel the same. When you are so full of problems, the idea that weight and food can solve them is like suggesting a plaster to treat a severed limb.

It is vital that before the person is asked to recover they are first acquainted with the side-effects and the problems the disorder has brought. Only then can healthy eating be reintroduced.

No one ever spelt it out to me in plain terms: that is, you won't be sleeping, you'll be constipated, unable to cope with emotions and so on as a result of anorexia. Silly as it may sound, I had no idea it was responsible for so much.

That established the first message that should be hammered home, which is that recovery can offer a better life. Don't bombard the patient with messages about food at the start: the disorder will be telling them that you are the bad guy in this scenario and it is vital to establish trust in the first instance.

It sounds so obvious, but when offering treatment I think this would be a useful tool of approach: it is very hard for someone sitting in a surgery with their life in tatters to believe that consuming a sandwich or chucking out the laxatives can really solve all their woes.

Not one of the anorexics I have spoken to who have consented to a quick-start feed-up programme in a hospital have spoken of that treatment as a favourable option. All those I know who have followed this course ended up coming out bigger people with the same problems. And for that very reason they fell back into the vulnerable position that allows an eating disorder to take over.

Any feeding that is done should be done in a healthy and positive way: I am extremely anti any kind of high-calorie diet plan. A diet plan must be a long-term plan and the sufferer needs to learn sensible, 'normal' habits which this mode will not encourage. It may also cause resentment. If the sufferer puts on weight too quickly, without adequate counselling about their feelings and how they ended up in that position, then any inclination to recover can quickly be surpassed by anger aimed at family, medical practitioners and inevitably themselves.

Inpatient/outpatient?

Inpatient care may be suitable for a younger sufferer whose condition is triggered by the home environment: but even in this instance it still leaves him or her vulnerable to that situation when they leave.

It makes no sense to me to try to help someone reform their life, while at the same time taking them away from their everyday environment. Overcoming an eating disorder is as much to do with readjusting to society so that one is able to cope more adequately with the obstacles in life as it is to do with finding a healthy relationship with food.

In many instances the 'jolt back to reality' is difficult: it may well have been something in their everyday existence that triggered the problem in the first place; therefore when they return to their normal life and find the same problems, despite their attempt at recovery, it can be easy to understand how so many turn their back on their acquired healthy behaviour they have picked up while under specialist inpatient care.

A supportive family or network is surely preferable. For older people, it can often help that they have to get on and deal with as much of their own life as they can. Certainly, I know that having to get to work was a big motivator to me eating at all at certain times.

There is one other point as to why I think inpatient treatment should be offered with care. Much is said about how sending criminals to jail can often be the wrong move: how they become a 'villain' by being in that environment, and how they often learn to refine their techniques of law breaking. I fear the same may be true of people with eating disorders: there is a chance that they will abuse this experience to hone their techniques.

Group therapy

I think that this is yet another form of treatment that should be administered with care, for many of the same reasons for which I oppose inpatient treatment.

Group therapy can be of wonderful benefit to outpatients who have no or maybe only a small outside network to rely on, to those that find the readjustment into the real world difficult, or to those who have little chance of contact with others, such as the unemployed, and so on.

However, for my part I found it a hindrance. Somehow it made me feel worse. I think it is because I felt labelled with an 'invalid' tag. I must be ill to be there. It didn't encourage me to let go, to move on, and this is the danger: if there is a difference in speed of recovery between individuals in the group then this may lead to an imbalance in the discussion.

On the positive side it did make me reflect on how ill I was at that time, as I could see how ill the others were. I liked to think that I wasn't as bad as them, but of course I was. The problem was that I felt that not all of the group were as keen as myself to recover, and this discouraged me from making the break from anorexia.

Coordination of care

This is vital to provide the sufferer with consistent advice. Inconsistency of advice at a time when a person is trying to re-establish themselves as something other than an eating disorder is confusing and distressing.

An example that happened in my own case arose when I was seeking both private and NHS treatment. This was in 1998, when my weight was so low.

I was coping as an outpatient with once-weekly visits to my private counsellor, appointments once every two or three weeks with my NHS psychiatrist and twice-monthly sessions with my NHS nutritionist.

I felt the need for the weekly help. It is natural that when you are going through so much upheaval, you both want and need praise and encouragement. However, because of this two-pronged approach, I received conflicting advice. The nutritionist advised me on upping my intake gradually, for example three Ryvita at lunch not one. Meanwhile my private counsellor was urging me to 'give it all up', to 'throw out the diet foods, eat five slices of bread a day'. True I would leave feeling inspired to do just that, but good intentions would last little more than 48 hours. Therefore, at first I chose to follow the nutritionist's plan: this was more attainable. However, it was also allowing the eating disorder to continue: this kind of plan is still giving in to 'faddy' habits that prevented me from leading a flexible lifestyle where food was not a big issue.

As I gained weight and realized this, I went back to my private counsellor for more help, and specifically advice on what kind of food and what kind of amounts I should be striving for. I felt more ready and willing to address this at the weight I then was (about 43 kilos, or 6 stone, 11 pounds). When I had weighed less I resented the emphasis put on food when I felt there were so many underlying problems to be resolved.

My counsellor's suggestions were to eliminate any kind of moderation in my diet. I was allowed no diet food, and he advised eating three substantial meals a day, including five pieces of bread. My NHS nutritionist favoured building on the amounts I was already eating, for example three crackers instead of two, four slices of bread instead of three. Despite both individuals' best intentions, the conflicting advice caused me distress and confusion at the time.

I needed everything written down. I was doing this on my own and was an infant at knowing how to feed myself. I felt that I needed one rigid plan that I could read and stick to at meal times. However, during 'wobbly times' the lack of a clearly defined plan seemed like a reason to me to give up. This is something that should be borne in mind.

Food tuition

Eating disorders and their treatment are surrounded by a lot of mystique: so much so, I think, that some of the basics go untouched. While we talk about eating plans and refeeding programmes there is scarcely any information for the sufferer about food education. And I'm talking basics.

I have found myself in tears at a supermarket, overcome with distress because I didn't know what a medium potato looked like, let alone how much of it I should eat a day and how much of that potato would be used by my body for natural metabolism and so on. Food re-education could be a small and valuable lesson for all areas. Simple lessons could be given about how much or how little we need to survive, what a healthy eating plan for our weight would look like: what about mock plates with food amounts on them for various BMI indexes? This would be a great help, especially as the patient struggles to readjust their patterns. To be able to visualize 'normality' would help a lot in many circumstances.

After-care

At her clinic in Montreux, Canada, Peggy Claude-Pierre uses a 'Wellness Scale' to measure recovery, but the scale ends not at 100% but at 86%. She explains the reasons for this in her book, *The Secret Language of Eating Disorders*, thus: 'This underscores our core philosophy at the clinic: our stress on human limitations. No one could ever be 100 percent anything; nor should we strive to be' (Claude-Pierre, 1998: 196).

This is one of the most encouraging bits of advice I have read with regard to my future recovery. It is comforting to know I don't have to scrap myself completely as I am, nor beat myself up, in so many words, if I don't behave exactly the way 'normal' people do as often as I would like.

Recovery is a bit like waking up over a long period: slowly the sleepiness wears off and you start to see things in clear focus.

So many things have to be learnt from scratch: my friends are tired of me asking them what they have had for supper. I'm still curious: what do normal people eat and when? What are you supposed to do on a 'lazy Sunday afternoon'?

Simply relearning how to live takes readjustment. I wasn't aware of how I had been breaking down my days, almost subconsciously, into 'rest' periods. The new-found energy that appeared from time to time was alarming and demanded I rethink my routine, which startled me a little. I would find myself drumming my fingers and raring to go after supper. Having spent almost three years having had little more than the energy to chop and boil a carrot at the end of my working day this was something of a shock. Although it doesn't sound unpleasant, it was enough to bring hysteria: I had no idea how to deal with this and felt useless and lazy.

It is a turbulent time. A time of throwing out old habits and exchanging the mantle of the person you thought you were for another, healthier one. Hence why I think the advice from Claude-Pierre is so valuable. Because at the same time there have been odd times when I have thought 'Hang on, that's not anorexia, that's just me: it may be strange, but it's me'.

Even feelings of happiness can throw you: they have become so alien. Ann Cox describes it as a feeling of having 'too much ice cream on your plate'. The patient will question what they have done to deserve this: should I be feeling this happy?

It can be very depressing to be told 'you'll never kick this completely', as one of my psychiatrists often does. That is why I think the Montreux 86% scale is such a good idea to work from. No one is perfect or normal: what is normal? The idea to foster is that recovery must mean a life that you are happy with, in which food is not the main issue, and where there is room for spontaneity. Within that, sufferers must know that there is room for idiosyncrasy, and holding up 'an ideal' for perfectionists, as eating disorder sufferers tend to be, is in the long run destructive and unhelpful for them.

Why fewer men?

Male eating disorder sufferers have had quite a lot of attention recently: fundamentally because they are so rare. Eating disorders affect 1% of the population, and of these only 1% will be men. These figures do not vary, whether taken in a controlled or random environment, such as a recent study involving a Native American tribe.

Despite the publicity, men still account for only 1% of sufferers. It is not a new phenomenon: history books indicate that the poet Lord Byron had an eating disorder, going through long periods of starvation followed by sessions of bingeing.

The reasons for this difference between men and women are, to me, obvious. In its crudest form an eating disorder is, for whatever reason, not feeling good about oneself and an inability to communicate this to others. When women feel bad, they blame themselves: they are the nurturers and must care; they do not expect others to care for them in a cerebral sense.

Self-punishment is a common form of expression for unhappiness for women. I mention this not to deride male sufferers, indeed, the only male in treatment for anorexia that I have knowledge of is a particularly distressing case. I mention it again for the reason of perspective: something that should be particularly borne in mind when deciding on the allocation of resources for treatment and especially if we are ever to investigate eating disorders from a preventative perspective.

What should we be doing?

My suggestions are made without any pretence to be fully recovered or to having knowledge of budgetary limitations and so on, but they are these:

Full-time nurse cover at specialist NHS clinics to be available as a first port of call for those who have not reached hospitalization weight but who, for whatever reason, find it impossible to go through their GP.
A reappraisal of NHS funding, with more resources being put into outpatient care (this done as a preventative measure to stop border-line cases from becoming potential inpatients).
Feeding programmes should be centred on healthy, well-balanced meals, with an eye to promoting long-term sensible eating habits – for example, no emphasis on high-calorie foods such as take-aways or cakes.
Food re-education programme offered as standard part of treatment.
A move away from traditional 'weigh ins' for patients: this can have a deterrent effect on a patient coming as they may be able to put on the weight but feel too distressed at seeing the scales. It can also cause an unhealthy resentment, especially in anorexia, that the professional is interested only in weight gain and not the healing process as an entirety.
A more flexible approach to individuals: remember each patient is an individual and what may be true for one is not true for another. Professionals must learn to trust the patient's judgement more than they do.
A 24-hour emergency hotline, fully manned, funded as a charity through government aid for those who need instant help or advice. At the moment there is no such facility, and the Eating Disorders Association, though it does its best, is open only during office hours.
Information campaigns to highlight the dangers and long-term effects of eating disorders: there is a need to educate the young that they are

not merely a case of 'I lost weight, I put on weight, end of story'. Perhaps campaigns similar to the 'skin care courtesy of heroin' might be an effective way to hammer this home.

Friends and family

Typical comments from friends were: 'Looking back, it was obvious. I just thought you were becoming very difficult. Got very irate about eating at certain times. I didn't notice at first that you weren't eating but then I wasn't eating with you'; 'It was so exasperating, especially as you used to be so spontaneous and so laid back: you loved cooking and entertaining.'

The more I ask my friends about me with anorexia, the more I am amazed that they are still my friends. I didn't realize how difficult I had become to be with, or how distressing it had become for people to see me, bones and all. My family, I think, felt universal concern and frustration: they so wanted to help but were afraid of doing or saying the wrong thing.

One thing is clear. Family and friends of those with eating disorders face an impossible task: to say anything or not; to take action or not; to be there to help, to offer the tissues through the tears, to put up with the tantrums and then hopefully to readapt to the new, recovered person, who must be different from the old, ill one.

I can speak only from my own experience here. All of the people close to me agree on one thing: it is better to say something than to pretend or ignore a problem.

Personally speaking, I wish people had been franker at the time. In a strange way I was grateful when for the first time someone asked me point blank if I was anorexic. I didn't know whether I was, but I did need to talk. I wish people had told me how distressing it was for them to look at me. The friends that spoke out of their distress are still with me, even though they upset me at the time. Without the help and support of them and my family, I doubt I would have had the courage or determination to continue and I will be eternally grateful for that.

Those that could not handle it, who did and said nothing – and my fiancé was one of these – are no longer a part of my life. Draw your own conclusions from that.

I understand that parents especially may not want to hurt or upset their children while they are obviously so unhappy anyway. But the choice they face is this. If that child is deteriorating, either you say something and maybe it is received well; or maybe you say nothing and maybe that child dies.

Chapter 4
Psychiatric nursing: The no-man's-land between patient and therapist[1]

BEN DAVIDSON

The idea of the collaborative, healing relationship between nurse and patient is, as Joy Bray (1998) put it, 'a cherished idea within psychiatric nursing'. Yet almost inevitably, it seems, patients act out, staff burn out and collaboration and empathy between them subtly drop out of the equation. What does this paradox tell us about the practice of psychiatric or mental health nursing, and what might be the nurse's role in such circumstances?

During my Registered Mental Nurse training, for the first six months I was placed on an inpatient eating disorder unit, immersed in a milieu where I had to try to fathom just such a scenario of acrimonious relationships between staff and patients. I had also to fathom what it was to be a psychiatric or mental health nurse in that situation – indeed, in any situation.

The ward was divided in many ways. On the third floor of a recently built L-shaped block, there was one side for eating disorders (10 patients) and the other side for another speciality service (about 10 patients again), with a few general psychiatry beds on each wing thrown in for good measure. Joe, a 60-year-old man occupying one of the latter beds, suffered from manic-depressive psychosis. At the time I worked with him he was destitute, following a huge spending binge in which he had blown his substantial life savings. He had clearly now swung to a depressive phase. Rather angrily, it always seemed to me, he would defecate where he sat, lay or, on occasion, just where he stood, insisting he could not help it. He made the staff angry, in any event, whatever *his* motivations

[1]Originally published as Davidson B (1998) 'Writing as a tool of reflective practice: sketches and reflections from inside the split milieu of an eating disorders unit', in P Barker, B Davidson (eds) Psychiatric Nursing: Ethical Strife. London: Arnold, pp.190–201.

might have been. If it *was* 'overflow' from chronic constipation, as some argued, he certainly did not make the situation any easier by standing, for example, in the medication queue in his pyjamas and allowing diarrhoea to spill down his leg on to the carpet, aware of the fact but uninterested. Yet I managed at times to find some relief in scraping him down and cleaning him off in the bath (he was too unmotivated and resistant to do it by himself), particularly after an hour-long session supervising the wrangling and antics of the anorexic patients at their meal table.

The 10 of them would sit around the table comparing and disputing the size of their potatoes and the unfairness of their portions, distressed beyond measure at how much butter was spread on their toast, cutting peas into improbably small pieces before forcing themselves laboriously, tortuously (and with considerable 'encouragement'), to swallow each bit. They would hide mashed potato in their trainers and knickers. After an hour's mind-warping effort of this sort of experience, something as earthy as cleaning down Joe could indeed be a relief.

It was an intense entry to psychiatric nursing – in at the deep end.

Although my main interest was in psychodynamic work, I was struck by the importance of having a range of interventions to offer, particularly as many people we looked after were at a dangerously low weight and required quite focused behavioural intervention in relation to their eating patterns. I participated in running the eating programme that formed an essential component of inpatient treatment, supervising meals daily and regularly eating at the table with patients. Twice I helped in 'force-feeding' a patient whose weight was at a dangerously low level. With the luxury of more time, once 'danger periods' were averted, and with help, I saw some patients change the patterns that comprised their 'illness', breaking through maladaptive habits into a greater understanding of their situation, into an experience of new feelings and into an ability to choose different ways of being.

A university lecturer in nursing taught my set one day early on in our course about academic pathways and career development in nursing (Ritter, 1989). The message she conveyed was that research is not distinct from what we do from second to second. It is merely a formalization of the ordinary human process of activity and reflection. We had surely been thrown into momentous experiences wherever we had been placed, she told us, and should try to write about them. By writing we could be reflecting. Regularly, daily, every evening after a shift if possible, reflect and write about what it had been like. Whether or not we felt interested in research, writing in this way could well keep us alive to the experiences we were involved in. All of us who were willing to write would be engaged in reflective practice, the essence of mental health nursing. It was good advice.

This chapter is the product of some such writing. Both in terms of the ideas contained in it, and also in the fact of its existence, it is also one answer to the question posed above: in circumstances where patients act out, staff burn out and collaboration and empathy between them subtly drop out of the equation, what can we learn about the practice of psychiatric or mental health nursing, and what might be the nurse's role?

Jeremy sits moaning and sighing, holding his head, complaining of a migraine as he stares at the mess on the table before him.

11.40am. Evaluation time. The enrolled nurse, Ulrike, is coordinating. She hears a report that Jeremy has vomited again over the dining table and the other patients are complaining. Someone snorts contemptuously and there is laughter. It is agreed that if the vomit is still there after the meeting, someone will offer him support in clearing it up. More contempt is allowed to haemorrhage into the air: for Jeremy, for the idea of giving him support, for the person who suggested it and for the system we all work in; this contempt is left to hang in the air as an animal noise while we leave the staffroom.

Two hours later, Liselle, a patient, interrupts the afternoon shift's planning time to report that Jeremy, still at the table, has again been sick. She is met with a courteous but abrupt response from a staff nurse, Jane, that we are aware of this, but busy at the moment. Liselle makes sure we know she feels something should be done. We let her know we have heard her. She leaves, exasperated, and the planning continues. The extent of our attempt to process Liselle's interruption is limited. It amounts to one of the nursing assistants, Daphne, wondering why Liselle 'don't go and sort something out, instead of bleating to us'.

More laughter.

Putting the most charitable gloss on these events, I privately observe that we probably do not get it across to Liselle that we want it to be an issue for the eating disorder patients to confront together with Jeremy, that they find his behaviour disgusting. But maybe there is no need to underline that; Liselle knows that it is ward policy for 'peer group pressure' to play an important part in treatment. I am a student nurse, anxious this time to understand before criticizing. I don't even know what my role is here, so I say nothing.

'Peer group pressure' seems to mean something like the process of Jeremy's peers making him feel bad for causing them distress and annoyance by his vomiting and other behaviour; accordingly, as Jeremy, like everyone else, needs to belong, to feel acceptance and approval, he will want to change his behaviour. Something as unsophisticated as this, however, seems unlikely to be effective with the inpatients here who are as low in weight as 4 stone and in some cases willing to starve themselves to death. The patients, too, seem unanimous in the view that for members of their group who do not want to eat, this sort of crude pressure is worthless.

I want to find a meaning for 'group pressure' that is a little more convincing if I am to believe that this is the first and foremost treatment of choice. I think about the sort of understanding of group process I am familiar with from my recent introductory course in analytic group psychotherapy.

From this viewpoint, eating disorders may acquire meaning seen against a background of complex intrapsychic, interpersonal and family dynamics (Palazolli, 1974; Crisp, 1980; Lawrence, 1989). For example, there are five patients here in whom it has become clear that there is a great desire to punish, as well as anger towards one or both parents. Where there has been sexual abuse as a child, painful marital breakdown and recriminations, or persistent neglect by alcoholic parents, these feelings are understandable to say the least. There is, at the same time, however, such terror at losing control and expressing this wrath, such unwillingness to look at these feelings (which would after all involve some degree of re-experiencing the traumatic events associated with them), that this anger and desire to punish gets expressed by way of a self-starvation programme.

The sense of control and self-determination afforded by adherence to such a starvation programme also, often enough, figures in an understanding of eating disorders (Duker and Slade, 1988; Moorey, 1991). One young woman on the ward, Madeline, has stated this explicitly in describing how her parents and siblings attempt to control so much of her conduct and her mental world that the only area where she feels she can exercise any autonomy is in her eating.

In group-analytic terms, whatever the specific complexities of these family relationships, the patient's interpersonal patterns of communication, the style of relationships between her and the most significant other people in her life, will sooner or later become manifest in her conduct and in the relationships she forms with others on the ward. This process, with other patients and staff (or indeed with the eating-disorder group as a whole or with the entire ward) having foisted on them a role or roles that the patient more or less unwittingly assigns in recreating her familiar relational world, is known as *transference* (Heimann, 1950; Kreeger, 1987). From this viewpoint it is of the greatest importance to allow, or even better to encourage, relationships between patients to develop. And it is essential that difficult issues such as distaste with another patient's behaviour when he vomits over the dinner table be aired and confronted. The hope is that this will contribute to the manifestation of transference, so that exploration and eventual resolution of the issues(s) underlying the eating disorder may take place in the context of the relationships on the ward.

This, then, I hope, is why Liselle is left, along with the other patients, to confront and deal with Jeremy's inability or unwillingness to keep his food down, even when he knows he will not be allowed to leave the table and must vomit there over his food while the other patients eat their meal and seethe, more or less silently, each in their own misery and isolation: They are developing relationships and allowing conflicts to arise which may eventually provide a basis for the understanding and resolution of whatever issues underlie the eating disorder.

I wonder whether Liselle understands all this. If she does, she may just about be able to see Jeremy's being kept at the table to vomit as some sort of therapeutic agent — compelling her and the other patients to express their emotions and relate (as well as encouraging all of them to give whatever support or censure is necessary to help him stop, thus conditioning Jeremy not to want to vomit). Without such understanding, however, it is impossible to see the same episode as anything other than vindictiveness and insensitivity on the part of the staff. If Liselle and the other patients see it only in this way, presumably they will be less inclined generally to cooperate in their treatment, and less motivated in particular to engage in whatever therapy is available. One needs to feel safe before risking 'opening up' in a therapy situation, and a patient here is not likely to feel safe if she experiences the regime or staff as vindictive and hostile.

Here follows the sum total of formal explanation of the crucial 'relationship-forming' component of the theory behind our 'peer group pressure' approach, given to patients on admission in a general booklet explaining policy on the ward:

> If you should have difficulty in finishing your meals or in eating, we have devised a group therapy approach which relies heavily on peer support and peer pressure to assist you to overcome your problems in a supportive manner. The supervisor's role during mealtimes is to facilitate this process by calling on your fellow patients to support and assist you.

The idea of the staff's role as facilitative of 'fellow patients' [mutual] ... support and assist[ance]' is included, but, as can be seen, only in the context of mealtime protocol, and even then in such a muddy way as to leave the notion of patient interaction and trust and openness in the group as prerequisites for therapy more or less obscure, so obscure in fact, that one may wonder if such issues are understood clearly by staff at all, let alone patients.

At the dinner table Ulrike is arguing again with Jeremy.

'So you're saying that because you've got a migraine you shouldn't have to eat, are you?'

'No, I'm not saying that.'

'And what about the last three days, then. I suppose that's your excuse for not eating then. If we listened to you, you'd never eat.'

'I'm not saying that, Ulrike. I know I have to eat. I'm just saying this migraine makes me feel even more sick. In fact I think it's this food that brought the migraine on.'

'Jeremy, just get on with your food and stop arguing, or am I going to have to feed it to you myself?'

A staff nurse, Clive, is inducting a new student, Emma, on to the ward. This is her obligatory psychiatric placement in the training she is doing as a sick children's nurse. It is evening now, quiet, the bustle of ward rounds and meetings and appointments for patients and staff over for the day. The staff room is relaxed, and while I browse through some patients' files, Clive tries to reassure Emma, who is unsure of her role, scared of mental illness and extremely nervous about meeting any patients. His reassurance is addressed specifically at qualms that may well arise in response to the disturbing events likely to unfold at her first mealtime encounter here:

> They're a manipulative lot, these anorexics. Be careful about trusting your first impressions, you'll see what I mean when you've been here a while. They'll go on about how ill-treated they are, but take no notice. They're wrong. We don't care the way they'd like us to but we care enough to keep them from starving themselves to death, no matter how bloody difficult they are.

Emma has already been told by another student that:

> They're very crafty; they'll take laxatives when you're not looking and make themselves vomit in the toilet, stuff like that. We have to inspect the contents of the bowl before they flush it away with some of them, and they have to ask us before they go to the toilet.

Emma seems reassured. I, too, feel some reassurance but also a considerable degree of unease. I am invited, welcomed into an attitude that forms an important bond among members of staff; there is an impressive cohesiveness within the staff group, and among them in the staffroom I feel a great warmth and security. But this bond and warmth seem intricately linked to, perhaps even founded on, a kind of oppressive suspicion and antagonism towards the patients.

Neither the patients nor the staff, it strikes me, are initiated into the theory of the therapeutic milieu of the ward, and a picture emerges of endless skirmishes and conflict between the two groups, taking place in a void, in the context of which it seems unrealistic to expect the patients to feel safe enough to 'open up', or even comply.

I feel in an unreal space between two worlds, each one trying to shield itself from the insecurity caused by a hostile 'them' in a sense of 'us'. The patients are undoubtedly manipulative. Presumably, like most people, they try to get what they want through devious means, subtly controlling, manipulating others' responses rather than asking straightforwardly. No doubt people who starve themselves to get a need or needs met could reasonably be said to be more manipulative than others, even if their conduct is 'the reasonable upshot of their life history' (Smail, 1987). But in *our* intense preoccupation with '*their* manipulativeness' I wonder just what else is going on. Why do nurses so want this aspect of patients' characters to be highlighted? Why does 'manipulativeness' need to be understood as a defining characteristic of anorexic psychopathology? And why does such an understanding form an intrinsic part of induction for new staff on the ward, to the extent even that an injunction is subtly made in the name of self-preservation to put aside all other perceptions? Why is there such neglect of the theory underlying this group psychodynamic approach, such lack of attention to the facilitation of patient-group cohesion, and such an obvious absence of a forum for the safe airing of feelings in staff brought up by the patients. The patients are sometimes and in some degree manipulative, no doubt, but equally, the staff are sometimes and in some degree angry and unsupportive to the people on the ward, particularly to those patients least in charge of their eating patterns and presenting the greatest management problems, as above. No one is perfect!

A short time on, after an evening meal, I help Jeremy clear the vomit from the table, restricting myself as much as possible to advice on strategic issues such as where the Dettol is kept, how to negotiate the doorway with a heavy bowl of water and when enough Dettol has been administered so that the table can be rinsed and dried. With such support, Jeremy manages to clear the mess without too much fuss and in reasonably good part. However, I am left somewhat jangled. Jeremy seemed in misery and I felt sorry for him. I was not very harsh with Jeremy, and even spoke to him in quite a kindly way. Have I thus exposed myself to staff and patients as too sympathetic and not sufficiently dispassionate to provide the firm boundaries necessary to become part of the team and to get these people better? Should I have shouted and bullied, just a little? Will I now be seen merely as a walkover and become a soft target for *manipulation*?

Two months later, 1.15pm, an argument rages around the dinner table. This time, though, it is between me and the anorexic patients.

'Oh c'mon, you two. Do stop playing with your food. What's the matter now?'

The words are barked from the comfort of some newfound confidence after learning that I can manage a group situation without anarchy breaking out. I have run the psychodrama group on my own that morning never having done it before, standing in for the qualified nurse who is on leave, and I managed to get everyone participating in some trust-building exercises and role-plays recently learnt in school. It went well and I feel strong.

'Well don't look so shocked. Tell me what's going on. What's the problem?' Irritation spills out. I do not want to be supervising the meal.

The two girls who are making games, one of mashing up her sponge pudding with the custard and the other of chasing it around her plate, do not know quite how to react. The sad-looking girl, Sally, who has occasional moments of quite astonishing fury, unleashes some of it in their defence:

'If you had to eat this mess like us, you wouldn't be so bloody smug.'

I am somewhat taken aback. I wonder whether she sported the same snarl just before she stabbed her mother with a pair of scissors. Normally such a forceful reaction would scare me, but, unusually, this time I do not much care. I have taken the plunge and may as well now start swimming.

'Oh do stop complaining and get on with it. It's not that bad,' I retort, unabashed.

Liselle is as sharp as ever: 'I suppose you're going to say that because we are anorexics our perceptions are distorted, are you, and really it's hot although we all think it's stone bloody cold.'

'I'm not going to say that, no ...'

'Oh, yes, lovely this is,' says Sally. 'I suppose Amanda's is really appetizing too.'

Everyone laughs and Amanda must feel the heat of it. She is faced with a plate of liquidized green mush, probably cold, and probably no easier for her to eat than the fish, potatoes and peas it used to be before someone got impatient with her complaints about being unable to swallow, and put it through the food blender. I feel a pang of protectiveness towards Amanda, who is currently beyond anyone's help, psychotic perhaps, and does not need, I feel, to be caught in this crossfire. It becomes obvious it is more than crossfire though, when Nigel makes some reference to green cowpats, and the uproar continues. Very little guilt seems to be around, although Amanda's nose is really being rubbed in it; the patients are as angry with her as the staff, it seems, just as they used to be with Jeremy before his discharge. It is some time before the baying and cackling abates. I feel the hurt dam up inside Amanda and wonder that her frailty can withstand it. 'Harvey's Bristol Cream,' she whimpers, unintelligibly, and I hear them laugh all the more. Take me on you idiots, not Amanda, I want to tell them.

I become placatory. 'If you say it's cold, you're probably right. I'm not going to argue.' Then, not wanting to seem too conciliatory, I quickly add 'So all right, it's cold. So what?'

'Would you eat it?'

'I've just had some. It wasn't brilliant but it was edible.'

'I suppose our perceptions are distorted if ...'

'Liselle, if you are going to say it's cold, no, I don't expect your perceptions are distorted. But if you say it's a cowpat then I think they are definitely distorted, deranged even. There's a difference between it not being very nice and it being inedible. Why don't you stop going on and eat the bloody stuff.'

Scott's plate is suddenly empty. He looks at me menacingly, defying me to challenge him, ready to protect Liselle's honour.

Two courses and a further 90 minutes on, Sally is still there, and wants blood: 'You've changed, just like the rest of them. You weren't like this when you started. Now you're bossing us around just like Malcolm and Sue. I think something must come over you, like you become power mad.'

Where can I go? Sally, the only reason I would be eating as much as you have to three times a day would be if I were anorexic, and if I was I don't know what I would feel. But I'm not. And unfortunately you are. But somehow I'm in it with you and someone is paying me a pittance to get you out of it and I am scared to see that I don't really know how to but I will try to love you and see it through together with you.... I do not say this though. I've gone in far enough for now. I try to show I have had enough.

I shake my head as it rests in my hands, elbows on the table. I imagine how I look and recognize the posture Jeremy used to adopt. 'Do stop this. I've said I'm not questioning your perceptions. The food may not be particularly nice. But it is edible. Eat it.'

'OK, you've had one portion now, but if you had to eat it three times a day with snacks in between, you'd be complaining just as much as we do.'

Sally is a 19-year-old girl having a tantrum, her fury unleashed is precise and powerful and she rattles me. I retreat into a defensive retaliation and, putting on my pedantic tone, begin: 'Sally, does it occur to you ...' Then I decide to open the field again and go for safety with a brash attack on them all: '... do any of you wonder whether it might not be you who have changed towards me?' After a moment's silence I soften my tone. 'Because it seems like this is the first time you've had a go at me personally for something to do with your food. The eating regime is obviously giving you a hard time, and these cock-ups the catering department keeps making must be infuriating. What was it the other day?

Jacket potatoes with lentil filling and boiled potatoes to go with them? I'd be going mad. But today is the first time since I've been here that you have given *me* a lot of shit because of it, directed at me personally. I'm sorry if my attitude seems to have changed but I don't see why I should have to put up with a lot of shit when it's not my fault.'

Which, of course, is partly not true, as it was me who drew the fire in the first place by being unusually brusque and petulant with Madeline and Jo who were playing with their food. This is not lost on Sally, who no doubt senses some mendacity afoot, and directs a parting shot my way.

'Oh let's just drop it, Ben. If I carry on you'd probably only go and tell Malcolm anyway, and then we'd all be in trouble. Just drop it.'

Not just caught in an unreal space between two worlds but wanting to be accepted and esteemed in both of these two camps engaged in the open hostilities described above, I am aware that I *have* changed. Two months back I would have held my counsel and bargained for everyone's approval, terrified of losing esteem or doing harm. Now I am willing to be drawn into these skirmishes and feel I have some grasp of what is happening. I try fumblingly to facilitate some willingness in the group to open up and talk, on this occasion, admittedly, more about food, but also about my relationship with the group. I am also drawing their anger and then showing I can withstand it. (If *I* cannot, then how can they be expected to trust in the safety of the group sufficiently to let out their feelings about each other?) I am modelling a willingness to engage in intense interactions in the group and survive. I am trying at some level to enhance group cohesiveness.

The theory goes like this: the more risk-taking is modelled and endorsed by the facilitator as a group norm, the more people engage in it in order to enhance their esteem and to belong. The more risks group members take in self-disclosure, the greater the esteem in which they are held. And the greater the ensuing mutual esteem in the group, the greater the cohesion. Yalom (1985) defines cohesiveness as 'the attractiveness of a group for its members' or 'the attraction that members have for their group and for the other members'. He says that:

> cohesiveness is a widely researched basic property in [successful] groups ... In general there is agreement that ... Group cohesiveness is not per se a therapeutic factor but is instead a necessary precondition for effective therapy, [and like] an ideal therapist—patient relationship [in individual therapy, it] creates conditions in which the necessary self-disclosure and intra-personal and interpersonal exploration may unfold. (Yalom, 1985: 49–50)

The cohesiveness which Yalom describes as a necessary precondition for effective therapy is in no small measure, in an inpatient group such as this, a function of the staff's willingness to disclose themselves and interact, as well as patients'. Indeed, perhaps the staff's input here is *more* important as their role is in large part that of role model; the limits they set for themselves are also the boundaries described for the patients in their eating and their interactions.

This highlights how nurses are in an odd no-man's land between patient and therapist. Although staff enforcing the rigid eating regime on the ward are caught up in the interpersonal dramas being re-enacted and inevitably become participants to some extent, they clearly need to be some steps back from complete patient involvement in the group. And yet not quite so far back that they adopt the role of therapist. Maybe the ideal role nurses can adopt is that of 'facilitator of group cohesion' as a sort of preparatory step towards the work which a therapist might facilitate in more formal sessions. This work (at least to the extent that it takes place within the inpatient twice-weekly group therapy sessions) is mentioned a little more explicitly in the ward brochure:

> The group aims ... to confront issues ... which are contributing [to] and perpetuating your eating disorder in order that positive change may take place ... The overall aim of the group is to provide a safe environment for you to explore ... your behaviour in a way that meaning can emerge.

And, of course, 'a safe environment' in this context has to mean, if it is anything more than an empty cliché, an environment in which patients really do feel safe enough to disclose and explore their condition. Presumably an environment which patients experience as one where they are bullied and hectored by uncaring staff does not apply.

It should be emphasized that patients do not generally object to firm handling per se. Out of some six patients whom I have heard complain at one time or another, all have confirmed that their treatment by the charge nurse Malcolm, whose reputation for noisy harangues is renowned, is not what they are referring to. All six have intimated this clearly, stating that his treatment of them is 'reassuring', 'it comes through that he cares', 'it doesn't feel like he's shouting for the sake of it', and, perhaps most significantly, 'it's different with him because you feel he knows what he is doing', which apparently he does, being the only figure on the ward with experience of analytic psychotherapy and training. One is left with the suspicion that the patients' objection is to the sort of 'firm handling' characterized earlier in this chapter as being based around an antagonism towards them, which emerges as the only thing the staff group can use as a focus for their own need for group cohesion and support. And as suggested above, this may be in large measure a result of the absence of any proper dissemination of the ward philosophy from ward manager level, around which staff cohesion could more usefully develop, and the spelling out of such a philosophy in terms of specific roles and functions for nurses.

It strikes me now how easy it is to be swamped and influenced by the culture of a place and by one's own inertia, resistance and bad faith, however much one would like it to be otherwise. My account above reflects some of my preoccupations over the six months in which I worked on the eating disorder unit, focusing mainly on group considerations, staff–patient dynamics and the procedures and structures of the ward. I may have avoided in this account the worst excesses of pathologizing patients with whom I worked, but I have nevertheless also avoided introducing any of them as people in the context of the distressing life stories they told. The final product centres, egoistically, on my recounting the story of my placement. As such, it is not just the culture of the ward or the permanent staff group that seems to have lost its empathic, collaborative heart, but myself too. I now wish to correct this imbalance.

While working on the inpatient unit I participated fortnightly in live, group supervision of a family therapist who would be seeing an eating disorder patient and their family for up to four sessions. Perhaps a good example of what is missing above is the material that came out of the family therapy sessions with patients, for example the sessions where the therapist saw Jeremy, his father and aunt.

Jeremy was 13, the youngest patient on the ward, transferred there after little improvement during his three-month stay on a child and adolescent unit. His mother was recently deceased and his father was fast becoming an alcoholic. Prior to being admitted, Jeremy had had on occasion to look after his father, getting him to bed when he passed out from drinking too much. He had had to shop, prepare meals and the like. He did not want to go back to boarding school, where he was bullied, but, equally, the situation at home must have been intolerable.

None of this was discussed in the patient group, either during formal therapy sessions or elsewhere. His eating patterns were so extreme that it was hard to focus on anything but Jeremy and his weight and his food and his vomit. What emerged dramatically during family therapy was that Jeremy had not been able to grieve properly for his mother, partly due to family taboo and partly because his role had changed in relation to his father from child to parent, as a result of his father's incapacity through drink. When the supervision group got the therapist to pass over the family's preoccupation with Jeremy's eating and push against their resistance to discussing the loss of Jeremy's mother, a well of blocked emotion was 'thrown up', both by Jeremy and the others in the family group (considerable emotion was also expressed in the supervision group), and progress began to be made. Jeremy subsequently stopped being sick, gained weight and was discharged to his aunt's care, while his father accepted treatment for his alcohol dependency.

Madeline's family therapy sessions with her domineering brothers and father were also revealing. The supervision group had at one point to help the therapist withdraw from conflict with the men of the family, who were speaking for Madeline. The therapist himself, although endorsing ideas that we knew Madeline held, had been drawn into doing exactly what the other men were doing, speaking for her rather than allowing Madeline to speak for herself. In discussion between Madeline and her primary nurse after the session, it transpired that the men's dominance included unwanted sexual attentions. Madeline could not finally bring herself to tell the whole family that her brother had raped her. However, the fact that she had told *someone* and the threat she made subsequently to her brother that she *would* tell the whole family, including her father, if anything like it should ever happen again, seemed sufficient for her to gain the sense of control of her destiny that she had previously said was missing in her life except in relation to food. Our intuition that she would not relapse proved correct.

Scott's family dynamics, similarly, were revealing. The family meetings were attended by his mother, two aunts, sister and grandmother, all of whom, like many of us in the staff group, were influenced by this attractive 15-year-old boy's charm. The subject it seemed hard to discuss was his delinquency. Talk of his forthcoming court case on charges including aggravated burglary, talk also of its implications, was persistently pushed aside out of greater concern for his illness. The only contact from his absent father was when word reached him of an intervention from the nurse Clive. The father stormed on to the ward threatening physical violence if ever again anyone suggested that his boy needed parental disciplining. The picture we were given of family dynamics could not have been clearer. Discipline and control of Scott and criticism of the men of the family in general were taboo, while an idealizing, doting love for him was powerfully endorsed. Attempting to restore some balance to this equation without jeopardizing our relationship with him, we subsequently focused a lot in work with Scott on *the court*'s likely use of its authority to 'discipline' him if he did not behave in a way that allowed us to report cooperation and progress, as we very much wanted to. We were surprised at how quickly Scott's eating disorder abated.

And what of the others? The 21-year-old Liselle's story remained unfathomed. Her parents' relationship never improved but her father's 'terminal' cancer went into remission. Liselle's forlorn devotion to him turned to anger when he announced that he was moving to the Far East with his new mistress. This turn of events, particularly Liselle's expression of hostility towards her father, seemed promising, but she had had numerous admissions before this one and it was felt, rightly, that there would be many more. Although many interesting facets of Liselle's relationships with significant others came to light, and possible links between these relationships and her eating disorder suggested themselves, we never quite found the key.

Amanda was in her mid-50s. She came out of her psychotic state to some extent, but remained depressed and unmotivated to eat, eventually being transferred to a general psychiatric ward.

Sally went back to live with her mother in the Midlands. She had not gained much weight and, particularly as sexual abuse had been disclosed, it was felt that insufficient exploration or resolution of her distress had taken place. Somewhat to our surprise, none the less, we heard of no further eating problems. She even came to visit the ward with a present of chocolates, which she shared, when she attended a follow-up group.

Nigel never really gained weight sufficiently, but managed to convince everyone he would be all right out of hospital. Like Sally, he too had been a voluntary patient. The following year he relapsed to a dangerous degree, finally admitting when he reached $4^{1}/_{2}$ stone that he was out of control. He asked for readmission. There were no beds. He died. As did the 32-year-old patient I helped to force feed, who had for some time in the months before admission driven around the area in her car looking like a wraith and frightening passers-by who happened to look in the window.

I planned to 'restore balance' to this paper by offering an empathic, collaborative account of patients' experiences. However, in the past few paragraphs I have again told as much of the story of our work with patients as I have of their own stories. And in rereading my description of Angela as a wraith, frightening passers-by, I recall the callous caricature of her final months that was circulating the ward a while after I worked there. Yet she had died. Perhaps callousness is inevitable in response to such relentless misery and distress. It is painful to stay with the experience of pain, perhaps ultimately even more so when it is someone else's. I suppose this explains a range of phenomena. It explains staff's need to take a distant, hostile, 'us and them' stance *vis-à-vis* patients, such as in the situation described above. It explains the tendency to move away from the raw experience of a situation into abstractions regarding structure and philosophy, as to some extent in my writing. It is certainly a strange experience for me now, eight years on, to be recovering memories of my contact with such a disturbed group of people in such awful states of distress. And then I recall how my own eating, as well as drinking and sleeping patterns, went haywire during this placement. I recall how patients' experience paralleled distress I was going through in my own life.

But that is another story, which, although inextricably interwoven with the above account, is outside the scope of this chapter. The question with which I opened this account, and to which, in conclusion, I now return, concerns the sort of circumstances detailed above, where patients act out, staff burn out and collaboration and empathy between them drop out of the equation. I asked what, in these circumstances, can we learn about the practice of psychiatric or mental health nursing, and what might be the nurse's role?

To summarize the above, it seems to me that as practitioners in any particular discipline we can attend to the counter-transference. Through reflection and writing we can struggle to get an authentic emotional take, and a conceptual grip on the situation. With a leap of faith we can open ourselves to honestly experiencing what is going on in our relationships. Even if the resultant understanding and experience is partial, it should yield a point of leverage where something that we can *do* is revealed. And if what we do turns out not to have the desired result, then at least we have new information with which to enhance our experience and aid further reflection. In the above account a useful role suggested itself to me increasingly, the more I struggled to understand what was going wrong on the ward to cause the antagonism between staff and patients. As mental health or psychiatric nurses, we may find ourselves often in the sort of situation described, where we are occupying a space, or a bridge, between patient and therapist. As far as possible in the above account I tried to make a difference using this space as a point of leverage. Such a role was, arguably (Davidson, 1992), little different to the role psychiatric nurses should adopt anyway: helping people and groups to communicate their experience, in the context of an authentic, honest relationship.

When we find that in our own relationships with patients collaboration and empathy are largely absent, then I guess we can at least be honest about that. The influence one has on others is in any event marginal, and the only small corner of the universe over which one has control is one's own being (Huxley, 1946). If, as I have tried to show, we can at least struggle to maintain an honest, authentic relationship with ourselves through reflection on and writing about our experience, then this in itself may make a positive difference to our approach and to the outcome of any intervention we make. We will have shown at least that we can communicate *our own* experience, as psychiatric nurses or otherwise, and perhaps others will follow suit.

Chapter 5
Reoccupying the preoccupied: Occupational therapy for sufferers of eating disorders

Laura C. Lock

People with eating disorders are indeed preoccupied. They are preoccupied in their thoughts, in their emotions and in their deeds. While other clinicians pay much attention to the emotional needs of eating disorder sufferers, the occupational therapist focuses on the sufferers' 'deeds'. Their occupational and social behaviour is the field of action (Breines, 1995).

The goal of this chapter is to explain what the occupational therapist does in the course of rehabilitating eating disorder sufferers in an in/day-patient setting, and how they do it. It will strive to expand on the underpinning approach and provide practical interventional detail. It will also meander down memory lane to put some flesh on the theoretical bones.

The occupational therapist's focus

The occupational therapist looks at what the individual is doing (or not doing), and how this impacts on their lives. She or he enables sufferers to acquire the skills they need to function effectively, free from the domination of their overwhelming preoccupation. The aim is, in essence, to 'reoccupy' them with lifestyles that provide more healthy ways of meeting their emotional needs, and to provide opportunities for sufferers to gain insight into personal obstacles that may prevent them from achieving such lifestyles (Harries, 1992; Giles, 1985).

To understand this process in more detail, let us first define exactly what occupational therapy is, and then look at some of the typical 'occupational' problems that arise.

Definition of occupational therapy

'Occupational therapy' is activity-based treatment designed to promote an individual's ability to function at home, work, leisure and in the community. It uses life-skill training, insight generating and social interventions and involves practical/experiential, psychoeducational, creative and recreational activities. It is action-orientated, aiming for action-orientated outcomes.

Typical occupational and social performance problems

(a) Bulimia nervosa

Here is Cheryl's account of an average day before treatment. Cheryl is 33 and has been bulimic since she was 19 years old. She weighs 60.8 kg (9 st 8 lb) and has a height of 169 cm (5 ft 7 in). Her BMI (Body Mass Index) is 21.3. Cheryl has additional impulsive features of self-harm, stealing, and drug and alcohol misuse.

> I would wake at 8.15am in time to see the last of my flatmates leave for work. I would have a coffee and four bowls of Frosties, then immediately vomit these. If my flatmates had left any food in the fridge I would polish this off in the same fashion.
>
> After 45 minutes in front of an aerobics video, I would begin my day.
>
> Having lost my job six months ago I had time to kill. My dad got me this latest job as a legal secretary but I struggled to cope with the pressure. My previous hospital admissions made people treat me with kid gloves, but it didn't stop them taking advantage of me. They gave me all the dogsbody typing – I was often there till 8.30pm finishing it. I got the sack after I exploded at my boss. This is the third time I've lost a job like this. I've tried working in a bank, as a holiday rep, advertising, journalism, I've even done some modelling but it has always ended in disaster. I start well and manage to impress them for a while but end up coming in late, going 'off sick' or just not turning up. I end up out of control – bingeing, taking drugs, anything to cope. Anyway, I never wanted to be a secretary. The trouble is I don't know what I want to do, or what I can do. I'm OK at interviews but I've never held down a job longer than six months.
>
> I would walk the familiar three miles to the swimming baths for a couple of hours in the pool. I wouldn't stop below 100 lengths.
>
> On the way home I'd visit the supermarket (one of three I frequented in rotation) and would buy the day's supplies. Today it would be two French loaves, a pizza, six cream cakes, three chocolate multi-packs, an Arctic roll, two tubs of ice-cream, a packet of Frosties and replacements for what I'd stolen from the fridge. This was by no means excessive as I knew I would most likely visit another shop this evening. After I got home I would binge on the food I'd bought, vomiting usually four times throughout the two-hour long episode, finishing off with half a bottle of wine.
>
> Later I would walk two miles to town to go round the shops. I would usually find at least one or two things to add to my wardrobe.
>
> I actually have three wardrobes: one for size 8/10 clothes, one for size 12/14 and one for 14/16. I was currently in the middle wardrobe: hence the

insatiable drive to exercise and diet. I can only feel confident in size 8/10 clothes, but I can't seem to stay at this weight for very long.

I'd already spent about £50 today, which would be added to my credit card debts. These come to £8500, which I am now paying off monthly after they threatened to take me to court. A year ago the only way I stopped myself buying clothes was to steal them. But I got caught so I had to stop. Anyway, I was getting addicted to stealing too.

I'll do anything that makes me feel good: binge, buy clothes, exercise, steal, drink, take drugs, and when I'm really desperate cut myself. I usually do this on my stomach where no one else can see the scars.

After my shopping spree I would walk home again and eat a salad for tea with one of my flatmates.

I would pop round to the local garage for some more supplies for the 7pm binge; usually junk food and Coke. I would then go down the pub with my friend to get suitably merry before hitting the club scene. I wouldn't go out if I didn't have at least four Bacardis inside me. I don't have a boyfriend at the moment, but when I do the bingeing gets even worse. At the club I'd usually dance and drink and do a bit of 'E' till 2am. My favourite way to end the day would be a bar of dark chocolate and what's left of the wine, which I would keep in my stomach to help me sleep.

Cheryl's account vividly reflects the extent of her preoccupation. It demonstrates some aspects of the 'occupational chaos' people suffering from bulimia nervosa get into.

To summarize:

- chaotic eating patterns – ritualistic time and mood triggered binge/purge routines
- excessive compulsive exercise – her present main occupational pursuit other than shopping
- interrupted employment history – unrealized achievement potential
- limited leisure pursuits – pubs and clubs which she can function in only if intoxicated
- non-existent budgeting skills – financial problems
- relationship difficulties – swings between passive and aggressive communication and struggles in managing her anger
- anxiety reactions in social situations.

(b) Anorexia nervosa

The anorexic's typical day is equally 'dysfunctional'.

Here is Teresa's day before treatment when her weight was 37.9 kg (5 st 13 lb), her height being 160 cm (5 ft 3 in). Her BMI was 14.8, and she has been anorexic for 15 years, since she was 12. She has been admitted to various hospitals on several occasions, twice needing to be tube fed when her weight was critically low. She has never worked and still lives with her parents. She was given a 'target' (recovery) weight of 52.2 kg (8 st 3 lb):

4am	Wake up. Smoke. Try to get back to sleep.
8am	Get washed and dressed. Drink black coffee.
9am	Exercise.
10am	Clean house.
1pm	Lunch: two tomatoes and a carrot.
2pm	Watch TV/write letters/go for a walk.
5pm	Have bath.
6pm	Supper: lettuce, carrot, tomato and celery.
7pm	Watch TV/sew.
9pm	Go to bed exhausted.

Karen's functional difficulties can be summarized as:

• severely restrictive eating habits – phobic reactions to all food other than vegetables
• negligible independent living skills – has never lived away from parents' home
• dysfunctional domestic skills – obsessionally hygienic, financially dependent on parents
• negligible employment history – only has experience of voluntary work at a library
• negligible involvement in leisure pursuits – main hobbies are sewing and TV
• dysfunctional 'community' skills – phobic of certain shops and public transport
• extremely limited social network – has only one 'pen friend'
• limited social skills – totally unassertive, conflict avoidant, severely shy.

The above accounts demonstrate the diverse spectrum of functional difficulties that eating disorder sufferers endure. Even the way they express themselves in these accounts reflects the 'out of control' chaos of the impulsive bulimic and the 'over-controlled' vacuum of the restrictive anorexic.

These patterns of behaviour have evolved to provide short-term solutions; ways of coping with negative or painful emotions fuelled by what they think or believe. These habits have become entrenched, self-reinforcing and are totally preoccupying. All such habits are extremely hard to kick.

The occupational therapist proposes that helping someone overcome their eating-disordered habit is not just a matter of getting them to 'give up something' but to 'take up something'. A large part of getting rid of bad habits is essentially about acquiring good habits. This is the occupational therapist's therapeutic function. Ideally this should happen at the same time as they receive help for their underlying internal dilemmas and emotional problems.

Talking of habits of a different sort, I recall the story of a convent novice. This northern woman had suffered from binge-eating disorder for years and was able to break free of its hold only by a complete change of lifestyle: she became a nun. The Mother Superior was surprised to find an entry in the new nun's spiritual journal that read: 'O Lord, at last I am Thin'. She gently pointed out that perhaps an 'e' was missing. Later she was even more surprised to read the corrected entry as: 'Ee, O Lord, at last I am Thin'.

While this story comes from an occupational therapist's joke book rather than a textbook, the principle of cure through change of lifestyle remains. In saying this, I am not in any way discounting the need to address and resolve inner emotional conflicts via psychotherapeutic interventions, but this alone does not guarantee enduring behavioural change. Both 'roots' and 'shoots' require attention. The reorganized lifestyle must be both internal and external. It must involve both perception and action.

In my experience, there often seems to be an under-emphasis on what the sufferer is actually *doing*. This is all the more surprising as it is the simplest measure of how far the individual is cured.

It is also important to note that this sort of therapeutic intervention is not the most popular with the patient. Getting the patient to *do* what will help them out of their eating disorder (for example, eating three meals a day, getting a suitable job or a hobby and so on) is very hard work. It is where the proverbial rubber hits the road. Because of this the severely regressed under-functioning anorexic may regard the occupational therapist as an 'occupational terrorist', whereas the 'I can do everything' bulimic often sees her as an 'occupational hazard'. Most patients lap up the opportunity to explore their innermost feelings, intensely painful though it may be, while they drag their heels to the occupational therapy kitchen.

But it is in the metaphorical 'occupational therapy kitchen' that true behavioural change can be made. Here together we 'cook up' lifestyles that help sufferers reach their full potential in life. Thus we help them to ascend the lofty heights of Maslow's hierarchy. We also strive to help them experience that just as it is true that what you think and feel affects what you do, it is also true that what you do affects how you feel and think.

The occupational therapist teaches them *what* they need to do to escape and avoid their eating disorder and *how* to do it.

I hear a number of non-directive die-hards among you gasp with horror at this potentially 'prescriptive' minefield. Let me reassure you: the occupational therapist offers the recipe while the individual chooses their personal 'ingredients'.

Let me demonstrate this in practice. At Springfield Hospital (SPH), where the St George's Eating Disorders in- and day-patient treatment service resides, the occupational therapy programme includes a therapeutic group called Relapse Prevention. In this group we use an acronym as a teaching tool to help patients memorize essential directives that will assist them to stay 'behaviour free'. Each letter stands for one of six directives – the 'recipe' for successful relapse prevention. The word is PLEASE:

P PLAN your time and meals
L LOOK OUT for 'triggers' (see glossary)
E EAT three meals a day, one cooked
A ASSERT your needs
S SEEK support
E EXPRESS your feelings.

In the group the patient is encouraged to choose her own 'ingredients' for the particular lifestyle change she requires. (I will describe this group in more detail later.)

Relapse prevention provides a good overview of the occupational therapist's main areas of attention in rehabilitating the eating disordered sufferer. The occupational therapist focuses on:

how effectively they feed themselves (food management skills)
how effectively they occupy themselves (occupational skills)
how effectively they manage themselves (intrapersonal skills)
how effectively they relate to others (interpersonal skills).

In a nutshell, the focus is on 'occupational and social performance'. This is an individual's ability to function in the tasks and roles needed for everyday living; the occupational therapist's bread and butter.

Already some common problems have been identified in Cheryl and Teresa's routines. Most patients present somewhere along a sliding scale between two polar extremes in their functional skills. Let's now take a look at how the occupational therapist does what they do.

Methods of intervention by the occupational therapist

The occupational therapist at AMH identifies specific occupational and social difficulties through an individual assessment interview. They identify the patient's perception of their domestic, self-care, intrapersonal, occupational and social skills. They ask the patient to complete a questionnaire on social anxiety and gain a detailed analysis of the individual's occupational routines. In the groups their abilities and motivation to participate are observed. It is important at the outset to define the problem accurately:

- Is it a performance difficulty? (That is, has the patient ever learnt the skill – or learnt it and lost it – and hence needs teaching?)
- Is it a 'habituation deficit'? Is the patient unable to make and sustain behavioural routines that incorporate differing social roles? – if so, they need training and practice.
- Is it a motivational problem? Is the patient able to perform the skill but simply doesn't want to? If it is fear that demotivates them, then exposure to the situation with support is what they need. If it is subconscious (or conscious) refusal then behavioural sanctions may be needed to assist motivation.

The occupational therapist works cooperatively with the individual at all times.

Therapeutic model

The treatment model that underpins the occupational therapy within St George's Eating Disorders service is Kielhofner's (1980) 'Model of Human Occupation'. This has both cognitive and behavioural components and also a systemic approach (De Silva, 1995; Martin, 1990). The basic foundation stone to the model is that everyone lives to achieve; to master their environment in all they do. It suggests that we all have an inner drive to reach our full potential and live purposeful interdependent lives. The model proposes that we need motivational, habituational and performance skills to function effectively, motivation being at the top of the hierarchy. Hence, the occupational therapist first identifies the area of 'occupational dysfunction' and then the skill deficit to work out how best to treat the individual.

The occupational therapist also identifies past or present occupational strengths that may be used to mobilize the individual in treatment. If the individual is motivated and able to organize their routines effectively but has a performance difficulty (for example, has never learnt to cook), the occupational therapist has the relatively simple task of teaching them and providing them with the opportunity to practise. The task becomes more complex when the problems are motivational, as they nearly always are with sufferers of eating disorders. It is then vital to explore the lack of motivation and to provide exposure to required behaviours. This helps to enhance motivation and overcome anxieties. The single most important ability required by the anorexic or bulimic is the motivation to eat a normal diet that enables them to maintain a normal body weight.

Treatment plan

After the occupational therapist has assessed the individual, he or she will discuss identified difficulties and strengths with them and formulate an agreed treatment plan. This is composed of both individual and group work. There are three treatment phases within the Adult treatment programme; an inpatient, a day-patient and an outpatient phase. Occupational therapy interventions are most intensive towards the end of the inpatient phase and throughout the day-patient phase. This reflects the need to gradually give back control to the patient and equip them for their new 'reoccupied' lifestyle.

Individual interventions

Every assessment is documented and includes a summary of the patient's functional strengths and difficulties. Specific goals are devised (with the patient) to help them function effectively and a plan to achieve these goals is then designed.

The occupational therapist sees the patient individually a minimum of four times: at assessment, before becoming a day patient, after becoming a day patient and before discharge to the outpatient phase.

Most patients require more individual sessions than the minimum and many need to be seen fortnightly or even weekly throughout the day-patient phase. Individual sessions always include 'lifestyle' planning: helping the patient to formulate a healthy balance of occupational activity. This will incorporate 'work' (paid or voluntary work, study, or any daytime activity), leisure, domestic, 'community' (shops, banks, transport), and 'support' activities. Patients are often at one or other end of the occupational spectrum; either filling every second of the day and night with frenetic activity or living like a hermit rarely stepping out of their home.

Other interventions range from making a weekly budget plan to how to enrol in adult education classes. One patient got a temporary position in the hospital shop to help overcome her fear of handling money. A student horticulturist got a voluntary job in the local ornamental gardens to give her work experience and increase her confidence. New leisure activities have ranged from Russian to rock climbing.

The choice of what to do and when to do it is crucial in ensuring the optimum recovery circumstances. Patients need a well-structured, stimulating (but not over-stimulating) and supportive lifestyle. The occupational therapist pays much attention to trying to get this balance right. But it is easier to lead the horse to water than to get it to drink.

The St George's Eating Disorder Treatment programme emphasizes expressing feelings through words not actions. For sufferers to be successfully rehabilitated, they need to find people in their lifestyle environment to whom they can express their feelings. Hence, it is all the more important to get the patient functioning in everyday social arenas. Ideally, they need people in their lives who will be supportive who are not all professional carers. They need to be with people who eat normally. It is also vital to get them linked into self-help support groups such as the Eating Disorders Association (EDA).

The occupational therapy groups are all designed to assist the individual to acquire and practise relevant skills, and to motivate them to use these skills. The more insight-oriented activities achieve this in a less direct manner and function in particular to assist motivation through greater self-awareness.

Therapeutic groups

The occupational therapy groups provided for adults are as follows: meal cookery; communication skills; assertion and anger management; relapse prevention; living skills; stress management; relaxation; projective art; and body image group.

Meal cookery

To help eating disorder sufferers recover, the first goal is to get them to eat a healthy diet that ensures weight maintenance. Three meals a day are prescribed, in many ways like 'medicine'. One of these has to be cooked (for both physiological and psychological reasons). Desserts are essential and are usually prescribed as three 'light' (under 250 calories) and four 'regular' per week, or vice versa depending on build.

The group aim is to motivate and equip individuals with the skills needed to prepare cooked meals that enable them to *maintain their weight*.

Objectives

(a) To overcome anxieties or difficulties in any of the following:

basic cookery techniques
using recipes
serving portions
eating with others
throwing food away
eating out in restaurants or pubs
eating 'high-risk' or anxiety-provoking food.

(b) To assist with any specific goals related to effective food management.

Method

Patients plan their meals to cook individually or as a group. They then shop for the ingredients and then cook and eat in groups no larger than four.

They have a 'menu' of different focuses for each session, each of which must be attempted at least once during their time in the group. These are:

basic cookery skills
cooking for one
low-budget cookery
eating high-risk foods
eating out.

Every meal must be planned in advance and be appropriate to the individual's income.

Motivating young women to cook for themselves can be an uphill battle. Cooking is often regarded as an alien concept, hence the importance of making this 'culturally' relevant. If the individual is not prepared to slave for hours over a hot stove (and just who is?) then heating up ready-made meals is fine. But each meal must contain the four essential components of protein, vegetables, carbohydrates and fat *in the right quantities* to ensure weight maintenance. This is worked out by portion size weights as set out by the dietitian in a booklet. In the early stages of recovery patients need to use these 'meal equivalent' measures religiously, as they are unable to guess accurate portion sizes by sight alone.

Of course, there is no magic cure in getting patients to eat cooked meals. But cooked meals do provide a number of curative factors. They usually contain the four basic components already mentioned to satisfy them physiologically. Each meal must include a dessert. This is both to ensure adequate calorific intake and, more importantly, to provide structured opportunities for eating 'pleasure' foods. Both are essential in effective binge and/or food phobia prevention.

Psychologically there are two goals:

1. Non-avoidance of 'high-risk' foods (usually carbohydrates or high fat content) that the restrictive anorexic cannot allow herself to eat and which the bulimic cannot allow to stay in her stomach.
2. Appropriate food-focused self-nurturing behaviour. Meal preparation involves: *planning* – avoiding impulsive mood/situation-triggered binges or refusal to eat through inability to choose and so on; *preparation* – training the patient in short-term delayed gratification and channelling 'food rumination' into productive time-limited behaviour; *appropriate controlled self gratification* – training the patient to allow themselves 'treat' food or previous binge foods.

Training eating disordered patients to cook sounds simple enough, but this seemingly harmless everyday activity can be torture for them. Often I have sat down to eat with a patient who has literally sobbed throughout the meal. Occasionally I have had outright mutiny; total refusal to participate in the session. I have had people running out, others cowering on the floor in the corner and others filling the air with colourful, high-decibel, uncomplimentary language accompanied by low-flying cutlery.

One skeletal anorexic vegetarian girl literally grated all her vegetables then steamed them into a pulp that resembled baby food. (Any takers for psychodynamic interpretations?) Another young woman took 45 minutes to eat a small pancake, constantly accusing me of barbaric sadism. One ebullient bulimic used twice as much puff pastry as required to make her Puffed Plum Parcels, which turned out with much more Puff than Plum!

The occupational therapist eats with the patient group (whatever they serve up!) to model healthy eating behaviour. During the preparation there is a lot of informal chat between patients and therapist. I particularly value this unstructured opportunity to get to know the patients and let them get to know me. We often have a laugh, about anything and everything, which helps reduce tension. Regularly patients ask about what I or other 'normal' people eat. I am frequently asked what I cooked the previous night or how often I eat chocolate. I see this as their attempt to conceptualize average healthy eating patterns and am happy to let them know. This is the one area I have consciously chosen to reveal about myself after thoroughly debating the 'transference' issues. I believe that the advantages of teaching (and inspiring hope) through modelling outweigh the disadvantages of muddying the transference in the therapeutic relationship. It is helpful being a therapist whose primary focus is behaviour rather than feelings in this respect.

Regularly, patients perform to absolute perfection in the occupational therapy kitchen. They are often far better cooks than I am but cannot bring themselves to cook for themselves in their own home. This is where the rubber very often doesn't hit the road.

Normal body weight maintenance through a balanced diet is a primary goal in overcoming an eating disorder. Physical hunger is a binge 'trigger' for bulimics and a 'reward' for anorexics, and can be easily avoided with a weight maintenance diet. This group tackles all aspects related to appropriate food management and hence is essential.

Interpersonal skills are also crucial for sufferers to acquire. They must learn to express their feelings and assert their needs appropriately. This will wean them off meeting these needs through food or weight-related behaviour.

The next two groups tackle this subject at different levels.

Communication skills

This covers basic social skills training. It provides communication and self-awareness exercises and is geared towards patients with more profound social skills deficits.

Many patients are totally incapable of even initiating a conversation. Stereotypically these are severely regressed restrictive anorexics. Many present themselves as mere shadows: hair over face, baggy dark clothing, sitting on chairs in the foetal position, voice in a whisper, absolutely zero eye-contact are all commonplace behaviours for these patients. The occupational therapist's job is to motivate and impart skills in relating to others, including basic assertion skills. This group is generally more structured and 'safe' than assertion and anger management.

Assertion and anger management

This group is geared towards the higher-functioning individual; stereotypically the bulimic. It provides specific input on appropriate expression of anger as this is a common problem for this client group. Many patients with impulsive traits have a tendency to explode or to communicate in an aggressive way. The group covers assertion skills and anger management theory (O'Neill, 1995a, b). It uses role-play and 'en viva' exercises to provide practice opportunities. Both groups aim to enable the individual to express their feelings appropriately using real-life situations to put theory into practice. Letters have been written to fathers expressing their anger at being sexually abused. Telephone calls have been made to mothers telling them they were not prepared to be dominated any more. There have been conversations with partners asking for help, with bosses asking for fair treatment, with banks asking for money and so on and so on.

Very often patients lack insight into their communication style, particularly if they communicate aggressively. Confronting such patients can be a delicate task, requiring both confidence and diplomacy. When they eventually gain insight as to how they are perceived by others, they frequently become full of self-loathing. The occupational therapist strives to avoid such demotivating responses by communicating unconditional acceptance while teaching alternative ways of behaving.

It is very important for individuals to recognize 'triggers' to certain responses (just as in relapse prevention) in order to empower them in changing their responses. Regularly, patients try out new communication skills on me, or other staff members. This is very much encouraged and rewarded. It often strikes me as a little bizarre that I go to great lengths to congratulate patients when they appropriately tell me how angry they are with me.

The group is also used for this purpose as well as to challenge patients. On one occasion a very shy anorexic was distraught at the possibility of having to share her room with someone else. The group exhorted her to assert her needs with the professor in the next ward round. This epitomized her worst fears. When she summoned every ounce of courage within her and rose to this horrific task, I had to restrain myself from applauding: but we did later in the group!

All such interventions are designed to develop patients' ability to assert their needs and express their feelings effectively. This is to prevent them meeting their needs and dealing with their feelings through abusing or refusing food.

Both groups use a variety of techniques – paper and pencil exercises, pair work, large group discussion and teaching. Both groups draw from the difficulties participants identify and use these as real-life scenarios to work on. They are active, educative, participative and (usually) fun.

Relapse prevention

This is a 'self-help' group based on the model developed by Marlatt and George (1984), which is used widely in the addictions field. The aim of the group is to enable participants to stay 'behaviour-free'. (The mnemonic 'PLEASE' has already been expanded earlier in the chapter.)

Individuals are encouraged to reflect on their preceding week to recognize what went well and what didn't go well in their recovery endeavours. They are also asked to anticipate forthcoming challenges and plan for them. When things have not gone well the group is invited to look at the memory word to see which aspect of their recovery they need to work on harder. A similar process occurs for participants facing difficult situations in the near future. Group support, advice and challenge are encouraged to assist the individual in the specific knowledge, skills and attitude required to ensure freedom from 'behaviours'.

The approach is adapted from work done in drug addiction. It maximizes the learning process in participants by encouraging them to complete 'Kolb's learning cycle' (Kolb, 1984: 63) assisted by peer pressure. This can be summarized as:

The approach is designed to empower the sufferer by providing self-awareness to personal behavioural 'triggers' and alternative coping strategies. It is the stuff of successfully 'reoccupying' the sufferer.

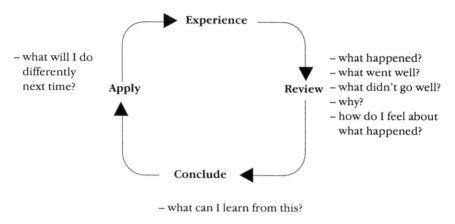

Figure 5.1. adapted from Kolb's learning cycle.

Living skills

This group addresses all aspects of independent living. It is modular in style (that is, a set number of sessions) and covers topics such as finding accommodation, budgeting, setting personal goals, leisure skills and so on. It includes talks given by the welfare rights department and the dietitian. A similar style and flavour is adopted as in the interpersonal skills training groups. Work sheets are also used to maximize the learning process.

Stress management and relaxation

Again this is a modular course covering basic theory on stress management. A weekly relaxation group is run in conjunction with this.

Projective art

The occupational therapy department provides a projective art session which helps individuals to gain insight into their functional difficulties through a non-verbal medium.

Body image

This session aims to overcome the individual's profoundly distorted body image. The sufferer's self-esteem depends on them looking like their perceived ideal. Because they can rarely meet this ideal, their self-esteem remains poor. This, in turn, demotivates, saps confidence and functionally disables them. The goal of this session is to help them accept their self-perceived inadequacies concerning their weight and shape. The session focuses on exposure work using mirrors and cameras alongside group discussion. Patients are encouraged to express their feelings about how they see themselves and to receive feedback and support from others. This can provoke similar levels of distress as meal cookery.

Evaluation of treatment

The occupational therapist reviews treatment at regular intervals with the patient to assess how far the treatment goals have been achieved. A variety of measures are used: a standardized assessment tool (Comprehensive Occupational Therapy Evaluation Scale) has been modified to record progress in food management skills. Self-evaluation questionnaires are given to the patient in a number of the groups at the outset and after set intervals. Together, patient and therapist agree renewed treatment objectives and priorities. The desired goals are personal independence and social interdependence. The occupational therapist regularly evaluates how well the patient is functioning.

Recording progress

The St George's Eating Disorder occupational therapy department has developed and piloted a recording tool called SCOPE: Situationally Categorized Occupational Performance Evaluation. This records the individual's functional difficulties alongside their strengths in the afore-mentioned categories: at home, at 'work' (employment, study, other daytime activity), at leisure and in the community. It also records intrapersonal and interpersonal functioning, and external/environmental influences. Outcome measures are rated on a scale of 0–5 (0 = goals not achieved, 5 = goals achieved).

Example case histories

Here's what the occupational therapist did with Cheryl and Teresa.

Cheryl was given individual occupational therapy assistance with:

cooking and menu planning
time management
lifestyle planning (career and leisure pursuits)
budgeting
assertive communication
stress and anger management.

Cheryl initially had a stormy relationship with the occupational therapist and expressed her anger to her frequently and floridly. Her ability to contain her angry feelings and express them appropriately steadily improved with plenty of practice.

Cheryl left the unit pursuing a new career in retail management: she much preferred a people-oriented job that was not office-based. She got a job in a department store as a trainee supervisor with day release for related study. This was quite a challenge for Cheryl as her previous lifestyle had been so chaotic, but she was highly motivated and found the stimulating, well-structured routine helpful in staying 'behaviour' free. She organized a monthly scheme to repay her debts, and had worked out a weekly budget plan. She joined an amateur dramatic society and attended an EDA group weekly. Temporarily, she got out of control with aerobics again, before succeeding in limiting this to one session a week.

Cheryl took a long while to submit to the benefits of cooking for herself. Several bingeing lapses and one or two in drinking helped her see the need to adhere to the diet structure. Cheryl gained valuable insight into how to express herself more effectively, and her relationship with her father matured considerably. A year after treatment Cheryl had managed to maintain a normal body weight and was 'behaviour' free. She had met a new boyfriend at work and had a leading role in *Gone With The Wind* with a local theatre company.

Teresa had individual occupational therapy assistance with:

desensitization to eating high fat/sugar content foods, especially in company
desensitization to the use of supermarkets and public transport
independent living skills
communication skills
lifestyle planning (career and leisure pursuits)
a behavioural programme to overcome obsessional cleaning.

Teresa found cooking and eating in front of others profoundly distressing but did eventually overcome her fears. She was able to cope with a highly structured weekly menu that was planned in collaboration with the dietitian to help her maintain her 'target weight'. She had several assisted journeys on the bus to the supermarket, then eventually managed this independently. Teresa learnt to manage her financial affairs on her own using community support agencies such as the Citizens' Advice Bureau. She returned to library voluntary work and began a course in librarian studies, and attended a weekly EDA group and evening classes in assertiveness.

When she became an outpatient she did drop below her target weight, but a year after treatment she had reached it again and was doing well. She made two close friends from the EDA group who accompanied her to a local restaurant every Friday night.

Conclusion

It is a challenge to successfully reoccupy eating disorder sufferers. Occupational therapy has a vital role in ensuring lasting freedom from this life-crippling preoccupation. Eating disorders don't go away purely by talking about them. Although individuals may be motivated to confront their internal conflicts and gain personal insight, the occupational therapist helps them *do* things differently. The proof of the therapeutic pudding is quite literally in the eating.

Glossary

Occupational performance is not restricted to a person's employment or job, although it includes this. 'Occupation' in this context is used in its broadest sense. It is an individual's ability to function effectively at home, work, leisure or in the community. This involves knowing what, how and when to do whatever is needed in these settings. It also entails the ability to establish and maintain fruitful routines. Most importantly, it requires the motivation to do what is needed.

Social performance refers to the ability an individual has in relating to others. It involves communication skills, self-awareness and sensitivity to others' needs. It includes the ability to behave appropriately in varying social situations and relate successfully to a broad spectrum of people.

Occupational therapy is activity-based treatment designed to promote an individual's ability to function, using life-skill training, and insight generating and social interventions. It involves practical/experiential, psychoeducational, creative and recreational activities. In essence it is action-orientated, aiming for action-orientated results.

Body Mass Index (BMI) is a theoretical measure used to estimate 'fatness'. It is calculated by: weight (kg) divided by height (m) squared. The normal BMI range is between 19 and 25. The International Classification of Diseases (ICD-10) gives a BMI of 17.5 or less in its diagnostic guidelines for anorexia nervosa.

Target weight is a specified weight in the normal range given to anorexics to attain in treatment and beyond.

A *'trigger'* is a term used to describe anything that acts as a prompt or catalyst that provokes a behaviour. This could be mood, time, situation or relationship related. For example: 'When I feel anxious I can't eat', or 'I binge every day when I get home from work, and whenever my mother phones me'. It is regularly used in the context of relapse prevention training.

Chapter 6
To eat or not to eat: The dietitian's role

Daphne Horder and Adriana Cuff

Dietitians offer expert help and advice on nutrition and feeding to groups, families and individuals of all ages. They are involved in many settings, such as hospitals, primary health care, the community, the food industry (both manufacturing and retail) and the media. In this broad spectrum dietitians are actively influencing and advising on policy making, provision of food, therapeutic diets and health promotion programmes, and participating in research. And this is in the context of the rapid change in many aspects of the society we now live in. Technological developments in food production and processing, transport and retailing, as well as changes in social and family structures and relationships, have radically changed the way foods are obtained, prepared and eaten, and their place in our lives.

Dietitians work as a member of a multidisciplinary team in most specialist units treating patients with eating disorders. But this covers only a small proportion of those whose lives are disabled, often seriously, by their preoccupation with food, eating, weight, body image and diet. Dietitians outside specialist units may be involved directly with these people with disordered eating, or they may be working with and through others such as parents, carers, health visitors, school nurses, teachers, primary care teams, homeless teams, hostel staff and caterers. So dietitians are likely to be involved at all stages of eating disorders – prevention, early stages of development, the acute phase and rehabilitation back into normal living after treatment.

Development of eating habits

Feeding is an activity essential to life from birth and is inextricably linked to making relationships. Survival is at stake if the mother and child do not get the communication right. Those who work with children (or indeed have their own) know the intensity of feeling generated in the mother and child around feeding. Habits develop very early and a child soon learns how to manipulate his or her mother's anxiety. Not only is the child learning and experiencing, but the mother is bringing her own early experiences, good and bad, to the relationship. Her ability to respond appropriately to her baby's need can have profound and lifelong effects. These early experiences stay with us unconsciously, and the link between feeding and good or bad emotional experiences resonates throughout life.

Learning and developing food habits goes on through childhood and into adulthood under the effects of many influences. Family patterns have changed rapidly over recent years. No longer is it the norm for families to have a meal together, and with this has gone a valuable learning experience of socializing, listening to others, being heard oneself and regular exposure to a variety of foods. Increasing numbers of children live with a single parent or working parents so there is much less time and thought available for food and meals. Cooking skills are not being passed on in families as an enjoyable experience and are taught less in a practical 'hands on' way in schools. Food technology and retailing have brought an undreamed variety of foods to supermarket shelves, and advertising reaches every corner of life. Choosing a healthy diet becomes more difficult as children become more independent earlier, with often fewer skills to make food choices for themselves.

Children now are on the whole better nourished and taller than they were earlier in this century. Many of the deficiency diseases and under-nutrition leading to illness which were the focus of nutrition planning and education have disappeared, but other concerns have taken their place. It is now recognized that many of the chronic diseases of adults with a nutritional component such as coronary heart disease, diabetes and hypertension have their roots in early childhood feeding (Barker, 1991).

There have been several studies of children's diets in recent years. Of particular concern are that one-third to one-quarter of girls have less than 8 mg of iron a day and 57% of girls have less than 700 mg a day of calcium (Department of Health, 1989; Doyle et al., 1994). The same studies show that 63–75% of children have fat intakes above the 35% of energy recommended by COMA (the Committee on Medical Aspects of Food Policy) (1991). As well as the risks of heart disease, high fat intakes can lead to energy intakes in excess of requirements. Coupled with less physical activity, this may contribute to obesity in childhood. This can be a factor in the development of eating disorders, which may start from dieting in response to being overweight.

Children live in a more and more adult world and are affected much earlier by the ideas, values, beliefs, prejudices and stereotypes of adults. One aspect of this is adults' perceptions of themselves in terms of body shape and image. For instance, the 'Twiggy' generation of the 1960s and 1970s have become mothers themselves and brought these values to their parenting. Surveys show that a large proportion of adults are dissatisfied with themselves. This cry meets its apparent solution in the dieting industry, but dieting is a far from benign activity. Repeated dieting (weight cycling) leads to fluctuating weight and makes it progressively harder to lose weight. Experts differ in their view of how much this is a metabolic effect due to change in body composition and metabolism (Brownwell, 1995).

Dieting feeds the dissatisfaction, misery and low self-esteem of those involved. Children growing up with these attitudes around them do not have the chance to develop a healthy and unrestrained approach to their own eating. Overweight is viewed as a negative quality, disliked above other disabilities by children. This leads to a distorted perception of themselves and a drive towards an ideal that is often unrealistic. Many want to be less than the ideal weight for height, responding to a perceived weight rather than actual weight. This precipitates dieting activity from an early age. Children as young as 9 years old are behaving in this way (Maloney et al., 1989; Hill and Robinson, 1991), and there is a clear link between dieting children and their dieting mothers (Hill and Weaver, 1990). This manipulation of food intake has serious consequences. It has implications for nutritional intake, and it encourages the restraint which leads to a lifelong struggle with weight, diets, and alternating starvation and overeating. This disordered eating bears no relation to the body's needs and internal signals and generates huge distress.

Dietitians in the community

Dietitians work with this background of food and belief, whether in acute or community settings. In schools, with teachers and school nurses, encouraging healthy eating is not simple. Dieting is considered to be normal behaviour in adolescence, with 70% of 15 year olds having already dieted to lose weight, and self-induced vomiting is used by many adolescents to control weight. Peer group pressures are strong and messages need to be positive, with an experimental approach to choice, which involves children in decision making and builds their ability to be responsible and affect outcome. Developing understanding of foods, labelling, advertising and manufacturing can empower the making of wise choices. School meals can also be a good learning opportunity. In the UK, Schools Nutrition Action Groups (SNAGs) have worked with the changes in school management to bring together teachers, pupils, parents and caterers in changing school meals and giving pupils a chance to participate in this decision-making process. Food is in danger of being pushed out of the curriculum or relegated to theory. Initiatives such as the Get Cooking Campaign have shown that practical cooking together can be fun as well as providing useful life skills. At the same time, children need to be encouraged to become aware of their own internal signals of hunger and satiety and respond to them – and be aware when other external or internal stimuli are the cue to eat – or not to eat.

Some countries have taken a different approach to the prevention of eating disorders. They have developed programmes based on helping students increase their self-esteem, and improving their communication skills and techniques for problem solving and coping skills. Dealing with obese children also needs to be done with care so that they are not stigmatized or set on a course of rigid diets but helped to make the changes they can achieve towards healthy eating. One secondary school has developed an alternative way of working with obese adolescents, instead of the traditional approach of giving them a diet and weighing them regularly, which had no success. Based on a questionnaire filled in by the child about their attitudes to themselves, the nurse looks with the child at how they can make changes in various aspects of their lives. This has enabled the children to be more positive about themselves and the issues they face and has also led to weight loss in some.

Staff working with adolescents have the dilemma, as with other adolescent issues, of how to try to prevent disordered eating from developing into clinical eating disorders. Secrecy, denial and confidentiality can make it difficult to know how to respond to children with problems. But supportive, helpful interventions by staff may help those negotiating adolescence to find other ways of coping before they get locked into a rigid drive to thinness.

Eating disorders and pregnancy

In primary care teams dietitians work with health visitors and general practitioners (GPs) with pregnant women and young mothers. Sometimes, when a woman becomes responsible for feeding her own child her own difficulties with feeding herself are revealed. Some women are diagnosed with eating disorders for the first time in this setting. It is a critical time when the mother's difficulties with food must be addressed, or the child is at risk of not developing properly physically, and the cycle of eating disorders can continue into the next generation. Working with these mothers and infants often has a similar feel to working in an eating disorder clinic, where there are the same high levels of anxiety and helplessness. Having her own child can be the impetus for a mother to move on herself, or it can reinforce the mother's own eating disorders, with a consequent effect on the child.

There are few papers written of studies done on pregnancy in women with eating disorders, and numbers recruited to these studies have been small. One such study (Stewart et al., 1987) showed that most anorexics experienced a worsening of symptoms, although the majority of those anorexics that had recovered before pregnancy remained well. A study of 20 untreated normal-weight bulimic women (Lacey and Smith, 1987) showed that during the pregnancy bulimic behaviour decreased but that symptoms returned and often worsened after delivery. Our experience of two pregnant bulimic women with a BMI (Body Mass index) of 18.1 and 18.9 was of almost no improvement of symptoms during pregnancy, although they were able to change the quality of food eaten after constant emphasis at each dietetic visit of the importance of good nutrition for their own and for their baby's health. They were also able to 'compensate' for their purging behaviour, to a certain extent, by having a smaller intake of nutritious foods in between binges without resorting to vomiting. A mother with a BMI of about 17.8 at the beginning of pregnancy, who had previously been anorexic, found it a great struggle to increase her food intake during pregnancy but managed to partly do so with constant prompting at each dietetic visit. The average normal healthy weight gain in pregnancy is about 12.5 kg (Hytten, 1980). Our three pregnant patients gained on average about 8 kg, with one women gaining only 2 kg. The babies' birth weights were between the second and tenth centile. All our mothers had healthy babies and breast-fed successfully for at least three months or longer. At weekly or fortnightly appointments, in some cases, the importance of eating well and need for an adequate intake to provide for the increased requirements of lactation (about 500 kcal) was always emphasized. The mothers were asked about the babies' weight and encouraged to see the health visitor regularly, and some liaison between the health visitor and dietitian ensured that the mothers had good support. All babies increased their weight and reached the fiftieth centile for weight within a few months.

There is an increased risk of delivering a smaller than average baby when the mother is underweight at conception and gains less than the average weight during pregnancy, and this was discussed with the mothers. The mothers found it a real struggle to do what was best for their babies and overcome the driving force of their disorder. Pregnancy is a time when patients with eating disorders are especially vulnerable and need much encouragement and support. All our patients saw a psychiatrist, dietitian and psychotherapist regularly, as well as their GP and attending antenatal appointments.

Early stages of eating disorders

Dietitians working in primary care will be seeing patients referred by GPs. Although it is not the dietitian's responsibility to diagnose eating disorders, she may well identify the symptoms in a patient who is referred with another diagnosis, and then appropriate treatment can be discussed with the GP. Some patients will be referred already having acknowledged their eating disorder. It is important to know what specialist services are available locally. When contracts are being set up the team need to be clear what can be offered within the constraints of time and resources in the practice. These patients will take more time per appointment as well as requiring regular long-term treatment. A team approach is essential, both ongoing and with good liaison. It may consist of any of the following: GP, community psychiatric nurse, practice counsellor, psychologist and dietitian. Initial assessment ideally will include physical, psychological and nutritional status. It may lead to secondary referral or treatment in the primary care setting. Dietetic assessment will be similar to that described later, and will include how ready and able the patient is to use nutrition intervention at this stage. The psychological issues must be addressed as well as the nutritional needs.

Disordered eating is an expression or symptom of underlying problems. It is one way of coping with what seem to be unmanageable difficulties. It is defending against and obscuring these other problems. Dealing with feeding issues alone, without psychological issues being addressed, can be a distraction leading to frustrating stalemate in making any changes. Alternatively, removing or lowering the patient's defences of the food issues may lead to further crisis without adequate support. Patients who have begun to address the underlying problems will need practical help with feeding themselves as they have often got completely detached from 'normal' eating. This is when a team which can offer different skills at appropriate times in treatment can be more effective than one practitioner on his or her own. Many patients, especially at an early stage, may be successfully treated in the general practice by the team in close communication.

Inpatient treatment

Patients in the acute phase of an eating disorder, or the long-standing chronic patient whose health may be severely compromised, can be referred to a specialist eating disorder unit, or, if this is not available, to a psychiatric or medical ward in a hospital. They may have been referred by a GP or another consultant.

Units vary in their approach to treatment, but there is a move away from the very rigid approach of some years ago when patients were on bed rest throughout the refeeding process and the aim was mainly to increase the patient's weight in a very short period of time. Force feeding or naso-gastrically feeding is used only if the patient's critically low weight or medical condition demands it.

Just restoring the patient to a healthy weight is not enough without psychological support.

A multidisciplinary team is the best way of working with these patients. Many dietitians outside specialist units do not have the support and the expertise of a multidisciplinary team and can be quite isolated. Professionals in the health service who do not have much experience of working with eating disorders may not understand the complex nature of the illness. Even if the dietitian is part of a large dietetic department in the hospital, she or he may not necessarily have appropriate support from colleagues, as eating disorders is a specialized area. Good communication with nursing staff, psychologists, psychotherapists, medical staff, occupational therapists, family therapists and other involved professionals in the care of the patient is necessary for good treatment.

These patients are often extremely ill, both physically and mentally. A multidisciplinary team can provide a service where the best care of the patient can be discussed and agreed, as well as individual members of the team being able to discuss their specific concerns about a patient. Usually dilemmas are not around what to do with the patient's nutritional intake but how to manage complex issues that are associated with these particular patients. It is important as part of the team to be able to discuss one's own frustrations about the difficulties of treating some of the patients.

The role of a dietitian is to devise a nutrition programme to restore normal weight and attain a healthy eating pattern for maintenance of normal weight. It also aims to enable the patient to stop binge-eating and purging if bulimic, and restore a structured eating pattern.

At the initial assessment, the dietitian will take a detailed nutritional and behavioural history. This includes previous dieting behaviour, family history of weight, attitude to shape, parents' and siblings' dieting behaviour, possible foods that would trigger binge-eating, purging such as misuse of laxatives, diuretics, self-induced vomiting, excessive exercise, use of appetite suppressant or other 'diet pills', and alcohol abuse.

The diet history will show calcium intake, which may be low, as dairy products (a good source of calcium) are often avoided. Because underweight patients who no longer menstruate are at risk of osteoporosis it is important to rectify nutritional deficiencies as well as promote weight gain in order to restore a normal menstrual cycle. Iron status can be low as a result of a vegetarian or vegan diet if these have not been balanced, and vitamin B12 levels can sometimes be low, especially if an inadequate vegan diet has been followed for a considerable length of time.

The decision to continue on a vegetarian diet or to avoid food because of the patient's claim of an allergic reaction is made by considering whether it predates the onset of illness. It is often the case that perceived food allergies and/or vegetarianism are related to restriction of choice, and the patient is asked to work towards reintroducing foods into their diets over a period of time.

When negotiating an eating plan, the emphasis is placed on establishing normal eating by having three balanced meals a day. Snacks in between meals are added to the diet as required to achieve the appropriate level of energy intake for the stage of treatment. Because having to make choices about food and order dishes can be difficult for patients, it is often necessary to prescribe an eating plan with little choice in the initial stages, but as the patients start to feel safer, they will be gradually encouraged to take more responsibility for their own choices.

Patients' energy intake will need to be between 2200 and 3000 kcal a day to gain 0.5–1.0 kg a week. Initial prescription should be based on recent intake, current behaviour, BMI and blood biochemistry results. This may be as low as 500 kcal/day if, for instance, the patient has been eating very little prior to admission. But it is more likely to be 1000–1500 kcal/day. Slow introduction to refeeding and hence resultant weight gain may help to lessen the refeeding oedema experienced by many patients. Energy intake will gradually be increased after one or two weeks up to the appropriate level of energy for steady weight gain. However, if anxieties and response to weight gain feel too intense for the patient, it can be more therapeutic in a few cases to continue at a lower intake for slightly longer.

Choice of meals varies from unit to unit, with some units allowing no choice at all and other units allowing patients to choose from a menu. Adjustments may be made according to the previous week's weight gain or loss, episodes of purging, and the patient's ability to cope with the programme. Supervision during meals is necessary to ensure that what has been ordered is actually consumed. Fear of weight gain will drive the anorexic to dispose of food. Food is hidden in napkins, pockets or thrown out of windows; butter is spread in their hair or under the plate. It is necessary to keep to certain boundaries and the nurse and the dietitian need to liaise and work closely with one another and be clear about each other's roles in supervising the patient eating or prescribing the diet. It can lessen pressure on the nursing staff to be able to say that the intake is prescribed by the dietitian and cannot be changed in the dining room; and it can help the dietitian, when dealing with complaints about abiding to the rules in the dining room, to be able to leave that to whoever eats with the patient at the time. Liaison is the key here, as patients often try 'splitting' the staff and are less likely to do so if they are aware that staff communicate with one another and are aware of each other's decisions.

Common physical problems associated with refeeding are post-prandial epigastric discomfort due to delayed gastric emptying in anorexic patients. This can manifest itself as gastric distension, commonly referred to as 'bloating' and 'feeling full'. Some patients are more sensitive to this feeling even when gastric emptying is normal, and vomiting may be triggered after meals even when the person does not usually have episodes of bulimia nervosa.

Constipation can occur because of poor food intake and also through persistent misuse of laxatives, which can damage the bowel muscle or make it 'lazy'. The diet can be adjusted to increase fibre content while taking into account the problem of a more bulky food intake which can leave the patient feeling 'fuller' but be less energy-dense and therefore provide fewer kilocalories.

Laxative and diuretic misuse, along with bingeing and vomiting, can lead to severe dehydration. Frequently this can lead to rebound fluid retention during the refeeding programme. Oedema can then occur mainly around the ankles, although in more severe cases fluid is also retained around the abdomen and other parts of the body. The most effective way to dispel fluid is to continue with the refeeding programme but, because of the distress it causes, it may be necessary to maintain a lower calorie intake for a short time.

The average weight gain patients may tolerate is between 0.5 and 1.5 kg a week. This may involve a long course of treatment for many patients and in some cases this leads to problems with funding, especially for patients with private health insurance. Patients will often ask what target weight they are expected to reach. Ideally, the decision to aim for a healthy weight is made between the multidisciplinary team and the patient. By forming a working relationship with the patient, she is more able to accept the advice and guidance on what weight she needs to reach to stop and hopefully reverse the damage incurred by being underweight and for menstruation to resume.

However, as a guideline, a minimum Body Mass Index (BMI) of 19 or 20 needs to be reached by the majority of females for menstruation to resume. The internationally accepted range of normal BMI is between 18.5 and 24.9 and is worked out by the equation

$$BMI = (kg)/height(m)^2$$

The patient may have an ovarian scan to see how near the ovaries are to producing ova, indicating the return of normal hormonal balance and the achievement of a healthy weight.

Although the issue of weight gain is very distressing for the patient, it is important that they are made aware that an important part of recovery is steady weight gain and that the agreement to increase weight must be kept to during treatment. Again, the backing of the team is invaluable to the dietitian, as patients often engage in real battles, because of their illness, in trying to avoid food choices that they associate with rapid weight gain. At times it is useful for the patient's key nurse to be present at some of the individual sessions between dietitian and patient to work with the dietitian in being firm while being understanding. Team meetings, where the patients are discussed, are also a good time for the dietitian to express his or her difficulties in trying to get a particular patient to comply with suggested food choices. Here, the consultant can feed back to the patient the team's decisions, which include expected compliance to issues such as food intake and weight gain.

Treatment programmes need to be flexible as most units are dealing with more than one type of eating disorder, including anorexia nervosa, bulimia nervosa and in some units binge-eating disorder and gross obesity. In addition, the chronically ill patients, who may have been ill for many years and unsuccessfully treated in the past, require special consideration during the programme, with a view to striking a balance between appropriate weight increase or maintenance of low but stable body weight and avoiding the use of self-harming behaviours such as purging, self-mutilation, drugs, excess alcohol and any other damaging substances. Sometimes it may be more productive to allow a patient to maintain weight, after some initial weight gain, while they are working on stopping self-harming behaviour. In most cases, however, it is possible to continue with weight gain during this process or return to it after a short period of time. When, in some cases, the patient is not able to reach or maintain a healthy body weight, it may be necessary to aim towards what is the best, most achievable weight and nutritional intake for them to allow a better quality of life.

Furthermore, the treatment is tailored, to a greater or lesser extent, depending on the unit, to the individual patient, taking into account energy requirements, anxieties, fears and ability to cope with the programme.

Bulimic patients are often a normal weight or slightly overweight or slightly underweight. To have a diagnosis of anorexia nervosa one has to be clearly underweight with a BMI of 17.5 or less. In an inpatient or day-patient setting there is often competition between patients wanting to be the 'sickest' and the most underweight. This can make it difficult for normal weight bulimics who find themselves surrounded by a very thin population, and often makes them feel even more overweight than they already feel. They may therefore be tempted to cut down on their food intake and increase their purging behaviour. It is important to continue with the plan of three meals a day and possibly planned snacks in order to avoid the relapse and perpetuation of the binge cycle, where patients will restrict their intake which leads to increased hunger and cravings for food followed by bingeing and then purging and restricting again.

In some severe cases of anorexia nervosa it may be necessary to feed a patient with a proprietary feed via a naso-gastric tube rather than giving food orally. This is a contentious issue, and people may feel it is not ethical to feed someone against their will. The decision must be taken whether to put a patient under a section of the Mental Health Act in order to save their life. This can be the case when the patient's BMI has dropped below 13, especially if the patient has lost weight very rapidly and/or if there has been prolonged and complete refusal to eat or drink.

At such a low BMI, it has been shown that the patient's cognitive function is greatly impaired and they are not always capable of taking decisions that they would usually be able to take if presented with the fact that they are in great danger of dying, nor do they usually comprehend how ill they really are. When a decision to refeed the patient against their will is taken, it is to give the patient a chance to recover and reconsider when they are at a less critical weight whether they really want to die. Although it is not always the case, many patients who have been refed in this way are grateful for this chance and have gone on to partially or fully recover. Refeeding via a naso-gastric tube is usually done on a medical ward and it is here that nursing staff and/or medical staff who are not used to these patients can feel very uncomfortable about what they see as 'force-feeding' and may also feel that one needs to respect the wish of a person to die by starving themselves. Close liaison and support from the psychiatric team, with preferably the provision of a mental health nurse, can greatly help in the patient's management. It is essential that the team that is in charge of the refeeding monitors the patient's blood levels, as there can be severe and rapid changes in fluid and electrolyte balance including low levels of phosphorus, potassium, magnesium, vitamin deficiencies and changes in glucose metabolism in severely malnourished patients. This can lead to cardiac, respiratory, liver, kidney, neuromuscular and intestinal changes, some very severe, and can even lead to cardiac arrest or heart failure. It is essential to increase calorie levels slowly and correct any electrolyte imbalances before and during the refeeding. Once the patient has reached a less critical weight they will be transferred or returned to the specialist unit to continue their treatment, and their food intake returned to the normal oral route.

During the programme, whether inpatient, day patient or outpatient, people are given practical nutrition education with the aim of helping them to find ways of addressing their fears and distorted beliefs about food. Although anorexics and bulimics are usually very knowledgeable about the fat content and energy value of certain foods, they are often very selective about the information they retain. False beliefs persist and are common, such as the conviction that carbohydrates such as bread, pasta and potatoes are very fattening, and these foods are often avoided altogether. Carbohydrates are foods that bulimics often binge on, feel guilty about eating and purge after eating them. Learning to choose balanced meals that provide adequate nutrition is important. Identifying correct portion sizes and what to eat at home and in restaurants is addressed, as well as increasing the variety of foods eaten. These patients often eat a very limited number of foods that they consider 'safe'. Increasing variety is not only important in providing all the nutrients the body needs but also satisfies the tastebuds. When a patient has been eating in a disordered way for a long time, she does not know what a normal portion is and feels very anxious about having too much or too little. Most units have a programme of pre-discharge shopping and cooking sessions with an occupational therapist in liaison with the dietitian, when balanced meals are prepared, from planning a menu, working out amounts needed, purchasing the food, preparing it and eating it together. This relearning process takes a long time and needs very practical help and support.

Liaison with partners and families is important, especially if the patient is living with them. It is especially indicated during the inpatient stay when people are approaching weekend leave and discharge. These are times when both the families and the patient feel particularly pressurized. With prior discussion potential problem areas around food can be identified and strategies agreed to deal with them.

Patients can be treated as outpatients or day patients if their condition is not severe enough to warrant inpatient admission. Also, not all units offer inpatient treatment.

Outpatient treatment

Outpatients cannot usually be worked with as intensively as inpatients or day patients as they do not have the same level of support from staff and they attend less frequently. Often it is a question of trying to work on one meal at the time, trying to increase intake and variety and stopping purging behaviours after that meal. Patients with an eating disorder frequently have only one or two meals a day, usually missing breakfast and not eating until late in the day. Establishing three meals a day and possibly snacks in between can often be achieved only over a period of several weeks.

Therefore their treatment can take longer, and for some patients this may be a better way as they can work within the setting of normal life.

Eating disorder patients should ideally be followed up for a long period of time, usually two years or longer. The discharge from inpatient to day patient or outpatient should be planned carefully and done gradually. Often it may start with one or two meals taken outside the unit per week, increasing gradually. It is useful for the patient and the dietitian to make a detailed meal plan for these meals, to fit in with the rest of the meals and taking into account the practicalities such as patients' cooking skills, availability of food and social activities. After in- and day patients have been discharged to outpatients, weekly sessions with the dietitian can be crucial for a while, as this period of transition is very difficult. Often patients lose some weight after discharge, when they or their families have to take complete responsibility for the provision of meals and their eating. Here, liaison with GPs may be important, especially if attendance is erratic or a weight decrease or bulimic symptoms become a concern.

A case study

An example of a patient with long-standing anorexia nervosa was Mona, an 18-year-old single woman who was living with her parents. Mona had been an inpatient admission as a matter of urgency, as she had lost a considerable amount of weight and her BMI was only 12. She had always been a 'fussy' eater but had not deliberately restricted her food intake until the age of 13 when she started dieting because she felt 'chubby' and started counting calories and limiting her energy intake to a maximum of 1000 kcal a day. From the age of 14 she had also started doing aerobic exercises for one hour every day. She had three previous admissions for treatment of extreme weight loss before her present admission. She had been a vegetarian for seven years but would eat eggs and sometimes a little fish. She gave her reasons for not eating meat and poultry as 'feeling sorry for the animals'.

Her list of disliked foods was extensive and included cheese, pastry, coleslaw, rice, pasta and any cooked dish apart from some soups, baked beans, boiled vegetables, boiled eggs, grilled non-oily fish, grilled fish fingers, tuna in brine and boiled potatoes. She avoided all fats as well as sugar and all foods that had any of these ingredients added to them. She had gradually restricted the variety of foods in her diet and by the time she was admitted to our clinic her diet consisted of:

Breakfast: 1 Weetabix, 1 banana and 50 ml skimmed milk
Lunch: Salad sandwich without fat
Supper: Marmite sandwich without fat.

This intake had been constant for at least three months. Her diet was both very monotonous and extremely low in energy and other nutrients. Some days she would also skip breakfast. She drank 2–3 litres of Diet Coke a day and 5–6 cups of black, unsweetened instant coffee. Mona said she felt safe with these foods and was very apprehensive about having to introduce other foods into her diet.

She ate alone and would usually have her meals in her room when living at home. She would never eat outside the home and when at college would go home for lunch.

Mona always cut her food into very small pieces as she maintained she had difficulty swallowing and said that this was a problem that was in her family. She also added salt and vinegar to her salad sandwich. As a child she ate with her family until the age of 11 when her mother had started to work full-time and Mona was left to make her own meals during the day.

Because of Mona's low body weight she was confined to the clinic but was able to move freely within the clinic on the understanding that exercise as a means of weight control would need to cease. An energy intake of about 1000 kcal/day was prescribed for the first week, with the aim of allowing her to settle in and not to feel too overwhelmed by the changes in her dietary intake and weight. This was based on the clinic's menu, which included at least one vegetarian choice but still had to be adapted to allow for Mona's great distress at the prospect of eating foods that she had avoided for so long. She was allowed three main dislikes, and decided on cheese, meat and coleslaw. However, there were many other foods that she still avoided, notably butter, margarine and anything high in fat or sugar. The main aim in the first few weeks was to slowly increase the energy intake and also introduce more protein into her diet. By the end of the third week the general choices made from the menu had increased to:

Breakfast: 2 Weetabix, 100 ml semi-skimmed milk and 50 ml orange juice
Lunch: 2 boiled eggs or tinned tuna or baked beans, 1 slice of bread (no butter), 1 low-fat fruit yoghurt
Supper: soup, 2 slices of toast (no butter), 1 low-fat fruit yoghurt
Evening snack: 1 sachet of Build-Up supplementary drink made with semi-skimmed milk.

Her intake of Diet Coke was limited to two glasses a day, outside meals.

Mona was very rigid about her choices and amounts she would eat including quantities of milk and fruit juice.

After the first two weeks, Mona was asked to aim to increase her weight by 0.5–1.0 kg a week.

Sessions with me were to be once a week for half an hour to discuss the week's progress and to decide on the menu for the following week. Progress was monitored not only on gaining a minimum of 0.5 kg a week, but also on increasing the variety of foods, and the ability to finish meals within the allotted time.

During the first two weeks Mona was knocking at my door daily and would stop me in the corridor asking to change things and complaining about the members of staff who dealt with her meals. While trying to reassure Mona, she was asked to keep to her weekly appointments and deal with dietary issues at that time. For the first month the sessions were fraught and often ran well over time. Mona would arrive, and talk non-stop about what choices she had made on the menu and tell me how well she had chosen and kept to the rules and that nothing needed changing. She would not listen to anything I said. She was asked to stop the chatter, which was very confusing, and would deviate from the purpose of the sessions. In fact, she was still trying to avoid ordering dishes on the menu and mainly asked for jacket potatoes with baked beans or tuna and omelettes with bread. Nevertheless, her weight increased by 3 kg during the first month, some of this due to oedema round her ankles. Her intake by the end of the first three weeks was about 1500 kcal/day.

During the following month Mona started losing weight and went down to her admission weight. She was still negotiating meals fiercely. It was found that she was exercising in her room. She was put on semi-bed rest and told she needed to increase her weight by at least 0.5 kg a week or she would be discharged. Mona had been very keen to be admitted and did not want to go home without getting better. By this time her intake had increased to 2000 kcal a day. Mona decided to be more cooperative and she asked for a small increase in her food intake. During this period her day programme was limited to meetings with her key nurse and taking part in the clinic's community meetings, as it was considered that she was too low in weight to be able to benefit from group therapies.

After three months she had started choosing more varied foods from the menu and her daily intake was about 2500 kcal. She was now having butter but was still avoiding cheese and pastry and most puddings. She had complained about constipation since admission and by the third month had an impacted bowel, which had to be treated with lactulose and then senna. As she was eating well at this stage and including a good amount of fibre in her diet, she was questioned again about previous use of laxatives. She admitted that she had been misusing laxatives regularly in the clinic until recently, confirming what staff had always suspected. Her weight was increasing by an average of 0.5 kg a week and there were no obvious signs of oedema.

Mona was an inpatient for a year, during which she participated in various therapy groups and also had family therapy with her parents and her disabled sister. Mona had begun to realize that she had been trying to keep her parents' marriage together whilst adopting a protective role towards her mother and disabled sister. She had gained 13.4 kg, reaching a BMI of 18. Because she had started to menstruate she refused to even contemplate increasing her weight any further for fear of looking fat. An ovarian scan and blood hormone levels confirmed normal oestrogen levels and that her ovaries were active. The multidisciplinary team advised Mona to aim to reach a minimum healthy weight that would give her a BMI of 19, but Mona was terrified of going beyond her present weight. Normally, she would have been discharged to day-care status to attend for meals and groups for another three to six months, but because she lived too far from the clinic she started spending some weekends at home after eight months at the clinic in preparation for her discharge. These went quite well. Her weight decreased slightly during the first two weekends, so her weekend menu was planned to include more snacks to compensate for an increase in activity. During this period her food choices improved further and she started eating pastry again although was still avoiding cheese. By the ninth month she was allowed to go to Greece for a week's holiday with an aunt and coped well as we had worked out an eating plan for the week. Mona felt she could only cope with 'safe' foods during this time and, although the menu was quite limited in choice, she managed to increase her weight by 0.3 kg during that week. Before final discharge, she had some sessions with the occupational therapist on home management. She remained quite rigid when planning and shopping for these meals, both with choices and amounts.

She was followed up at the clinic as an outpatient attending appointments with the psychiatrist and with me monthly. She lost a little weight initially, but managed to regain it. She was eating a balanced diet and felt comfortable eating with other people. However, she remained quite inflexible about her weight and maintained a BMI of 18. She needed to control the amount of food she was eating and therefore still needed to work on trying to leave the anorexia behind with our help and that of a local psychotherapist that Mona was seeing once a week.

Obesity and disordered eating

The most recent DSM IV criteria for eating disorders recognized the complexity of many cases of obesity in introducing binge-eating disorder as one of its categories under eating disorders not otherwise specified. A high proportion of patients in obesity clinics suffer from disordered eating, with restricting and bingeing preventing weight loss. Obesity is a serious problem and its prevalence is increasing worldwide. It is well documented as a risk factor in the development of many serious, chronic diseases such as non-insulin-dependent diabetes, coronary heart disease, stroke, musculoskeletal and respiratory problems. It leads to increased costs in health care and much reduced quality of life.

Much has been written over the years about it and the difficulty of long-term treatment. A multimillion pound industry has grown up to respond to the desperation of many people and their hope for a cure. It often only succeeds in maintaining an obsession with diets rather than treating obesity. Overweight and obese patients are part of a dietitian's caseload from the day she qualifies. Variable success rates have led most dietitians to review their practice and explore different ways of working with these patients. The obesity or morbid obesity of most patients presenting in clinic is complex in its development and the factors maintaining it and preventing weight loss. The physiological factors in its development are known to be increased sedentary lifestyles and high-fat, energy-dense, palatable foods available easily and cheaply, and the body's difficulty in adapting to these changes. As more research is done, there is growing understanding of the many metabolic processes involved in energy regulation in the body. The psychological causes are more complex and maintain a resistance to treatment which is now being recognized. Offering too little or not understanding where the patient is in terms of readiness to change can risk only reinforcing the patient's experience of failure again. It is clear that nutritional advice alone will have little effect, unless these things are addressed also. Like anorexic patients, obese patients often know the calorie content of foods but are unable to use this knowledge usefully in the face of being driven by concern about weight and shape. So dietitians have begun to develop their own skills in helping people to change long-established habits through using more cognitive behavioural methods in combination with dietary counselling, and exploring with the patient what steps they feel are possible so that treatment becomes a joint process and not something imposed by the 'expert'. Goals decided together should be realistic, not just in terms of weight, but taking other lifestyle changes into account. Research shows that while behavioural, dietary, exercise and drug treatments have all been shown to be effective to some extent, using two or more approaches in combination is more effective (NHS Centre for Reviews and Dissemination, 1997). As is the case with other eating disorders, working with other professionals such as a psychotherapist or a psychologist also can provide a more effective treatment.

Because patients with binge-eating disorder and compulsive eating require such lengthy treatment and support, it is getting more difficult for treatment centres to find the resources to fund such treatment. Outcomes are still often poor, but are too often judged only by weight and not improvements in psychological health and social function. It is now recognized that even a modest weight loss is associated with health benefits and should therefore be encouraged (NHS Centre for Reviews and Dissemination, 1997). The timing of intervention is often crucial in offering help when the patient is ready and motivated. Multidisciplinary teams can work more effectively together than one professional.

An example of this is Sophie, who had been seeing a therapist for some time after a major depressive breakdown. As she also had a problem with her long-standing obesity, the therapist offered referral to one of us (DH) for help with her weight. At first this was dismissed, as diets had been tried frequently before without any long-term success. Two years later she asked for the referral herself when she was in one of her periodic depressions.

At the first session we explored her current eating pattern, which included large quantities of food and a high fat content. Her resistance to dieting was very clear, as was her attachment to food which, together with travel, for her represented freedom. She would binge-shop and binge-eat. Her weight was clearly a source of great distress which she felt very hopeless about.

She came from a family with a mother who did not like food herself and associated it with greed and laziness and put Sophie on diets from the age of 11 years onwards. She was experienced by Sophie as very depriving. In contrast her father was very indulgent, both to himself and others. Mealtimes and food had always been an area where family conflicts were played out, and still were.

We discussed what steps she thought she was able to take to begin a process of change. She decided on three things:

1. To put boundaries around eating occasions; i.e., times, places, not at the same time as other activities.
2. Plan to have an evening snack of cereal.
3. To have a little less butter on her bread.

She came back for the second session still greatly astonished that I had not put her on a 'diet', and cynical that this would help her lose weight. To her surprise she had lost half a kilo in the week.

She told me later that if I had told her what to do, she would have come back spoiling for a fight with me and set herself up for yet another failure. She gradually began to realize that she dealt with many other situations in life in the same way. 'As it was, you (and my therapist) would not play ball.'

From the start she slowly began to make changes. Eating always included some foods that 'felt like a treat', and what was important was that no foods were banned. She began to lose weight without feeling deprived, and reduced quantities at her own pace. We had some fairly dramatic ups and downs during the process – sometimes taking quite a long time to work through when it all seemed to fall apart.

The dynamics of her parents that she had internalized came fair and squarely into the consulting room. They got worked out between us or put into her therapist and me. It was very important that we were able to work together too. In the consulting room I was occasionally seen to be the indulgent father but far more often represented the depriving mother. When she had had a difficult time and binged she would come to a session inviting me to respond by telling her to eat less of this and cut out that. Sometimes I fell into the trap, but it was always more helpful when we could understand together what was going on. As time went on, she was more and more able to see and accept responsibility for this process inside herself. Fear of failure was a big issue in her life and she would work herself to the bone at times to avoid it. Over the months she gradually learnt how to negotiate the times that things went wrong foodwise so that she did not bring the failure down on herself.

Over 18 months she lost 21 kg, from a BMI of 35 to 28. During this time her relationship with herself and food has changed, and she is still surprised how 'different' it feels. Her body image distortion has also changed and she has been working through a lot of this recently in art classes.

Conclusion

Although the difficulties with food are the symptom rather than the cause of the problem, for patients with eating disorders working with the food issues at all stages is an essential part of treatment. Timing of interventions is often crucial, and activities, often very practical, need to be appropriate to the stage the patient is at. But our role is to help the patient to take back the skills and responsibility of feeding and nurturing herself or himself rather than feeling she or he is constantly living with an enemy waiting to pounce; to find the enjoyment of food together with the health and social interaction that comes with it. This is likely to be a lifelong process to a greater or lesser extent.

Note

[1]The Get Cooking Campaign can be contacted at the National Food Alliance, 3rd Floor, 5-11 Worship Street, London EC2A 2BH.

Chapter 7
Systemic family therapy in the treatment of eating disorders

LORNA ATKINS AND BARBARA WARNER

As an intervention in the treatment of eating disorders, systemic family therapy is a later arrival than many other therapeutic models discussed in this volume. However, it is now well established in most specialist centres. Practice on which this chapter is based spans the family therapy services in:

- a national specialist inpatient and outpatient service for adults – the St George's Eating Disorders Service in South West London and St George's Mental Health NHS Trust – receiving both local and national referrals;
- a national specialist inpatient and outpatient eating disorders service for children and adolescents in South West London and St George's Mental Health NHS Trust;
- a specialist family therapy unit – the Prudence Skynner Family Therapy Clinic, in South West London and St George's Mental Health NHS Trust – receiving general adult referrals and specialist referrals, including referrals from the St George's and other eating disorders services;
- a private sector hospital, which has a specialist inpatient and outpatient unit for the treatment of eating disorders – the Roehampton Priory Hospital.

All services communicate with relatives of the individual patient at a number of levels – from involving families in information sessions and consultations with psychiatric medical staff, key nursing staff and dietitians, to minor contact with the patient's visitors. In all of these settings referral on to the family therapy service is made when the treatment team decide that family dynamics are influencing the individual in treatment.

The position of partner, parent, sibling, other relative or person close to an individual with an eating disorder is inevitably imbued with many emotions, some positive and some very difficult. Once a person is in the grip of an eating disorder, family members may have become alarmed and very wary of saying anything that might trigger episodes of bingeing or starving behaviour. Meanwhile, a father may blame a mother for previously encouraging dieting in the daughter[1] and there may be covert conflict between the parents, sensed by the ill person. She may become worried about her parents' marriage and consequently reveal less and less of her worrying feelings – bingeing or starving more to rid herself of the worry and self-loathing. The more ill she becomes, the more frightened parents and other relatives become of saying things directly, or taking action. Although outwardly desperately trying to please, evasion becomes second nature for the young woman. Family members gradually become organized around the symptoms and often describe themselves as 'walking on eggshells'.

The eating disorder sufferer who decides to become the patient of a specialist team commits herself, for some considerable time, to withdrawing from the way of life she has been following. Making this decision as an adult, particularly to undertake inpatient treatment, can often mean risking losing a home and/or a job, jeopardizing a relationship (which may have been founded on the basis of one partner being ill), and, heart-wrenchingly, leaving young children. For a younger person, education is often put on hold, unless there is a facility for tuition in the treatment service. The patient may be away from their family for the first time, leading to homesickness, a sense of no longer belonging, or even being replaced.

After years of diverting feelings through eating disorder symptoms, the patient learns how to access underlying thoughts and feelings and begin to express them in more functional ways. This can be a terrifying experience for the patient, leaving her feeling exposed and vulnerable. However, with the consistent input of the treatment team, risks begin to be taken and an awareness of personal resources and abilities begins to replace the previously dominant story that life held nothing without the anorexia or bulimia. A change slowly occurs in the belief that using the behaviours typical of anorexia or bulimia is the only way to cope.

As this process develops, the patient becomes closer to, and more reliant on, the therapy team. With this change, family members can feel distanced and excluded; uncertainties that arose during the development of the illness can become compounded and give rise to complex emotions, both positive and negative, in the patient and other family members. Similarly, members of the treatment team can develop strong emotional responses to the individual patient and her relatives.

Discussions about beginning family therapy often engender a high level of anxiety in a patient and feelings of betrayal and disloyalty towards partner, parent(s) and other family members. There can be unrealistic idealization of the family and a belief that the eating disorder is the problem of the individual, who is responsible for resolving it through individual therapy. Alternatively, the patient may be aware of long-standing family problems, which she believes cannot be changed or would result in a family disaster if they were explored.

From the parents' perspective, there are often high levels of concern, anxiety, self-blame (especially in the mother), guilt and anger. Siblings, partners and children of patients will have similar complex feelings. Consequently, anxiety and uncertainty may hamper initial sessions. By the time someone has reached a specialist treatment service the individual and their family have been seen in different settings by a variety of agencies and professionals – and may come with preconceived ideas or expectations of family therapy and its usefulness or otherwise. Those who have found family therapy effective in the past may attend with an open mind and less anxiety. Those who have had painful experiences may understandably be hesitant, reluctant or hostile. Members of some families may be aware of events and family circumstances with which they believe therapy can help and are keen to begin. In other families, members may be concerned that difficulties they have managed to contain may need to be revealed and discussed.

Usually, however, there is a great deal of goodwill and commitment on the part of partners, parents and wider family members to help the patient recover in any way they can, even if this involves putting themselves through what might be an unsettling and, at times, distressing experience.

The family therapist and the specialist treatment team

Responding to these referrals requires that the family therapist consider carefully her position in relation to both the team treating the individual and the family of that individual. The family therapist has the particular task of constructing a safe space in which the two systems of which the patient is a part – that is, the family system and the treatment system – can be brought together in a therapeutic manner. This requires an understanding and acceptance of the treatment models employed by the treatment team and sufficient independence in the system to ensure that all family members are heard and feel involved in family therapy sessions.

The family therapist will need to establish her own position as separate from the treatment of the individual but also collaboratively connected to this treatment. In the NHS inpatient service and the private sector unit this means contributing to multidisciplinary notes, reading those notes and taking part in discussions. In the outpatient services this means making written reports on the therapy to the team(s) involved in treating the individual and taking part in discussions with team members. This level of collaboration must be explained to, and accepted by, the patient and family.

The diversity of expertise and information available in the specialist treatment team is considerable. It can be a complex problem for a lone family therapist to retain a stance of 'not knowing' and 'curiosity' about the patient and family in the face of so much information, much of which can be presented as 'the reality'. There is the potential for the family to be deemed the source of 'pathology' and for 'blame' to shift from one person to another.

At times, members of the team may, in the interests of the patient, ask the family therapist to deal with issues in a particular way. Such requests, and the potential for family members, team members and the patient to have strong emotional responses to each other, require that the family therapist take great care with issues of her own neutrality, both in the therapy room and in discussions with members of the treatment team. In order to maintain her own neutrality and systemic perspective, it is essential that the lone therapist consult regularly with another systemic therapist about her work. For the family therapist working in a family therapy team this consultation is built into the therapeutic process.

The family therapy team

It is common family therapy practice to work with a team of several people using a one-way screen and videotape equipment, all of which may at first generate considerable anxiety for the patient and her family. This method of work may seem voyeuristic, be a reminder of former powerlessness, or feel intrusive into family matters. However, it can also be perceived positively, in that the session is both audible and visible to several people, making it less rather than more threatening. The aim in this model of working is to create a positive experience, providing therapist and family members with the knowledge and input of several minds, thus adding to the diversity of ideas available to the therapy and giving witness to a family's experience and work towards change.

When working with a team it is possible to include a member or members of the specialist treatment team in the family therapy team. This helps to keep communication open between family and treatment team. This level of openness, either through the family therapist's contact with both team and family or the presence of team members at family therapy sessions, can be used to deal directly with the emotional responses of family and team to the patient and to each other.

Using systemic family therapy models and theory

Models of family therapy have developed rapidly in the four decades since psychotherapists began to explore methods of working with the families of individuals who were displaying psychological problems. This chapter is not the place in which to provide a detailed discussion of systemic theory but it will be necessary to mention a number of theoretical concepts in describing the therapists' work.

Our own practice is informed by the developments in family therapy, from the early work of structural, strategic and transgenerational therapists and the powerful influence of the Milan therapists, to current ideas of co-constructionism, narrative and solution-focused approaches. We also value highly the influence of psychodynamic models and attachment theories on the development and practice of systemic family therapy. We especially make overt use of both the Milan model and the transgenerational model and have given brief comments on these below. A useful text providing coverage of all these models is Jones (1993).

Working systemically contrasts strongly with working purely psychodynamically. The psychodynamic model aims, through interpretation and insight, to make the unconscious conscious, and in this way enables people to confront concerns more directly, thus undermining dysfunctional behaviours.

The family therapist's task is to search together with family members for differences of meaning which can then alter the understanding of behaviour, and bring about changes in ways of interacting and in the fundamental beliefs and rules in the family system. This can best happen through a collaborative approach with family members, exploring what is important to them.

The Milan model

In this model there is little interpretation and much intervention, often in the form of questions to different family members about their own and others' thoughts, beliefs, relationships and behaviours in the past, present and future. Such questions are challenging and aim to provoke new thinking and behaviour. These forms of questions focus on family connections rather than an individual's symptoms. For example, Steven, brother of Anna, an adolescent anorexia sufferer, was asked what difference it made to his father when Anna had been able to eat her meal on a weekend at home. 'Dad was more relaxed.' ... 'And when your father is more relaxed, what difference does that make to your mother?' ... 'She is more relaxed too and nags less.' ... 'And if there's less nagging?' ... Anna interjects with, 'I'm more likely to be able to eat!'

Circular questions aim to broaden the context while focusing on significant family issues, as in the above example where the problem moved from being specifically about a daughter's ability to eat with the family – 'the problem' – to one where patterns of interaction were tracked and which provided possibilities for change. New information is discovered about the part each family member plays in perpetuating the status quo. They connect symptomatic behaviour and the family's responses.

The focus for the questions is arrived at by hypothesizing ideas in advance of the therapy about what might be maintaining the problem. Questions are formulated to discover the usefulness or otherwise of the hypothesis in understanding how the family is organized around the symptom or problem. Questions, such as 'If your mother were talking to your father about you and the eating disorder you have been suffering from for some years, what would she say?', help to clarify and verbalize family beliefs, expectations and roles – and to question their usefulness or appropriateness. Questions of this nature, and their replies, begin to develop a belief that there are possibilities for change and enable different perspectives to be identified, interactions to be examined and changes in behaviour to be considered.

The transgenerational model

Families pass on family history, culture and beliefs from one generation to the next in both overt and covert ways. By following family traditions, telling stories, and ascribing likeness to and difference from siblings, parents, grandparents and wider family members induct children into a sense of themselves and their place in the family. By hiding past events from children, parents and grandparents may wish to protect them from painful knowledge or prevent them from following difficult or proscribed pathways. Children learn patterns of behaviour from family members and adults pass on these patterns or attempt to alter them for their own children. The transgenerational model of systemic therapy explores these areas of family life, developing an understanding of family history and helping family members find ways in which they may understand their unique family and individual stories, reorganize their relationships and create new pathways for the future.

A family genogram (for an example, see Figure 7.1, p. 127) is a useful tool around which the family story can be told, re-evaluated and projected into the future. In working in this way the therapist will use the whole range of therapeutic models available to her. The use of the transgenerational model has the value of developing the family story over at least three generations. This can often provide family members with a longer view of their situation, locating themselves not only within the history of their immediate family but within the social and political history of the family and their culture. One young woman and her siblings were helped to relate differently with their father when they learned that he had been four years old when he first met his own father. Their grandfather had been involved in the trauma of war and had never spoken about this to his son. Discussing this together helped father and children to understand his difficulties in relating affectionately with them and in sharing his deep thoughts and feelings. They were enabled to develop new ways to communicate.

Explorations with families using a combination of models will reveal each family's unique story, the significance for them of particular life events and provide the context in which therapist and family can collaborate in working towards change.

Therapeutic techniques: structured changes, tasks, rituals, sculpts and role-plays

Talking therapies can lead to the intellectualization of problems without change occurring, and family therapy is no exception. Using the techniques of task and ritual planning, family sculpting, or role playing, can help to facilitate change that is otherwise hindered. Some families find that in order to move on to new ways of relating and behaving together they prefer to make deliberate changes to sequences of behaviour or to hold more structured conversations about family difficulties. The family therapist will be able to suggest concrete ways in which family members can make changes within or outside the sessions. This may involve all or some family members.

Parents whose own families of origin have been very different may find themselves in open or unacknowledged conflict over setting standards for their children. This conflict may be expressed in differences about how boys and girls should be treated or behave. For example, on eating, boys being expected to 'tuck in' and girls being expected to be more restrained. Such differences may originate from the different cultural origins of the parents; the special difficulties of moving from, say, an Eastern to a Western culture, or perhaps from parents being from same-sex sibling groups, or only children where they have little experience of the opposite sex.

Many of these differences can be discussed and changes planned in the whole family group. Some differences may need to be discussed with just the parental couple. This will be particularly so where issues of belief may be at risk and parents are concerned not to share their uncertainty with their children. Independent travel may be one such issue: parents can have different views about when the eldest daughter in a family should travel by bus and tube in central London, but may already have allowed her younger brother such freedom. Discussion in the session about each parent's view, and decisions about first steps (maybe mornings rather than evenings), will not only move the family towards change but will also help parents give voice to views of which they may unaware.

Adolescence brings with it the life stage of releasing children from parental constraints into taking responsibility for themselves. This can be difficult for some parents to negotiate and small, structured changes in which the family negotiate new behaviours and try these out between sessions, bringing back results to discuss with the therapist, can be a useful way of moving forward.

Rituals are an important part of social and family life, denoting life-cycle stages such as 18th or 21st birthdays, stages in religious life, marriages, anniversaries and funerals. These events facilitate times of transition and change.

Developing specific tasks or rituals may be useful in helping families to move forward. For example, a series of miscarriages may have been largely unacknowledged in the process of building a family, but may be highly significant in one or both parents' extra protection of, or difficulty in bonding with, the living child. These factors may play a part in the development of an eating disorder. A whole family, or the parental couple, may need help to develop their own mourning ritual for lost family members, enabling them to be acknowledged as part of the family and laid to rest.

Rituals can also be used to help families resolve past injustice, allowing new perspectives and enthusiasm for change to develop. In other circumstances a ritual may be suggested as a way of promoting less confusing interaction or less rigid behaviour patterns, and can be about retaining the useful and abandoning the less helpful. Both rituals and tasks should be carefully planned in collaboration with those family members who will be undertaking them.

Another intervention, which has the benefit of being active rather than verbal, is the use of a family sculpt, in which family members take turns to be the sculptor, placing other members in positions and postures that represent the relationships between them and their ways of communicating. A sculpt can be used to help family members express feelings in a non-verbal manner and can make issues of power clear. Making changes to positions in a sculpt can provide family members with the opportunity to experiment with new ways of behaving or relating. This technique can be particularly useful with a patient and her family when she is at a transitional stage of the treatment programme where some psychological change has occurred in how the eating disorder is perceived. This may be demonstrated by the patient positioning herself half-facing her parents and half-turned away from them. This can be symbolic of not wanting to return to where she was previously, both with the family and the eating disorder, but also not knowing (and being frightened by) where she is heading and what will fill the void left by giving up the eating disorder.

A development on from the sculpt, or a separate event altogether, would be a role-play in which family members act out events as they happen at home for the therapist to experience, or act out proposed new ways of behaving within the safety of the therapy room. These interventions, as in psychodrama, can provoke new information and experiences and new behaviours and outcomes.

Family therapy is, however, more than the application of techniques: it is the arena in which relationships can be explored and redeveloped between the individual and her family and may require work with a number of different family groupings.

Working with the whole family, parts of the family, couples and the individual

Our own experience accords with the research and clinical practice explored in the literature review. We approach each family in an open and collaborative manner, inviting those of most significance in the family system to attend. This may well be all those living in the family home, but could include others, for example a remarried parent, grandparents or other members of the extended family. We accept whoever arrives for the first session, enquiring how decisions were made about who would attend and always leaving open the possibility for others to join the sessions later. The systemic therapist seeks ways in which to intervene in the family system which will stimulate changes in relational patterns and behaviour, generate the sharing of new information between family members and create space for each family member to have a voice.

In general, we would consider those family members living in the same household as the eating-disordered family member to constitute the significant family. However, by the time that the treatment team decide to refer on to the family therapist they may also be aware of siblings no longer living in the family home, grandparents, step-parents and half- and step-siblings, other members of the extended family, close friends and significant others. Our usual aim, if possible, is to convene all significant people for the first session. We explain to reluctant members, often the person with the eating disorder, that we believe this will be the most useful beginning and that we will work slowly and safely to engage with this initial family group. The first session will usually provide an opportunity to discuss how to proceed, which may mean continuing with the whole group or planning sessions with different subsystems in the family. Particular family circumstances may also dictate the need to work creatively with the absence of some family members from sessions. Fathers working abroad create the opportunity for sessions with mothers and children, which can then be balanced with sessions including fathers. Siblings away at boarding school or university or living away from the parental home may also only be included on an irregular basis.

Work with the parental couple

In some family situations it is important to spend some sessions working separately with the parents of the eating-disordered person. Difficulties in the parental marriage – for example, sexual problems, feelings about a past or current affair which have not been discussed, past family events that have not been shared with the children, continuing conflict between divorced parents – may require separate exploration with the family therapist combined with meetings that include the ill family member.

Another model of work that can be effective is for the same therapist to see both the individual and her parents, but separately rather than together – what the Maudsley trial 3 (see page 133, where this research series is discussed) called 'family counselling' (Colahan, 1995). This can be a useful way to proceed when one or more family members refuse to be seen together, but all wish to have the opportunity to discuss ways of managing their relationships and the eating disorder differently.

Work with siblings

In some situations it is useful to see the eating-disordered person with a sibling or siblings. Some sibling groups may have old issues of rivalry, feelings of rejection or injustice, or shared losses or traumatic experiences which can be resolved with the family therapist. These sessions may be combined with sessions including parents and/or partners.

Siblings being seen separately can offer a place where feelings, thoughts and experiences from each person's perspective can be offered more freely, without the constraints of worrying about upsetting or shocking the parent(s). Sharing the difficulties and new information can increase understanding and may produce increased closeness between them.

Previously, siblings may not have felt that they could express their own needs or anxieties to their parent(s) because their sister was suffering with an ever more serious illness, leading to resentment and more worry. The therapist can help siblings realize that their perspective and views are important too. A sibling who has effectively negotiated the leaving-home stage of the life cycle, and is getting on with their life, can offer hope and an example to the stuck, unwell person.

Twin pairs have a special experience, particularly when both are suffering from an eating disorder. Joint work, together with individual and family work, is usually indicated.

Working with couples

In the same way as the benefit of working with the wider system of the family is recognized as an important aid in the recovery of some individuals, couple work can also be an influential component of the treatment programme.

Most partners, whether heterosexual or homosexual, are generally willing to attend and are often clear, at the theoretical level at least, in their desire to help their partner in whatever way they can. However, as with families, the chronic and inexorable progress of the illness has ultimately rendered them paralysed, frustrated and often the main carer for the family, with duties greater than would normally be expected. Sometimes the well partner assumes quite a burden of guilt about being a trigger for more symptoms, or, on the other hand, they may be totally unable to recognize the part they play in maintaining the status quo. In some cases it can take months before the non-ill partner becomes aware of their role in the painful dance that has become their relationship.

The predominant problems for the majority of couples seem to be in the area of communication. The non-ill partner feels bewildered and struggles unsuccessfully to understand the illness, often giving up in exasperation, at times resorting to inferences of madness; whereas the eating disorder sufferer is desperate to be understood and accepted as a person.

As with couple work generally, one partner will often attempt to make the therapist into the judge and jury, form a coalition with her against the partner, and be very keen to reiterate past problems and perceived hurts in great detail. The expression of this can be vital, especially for those suffering from anorexia who have previously been unable to find a voice strong enough to say clearly how things have truly been for them, but too much can lead to feelings of hopelessness and failure. It is therefore important that the therapist helps the pair search for the strengths in the relationship and exceptions to the problem-saturated picture they present in the early stages of meeting, making sure that equal attention is afforded to each of them. It may not be possible for them to ultimately find enough embers of hope to believe in a future together, in which case the therapist needs to open up discussions about separation, if this has not already been talked about overtly. Understandably, these discussions and the therapist's questions can be challenging and distressing, but reaching crisis point can sometimes, paradoxically, lead to an increased willingness to let go of endlessly airing the problems and to begin to look for solutions.

As the sufferer begins to recover physically, to develop increased self-esteem, to make tentative steps towards being more assertive, and to see herself as a unique and worthwhile person, adjustments and changes in the dynamics of the relationship occur. Talking about these changes and practising some of the newly acquired or revived skills such as assertiveness can happen in the safe environment of the therapy room. However, these changes can be irritating or threatening developments for the non-ill partner, who may have had the role of major decision-maker for some time. Exploration of early and current expectations of the relationship, letting go of unrealistic expectations and the development of new goals are necessary.

Intimacy is usually a further significant issue for a couple where one partner is suffering from an eating disorder. For an individual it may seem that promiscuity is a way of proving they are wanted and needed, but in an established partnership sexual relations have often ceased or become very infrequent. This may be partly through the distorted body image of the sufferer, who feels fat and unattractive, the physiological effects of starvation on libido, and unpleasant feelings of rejection – actual and perceived – which are present for both partners. Eventually, any attempt at intimacy becomes too risky and any change from the status quo can be frightening. It is important to respect the couple's wishes about how much to discuss their sexual relationship. A 'go slow' approach may well be recommended, which again can have a paradoxical effect. Issues of violence and/or sexual abuse in the relationship or in the family of origin may necessitate working differently with the couple (see below).

We have referred to the ill person and the non-ill person, and when there is clearly an identified patient (because they have been diagnosed as suffering from an eating disorder), then the assumption can be that she is the one in need of the help – that is, the only one. However, there may be another unidentified, untreated patient in the system, such as a depressed partner or an alcoholic parent, and when they decide to seek treatment for themselves, the identified patient may be more able to recover.

Systemic therapy with the individual

The family therapist is most usually involved in working with the patient and all or some members of her family. However, systemic models of therapy are very useful in working with individuals. Systemic therapy with an individual would be appropriate for those patients who do not seem to have significant others in their lives, who are resistant to the idea of family therapy or whose relatives refuse to attend. The last situations may arise from profound reluctance to begin talking about previously avoided subjects, or from intense feelings of loyalty giving rise to anxiety about family members being blamed or judged in the therapy. Alternatively, such reluctance may be generated by anger between family members or from the patient towards her partner or relatives. A patient's anger may result in excluding her family members from contact with the hospital and treatment programme and is not uncommon at certain stages of treatment. However, while working with an individual the systemic family therapist will keep open the option for others to join the therapy at any time. Therapy is conducted in a manner which metaphorically brings significant others into the therapy room, whether from the past, present or future. Whether seen alone or with family members it is critical that the patient begins to experience herself as competent and able to move forward. Using a solution-focused approach can begin to alter the dominant story held of herself as a victim in life. A problem-focused approach runs the risk of perpetuating this dominant story. One way of beginning to change this story is by exploring differences the client has been able to make to her circumstances. Future-oriented questions such as 'What would you be doing that you are not doing now if your parents got along better together?, 'What fun thing could you do as a family before we meet again?', 'What would make it more possible to share feelings in the future?' help to generate ideas and new perspectives around the possibilities of change.

A dilemma for some eating disorder sufferers is to know when one person (often the mother) ends and they themselves begin. The behaviours associated with eating disorders allow for private space where certain feelings can be felt. The compartmentalization of self and family can become habitual and distress is caused when, either by design or default, two worlds merge, such as the necessary use of a group therapy room for a family therapy session. This can feel very unsettling and intrusive to the patient but can also be seen as a useful – though upsetting – transitional step back to life in a non-hospital environment. In either case it is important for the therapist to acknowledge the situation and provide an opportunity for discussion.

Clinical practice

Enquiring about the family experience of the development of the eating disorder is often an acceptable place to begin and can be a source of new information for each member of the family. The development of an eating disorder is a distressing event for family members and may well not have been talked about by the whole family together before attending the therapy session. The concerns and experiences of siblings, as they watched their sister becoming increasingly ill, may be voiced for the first time in a family session.

Moving on to the development of a genogram during the first or a subsequent session may provide a useful focus for family members as they make the move from visitors to the ill family member to participants in the treatment. Some family members may readily accept that family relationships are an appropriate focus of therapy whereas others may firmly believe that the illness is located within the individual but are willing to help in the therapeutic process. Often both views are held by members of the same family or by the same person at different times in the therapy. The family therapist needs to be sensitive to all these positions: enquiring thoughtfully into the different views of family members; giving them equal weight; encouraging and containing emotions; challenging and reflecting; unravelling family of origin histories and blending these with the social and cultural context of past and current times. An example of the cultural context would be the fashion industry's continued promotion of the ideal female image as being corpse-like, despite the very serious health implications involved in trying to maintain such a low body weight.

These early enquiries will begin to show the therapist some of the areas of strength and pain in the family, and she will be able to acknowledge these and convey the possibility of discussing them.

An important area of exploration with families is their place in the life cycle and their experiences of life-cycle events. The genogram will often be a useful tool for enquiries about family experiences of birth, maturation, leaving home, partnership, parenting, work, retirement and death. As listed, these events take on the attributes of 'normality'. However, each family, and each individual in each family, has a unique experience of life events, which will contribute to their development as individuals and family members.

Anorexia is often viewed as a response to the developments imposed on the individual and her family by the onset of puberty. Certainly, progression through this life stage can be severely disrupted by an eating disorder.

The combination of a number of life events at particular points in the life cycle will provide a context in which the family will have to function and which may prevent them from negotiating the current stage in family life optimally. The late miscarriage of a much-wanted first baby may create a context of higher anxiety and concern for the subsequent child who may themselves be ill or born at a time when the family are dealing with the loss of a grandparent. Events such as these may result in a stronger bond between mother and child and a weakening of the parental couple relationship. Later life events may lead to a rebalancing of relationships but can also lead to a consolidation of these patterns to a point where a family may lose its potential for flexibility at a time of difficulty or a new life-cycle stage.

Parents who are moving through middle age with the prospect of children leaving home and who have negative views of the latter stages of life may unconsciously inhibit their daughter from moving through adolescence into young adulthood. Her growing independence and individuation will be symbolic of their own ageing. Their daughter may then struggle with moving from one developmental stage to the next. Restricting food is one way of slowing down or stopping the developmental process. This may then result in anguished struggles for the young person between the need to emulate her peers in entering higher education or work and making new relationships and the need to remain her parents' child.

In considering these issues with families the systemic therapist can invite new thinking and behaviour and new approaches to the life events. The therapist will ensure that she remains aware of life-cycle stages and events throughout her work with families.

Working with family experiences

Family emotions

The experience and management of human emotions differs from family to family and is understood and thought about differently depending on the family members' culture (both ethnic and familial) and religious beliefs. The role and expression of the major emotions – love, humour, anger and grief – in a family will have been affected by the experiences of parents in their families of origin and have developed in their relationship together. Careful construction of a genogram, in which attachments and losses are explored, will reveal the unique experiences of families and their patterns of management of emotions of various kinds. Children will have learned about these aspects of family life as they have grown and will have contributed their own unique responses to feelings of attachment, frustration, hurt and loss to the family repertoire. The development of an eating disorder in a family member will have profound repercussions on the experience and expression of emotions in the family. The emotional life of the family may also have had some influence on the development of the eating disorder. Exploration of the major emotions (love, anger and grief), and the unique expression of these in each family, is part of the task of the family therapist. The therapy session will often become a forum in which these emotions can be expressed or are provoked by the process of therapy.

Love

This emotion is not often written about in clinical literature but is often discussed in the therapy room. How family members know that they are loved or not, how they express their love or antipathy to each other and what they mean by love will be explored by the therapist throughout the therapy. Discovering with family members the patterns of loving in the family, how these have been expressed before and during the illness, and finding paths to the restoration of old patterns or the development of new ways of expressing love are all areas for the family and therapist to explore.

When appropriate these discussions will also include family members' attitudes and beliefs about marriage and divorce, the expression of sexual love and beliefs and feelings about heterosexual and homosexual relationships. In some families these issues have become matters of secrecy (see p. 126); in others they are arenas for abuse (see p. 128).

A belief we sometimes hear expressed by the anorexia sufferer is how difficult it is to believe that love can be shared with others with enough left over for oneself. The sufferer wants desperately to be special and may experience intense jealousy and disappointment when she has to share an attachment figure. This may be a parent but can also be a therapist or key worker.

Humour

This is another emotion, infrequently written about but a major currency in family communication, which can be usefully explored by the family therapist. In many relationships and families shared humour is a major asset in managing the expression of both positive and negative feelings. However, differences in the use of humour between partners or parents can lead to misunderstandings or hurt feelings. Making use of family humour or exploring misunderstandings can help in the development of new patterns of communication between family members.

Anger

Anger and its expression and management, like love, differs from family to family. In some families there is an unwritten rule of 'no negative feelings'. This poses dilemmas for a person who feels angry, dispirited or jealous and who may believe that they are different from other family members or may fear rejection if their feelings are expressed.

Although feelings of anger may be generated by the behaviours developed around the eating disorder, by both the sufferer and family members, discord in the family of an eating disorder sufferer is usually avoided at all costs. Fear of escalating an already precarious situation prevents any challenging of the sufferer's behaviour. Problems can become self-perpetuating as family members or partner are caught in this pressure cooker of suppressed emotions, and for the patient feelings become even more channelled through the illness. In other families anger may have become difficult to control and its expression may have become unpredictable and extreme. Again the family therapist's task will be to explore the meaning and expression of anger in the family and discover old and new ways of managing the emotion. In some relationships violence can become a major feature (see p. 130).

Grief

Bereavement experiences, and the stories associated with them, will have repercussions in the immediate family and across the generations. Within the term bereavement we include not only the loss by death of family members and significant others, but also loss through miscarriages and abortions, physical illness and disability, learning disability, mental illness, failure to meet academic expectations, loss of work, separation, divorce, migration, losses associated with traumas such as sexual abuse, accidents, war, and so on. The therapist can construct questions aimed at seeking the different beliefs family members hold about these events. Questions can also be posed to consider the possible views that might be held by family members not present in the session, because of non-attendance or because they are dead or not yet born. Responses to these forms of questions provide a richer pool of possibilities for family members to consider, and alternative ways in which to construe their experiences and understanding. Where family stories have become imbued with a dominant narrative of failure and disaster the therapist can seek out the alternative narrative of perseverance and strength.

An example of the influence of loss is demonstrated in the family of a young woman, whose parents both lost a parent during their own childhood, one through divorce and the other through death (a shared experience which may have drawn them together as partners). This experience led to difficulty in successfully negotiating the life-cycle stage at which the grandparent died or left and at which the young woman should have been moving into adult life. The family had no clear models about how to move forward without parents becoming divorced, redundant or dying or without children 'going it alone', a daunting and frightening task which may contribute to the development of an eating disorder. The exploration of these stories and alternative possibilities can release new energy in a family.

Both anorexia and bulimia, in advanced and chronic stages, can bring patients close to death and do result in the death of some individuals. The impact of the eating disorder on family members or partners of the sufferer is profound. In situations where the patient has been chronically ill for many years, partners and family members may well have felt tyrannized by the eating disorder. This mirrors what has occurred for the sufferer, although her ability to perceive this is limited until considerable psychological change has occurred. As problems escalate, so the prospect of death moves ever closer, whether by starvation, through the binge/vomit cycle which disrupts the balance of body chemistry as it continually attempts to adjust and adapt, or by acts of self-destruction.

There may well have been one or more critical episodes resulting in hospitalization and tube-feeding until physical stability has been established. The experience of seeing one's offspring or partner close to death is profound. The pattern of communication and interaction from involved relatives or partners following such a crisis once more becomes organized by the illness. The understandable desire is to protect, nurture, control (but how?) and refrain from any hint of criticism, in case the fragile state of the eating disorder sufferer is rocked again.

The paradox is that the sufferer seems impervious to how life-threatening the illness is, even after having been tube fed. The horrors of weight gain and intolerable feelings continue to take precedence over the fear of dying. Having survived against difficult odds, she can begin to feel almost omnipotent and blasé about potential collapse. Experiencing this perilous state can also reinforce the belief that sufferers frequently hold that the only way of receiving what they need emotionally from significant people in their lives is by being ill. While in hospital family members (mother especially) or the partner may have shown a level of tenderness and nurturing usually reserved for newborn infants.

One task of the family therapist is to begin to introduce the taboo subjects, which have so carefully been avoided, sometimes for many years. It can seem very threatening for partners and family members, who have lived through the frightening experience of almost losing their relative, to get in touch with their own potentially negative and less safe emotions such as anger and disgust. There is naturally a wave of relief that the danger has passed and they are not willingly about to jeopardize the improved situation.

However, this lack of congruent emotion can be confusing to the sufferer, who is puzzled by the one-dimensional expression of emotions such as compassion and sadness. Unresolved issues of blame, shame or guilt can seriously inhibit the development of healthier relationships.

The family therapist begins to explore these near-death experiences sensitively from each person's perspective. There is frequently ongoing concern from family members, partner or therapy team for the well-being of the sufferer who continues to lose weight, over-exercise, binge or vomit. Again, a sensitive but clear discussion about the meaning and consequence of this deterioration is vital. Questions around what would happen in the event of further collapse, who would be informed, what if the sufferer died, and discussion around the funeral and inquest, all highlight the severity and potential hopelessness of the situation. The refusal by the therapist to give false reassurance can sometimes have a paradoxical effect on the patient, who may shift to introducing more positive ways of functioning into her life.

The eating disorder sufferer has often experienced intense feelings of rejection, loss and abandonment, and at a conscious or unconscious level may try to do the rejecting or abandoning first. This may be by leaving therapy before it can be concluded, or by dying so as to prevent the terrifying feelings being triggered again. Other family members may experience similarly intense feelings and indeed there may be a trans-generational pattern of dealing with the fear of abandonment by acting first. The family therapist will be sensitive to these possibilities and will explore them during the sessions.

If the sufferer dies, the family therapist can continue working with the family members, providing they wish it, on issues of bereavement, facilitating some of the more difficult and unacceptable feelings such as guilt, anger, blame, powerlessness, inadequacy, shame and even a sense of relief. This work will also aim to review the whole life of the deceased family member and help the survivors towards a resolution of their grief.

In the event of a patient's death the family therapist and specialist treatment team will face some of the same emotions engendered in family members. Each person's own experiences and beliefs around dying and death will influence their work with the individual and her family. These emotions and concerns must be dealt with effectively in the team as a whole, and individually through discussion and supervision.

The death of a fellow patient will also have a profound effect on other patients and their families, and the treatment team and family therapist will need to address this in their work with individuals and families.

Secrets

The management of secrets in families differs widely. Some families contain dark secrets, such as violence or sexual abuse, known only to abuser and abused. Often these secrets are maintained by threat, fear, shame or love. Other families may contain secrets of previous events, which are known to some family members and not others or known to many family members but not spoken about. The more forbidden a subject, the more communication can become inhibited. Keeping secrets about one's self, as occurs in restricting or bingeing, is one way of experiencing uniqueness as an individual, and can confer power, but can also become a burden.

In the treatment of eating disorders, secrets may emerge at any point during therapy and be shared with any member of the treatment team. At times the family therapist may be aware of a secret but is unable to bring this into the family session unless the individual who holds the secret has given permission for it to be discussed or feels safe enough to raise it. The capacity for the therapist to maintain a safe-enough space may well be tested several times by family members and treatment team before the secret can begin to be shared. Secrets may well have strong influences on the lives of family members and reverberate over generations. If they remain undisclosed and unresolved throughout a generation, bewildering and unidentifiable feelings can be created in an individual. A consequence could be a retreat into ill health, such as an eating disorder, or depression.

Case example

Sheila M, an only child of 15, and her parents were referred for family therapy because Sheila had been suffering from bulimia for a year, and there was difficulty in cooperation between family members. Sheila had formerly been a keen student, but was no longer motivated. The family had suffered a bereavement 19 months previously, which had seriously affected Mr M, who had become depressed. He had recovered from the depression, but assumed that his daughter's illness was a result of his changed behaviour while depressed.

However, in consultation with the parents alone, it emerged that Sheila's mother had had a child adopted before marriage, whom she had managed to trace two years previously, but who had not followed up the contact Mrs M had attempted. Sheila had no knowledge of this child, but continually felt unacceptable and never good enough to meet her parents' expectations. The therapy enabled Mrs M to begin to talk about her earlier years, the child she had borne and lost to adoption, and her subsequent search and desire to see her again. Though initially shocked, Sheila came to terms with the knowledge. The family members were able to relate more openly to each other, to recognize Sheila's unique place in the family and to talk together about the lost family member. They were able to explore together the possibilities of contacting the lost child or accepting her right to remain unknown. Sheila's recovery from bulimia proceeded.

When working with secrets, the task of the family therapist is to help family members develop more open ways of communicating, create new experiences together and develop new relationships and stories for the current family and future generations. These new stories will come from the experience of sharing the old stories and the responses to new questions and conversations about the future.

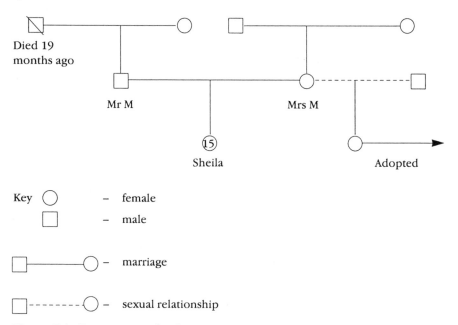

Figure 7.1. Genogram – M family.

Violence against the self

Those suffering from impulsive anorexia or bulimia feel compelled to manage their distressing feelings in ways that are more overtly self-destructive than the self-starvation strategies of the person diagnosed with anorexia nervosa.

The violence to the self may take the form, for example, of head-banging, throwing oneself down the stairs and, more commonly, self-harming by cutting. The last behaviour can serve as a punishment when the sufferer feels so worthless and full of shame that the pain must be inflicted. It can also function as a way of obtaining relief from pent-up, explosive emotions that have not been expressed in more effective (that is, less harmful) ways.

The knowledge that their daughter or partner is harming herself can be frightening and distressing for family members and can induce feelings of inadequacy at the inability to provide enough of some mysterious, so far elusive commodity, which would prevent their relative performing such painful acts. The physical scars often remain as a permanent reminder of the unhappiness and despair experienced and self-harm can be perceived as a powerful method of communicating that anguish. In this way it becomes self-reinforcing.

Families and individuals very often continue to repeat the same ineffective formulae as a way of attempting to resolve problems. If this has been the pattern, doing something different can reveal new possibilities for alternative and effective solutions. In the case of self-harming, exploring the thoughts and feelings, and gains and losses from the harmful actions in the calm and safe context of therapy is already 'doing something different'. As sessions progress more open and honest communication develops, understanding of different perspectives grows and brainstorming for alternative strategies can be undertaken by the family as a whole, or by the individual, to find and begin to implement safer and more effective ways of coping with difficult emotions. The benefit of searching together for solutions that fit for the individual who is harming herself is that the self-harming becomes the problem instead of the person herself. The family members are then on the same side trying to find answers.

Sexual abuse and violence in the family

Both violence and sexual abuse can be present in family and couple relationships and may be carefully guarded secrets surrounded with guilt, fear, shame and threat in relationships where love and interdependence are also present.

Sexual abuse

There is growing evidence that unwanted sexual experiences or early sexual trauma may well trigger the onset of an eating disorder. There also seems to be a link between recurrent abusive experiences and bulimia.

Current abuse, sexual or physical, of a minor when disclosed during treatment is dealt with in all settings by involving the local authority and police investigation teams and dealing with the repercussions for the client and family as professionally and sensitively as possible. The family therapist may have an important role to play in helping family members to negotiate this experience.

Current adult experiences of abuse or memories of childhood abuse will be difficult to manage both for family members and treatment team, but may not involve investigation by local authority and police, at least immediately.

Collaboration between family therapist and treatment team will need to be carefully managed to enable the patient to work within her individual therapy, the therapeutic groups, family therapy and with the staff team in safety and confidence and at an appropriate pace. Team members will need to know that, as with any other painful human experience, changes in feelings and beliefs occur over time and that they can help the patient and her family to negotiate this difficult experience. Their own responses to abuse experienced by the patients they are treating will require acknowledgement, understanding and discussion. They will need to be alert to the part their own beliefs and values and, perhaps, personal experiences of abuse, play in the therapeutic interventions selected and how they manage the situation. Attention to these issues is essential if a therapeutic and professional environment is to be maintained for the patients, their families and the treatment team.

Issues for an abused person often run parallel to the issues for a person suffering from an eating disorder – those of secrecy and secret-keeping, powerlessness, beliefs about gender roles, isolation, low self-esteem, self-loathing, repression of overwhelming feelings, emotional withdrawal, problems about the boundaries between people and gender-appropriate behaviour. A person who has experienced abuse often feels responsible and blames herself. Remaining trapped in this position of victim may be connected with a need for approval or control. Or she may believe it is helpful to her family, or partner, for her to be the 'problem person', providing a safer focus than perhaps differences between parents, across generations, or in the couple relationship.

When the abuse has been in the family, feelings of loyalty and ambivalence, in the sense of experiencing fear, anger and love towards the offender, become very confusing. Anger is often directed at a mother who has not provided protection, rather than at the perpetrator (assuming the perpetrator and the mother are not the same person).

The important task for the family therapist is to create an environment in which members of the family, not necessarily all together, are enabled to hear of the experiences of the abused person; to accept these experiences and to voice their own responses; and then to work through the complexities of emotions and behaviour raised by both physical and sexual abuse.

The revelation of experiences of abuse may allow other family members to tell of their own experiences with the same or a different perpetrator, or may explain behaviour and events which have been puzzling or difficult. Guilt, anger, blame and disbelief are as likely to be evoked as belief, understanding and empathy, and all these feelings may be interchangeable at times, both in the family and in the treatment team. The capacity to retain a level of neutrality, without condoning the abuse or poor protection of the abused, will be essential if the family therapist is to maintain the therapeutic environment.

A survivor of abuse and her family can be helped to think about the wider systems, such as family of origin and the patriarchal culture in which we live. Exploring these areas of gender and family patterns allows family members to begin to think about the broader picture of how and why the abuse may have occurred, and possible links with the eating disorder. The therapist can enable the individual and her family to view her childhood experience from an adult perspective and to see that the offender was responsible for the abuse. Patients and their families can be helped to access suppressed feelings – anger being one of them – and to channel these constructively. This may include the reporting of a crime and subsequent legal proceedings. As therapy progresses, these feelings can be explored in depth and can move on to include acts of reparation and forgiveness.

Recovered memory

Currently, there is much discussion and controversy on the issue of recovered memory of abuse. As systemic family therapists it is our practice to take seriously an individual's memories of abusive experiences and to explore these memories with the patient and her family. However, we do not seek these memories by suggesting that abuse has occurred or by using interventions such as hypnosis. We believe it is vital to use non-leading language in the conversations we have with families and in the letters we may write to them.

Violence in couple relationships

For the most part we have experienced parents, partners and other family members as wanting to help the sufferer but no longer knowing how, or unable to believe in their abilities to do so. However, the reality is that there are also violent and abusive relationships and there seem to be links between recurrent abusive experiences and bulimia. In these relationships the needs of the abusing partner are paramount to any needs their partner might have. Both people in this scenario are struggling with intense feelings of powerlessness and seem to be at the mercy of unbearable feelings. To try to gain control of the powerless and intolerable feelings, the abusive partner resorts to violence and the abused person relies on the temporary relief of bulimia to assuage the worst of the distressing feelings. Both attempts to gain control lead once more to being out of control, with an associated diminution of self-esteem and self-worth coupled with an increase in shame and guilt. Paradoxically, the eruption of violence can be perceived as one way of becoming closer, especially when it leads to contrition and forgiveness.

Our thinking on this topic is influenced by the work of Goldner et al. (1990), who have developed a therapeutic approach for couples experiencing this form of relationship. Conjoint therapy may or may not be the most appropriate form of help. The use of peer groups for the violent partner and support groups for the victimized partner may be more effective, which can then be followed by conjoint work. This approach would allow space for exploration of earlier abusive experiences that may have been endured. Conjoint work that is carried out before these areas have been worked through may mean that the person being abused continues to be at risk of further abuse. They will take the blame for having provoked the attack, will also believe that they deserve to be beaten, will minimize the significance and seriousness of what has happened, and may even not want to attend therapy at all. The abuser is then able to avoid the seriousness of their behaviour.

However, some couples strongly wish to be seen together, in which case the therapist may help them make a contract of safety for the duration of the therapy, or to temporarily separate to reduce the possibility of further abuse occurring. There are dilemmas for the therapist when carrying out conjoint work without peer group work or individual sessions first having taken place. Attending together may be understood to mean that there is a combined responsibility for the problem. However, the therapist cannot ethically adopt a position of neutrality, which may inadvertently give a message of approval to the abusive partner and perpetuate the status quo. She will explore the couple's beliefs about gender and power in the context of their relationship, their families of origin and more broadly in society. The different threads will be disentangled, separating out feelings experienced before, during and after the abusive behaviour has occurred.

The relationship is more than just the violence, however. The abuse is followed by forgiveness and reuniting – and hope that it will not recur. The strong attachment between the couple must also be explored, valued and developed.

The added dimension of the eating disorder should not be forgotten, as the sufferer may be severely under threat not only from the physical abuse, but also from the effects of the constant bingeing and vomiting cycle on her vital organs. She will also be prone to severe mood swings which are disturbing and provide her with yet more evidence of being out of control and worthless.

As couple therapy progresses in parallel with an eating disorder programme, space is opened up for new possibilities of relating and alternative strategies for managing feelings. Both partners have an increased sense of gaining back control and of having choice – which might mean staying in a relationship or leaving it. The family therapist may have a role in helping the couple to explore this option.

Literature review

It will have become clear from the foregoing descriptions that the multiple challenges and stresses an eating disorder brings to family dynamics and the effect of family dynamics on the eating disorder are a complex combination of interactions and emotions, emotions and interactions. We have selected recent publications which have reviewed previous literature as a guide to the research and writings on family therapy and eating disorders.

The best starting point is an authoritative overview of eating disorders (Bryant-Waugh and Lask, 1995: 13), which can point the way to the literature on eating disorders as well as family therapy. It contains 62 references from 1970 to 1994, concentrates on defining 'eating disorders' and covers the incidence, causation, clinical course, management and prognosis, especially of anorexia nervosa and bulimia nervosa. Family therapy for eating disorders is contextualized and critically analysed. A counterbalanced overview (Speed, 1995: 1), which concentrates more on theoretical concerns, includes a discussion of the appropriateness of family therapy, gender issues, postmodern approaches and the role of the therapist.

Clinical observations have often led to the creation of untested theories. The attempt to apply the 'invariant prescription' in family therapy on an inpatient ward in Spain (Vaz-Leal and Salcedo-Salcedo, 1995: 97) is an example of the way in which theoretical beliefs must be tempered by practical observation. The 'invariant prescription' was developed by the Milan team (Selvini Palazzoli and Prata, 1982) as a model of family investigation and treatment for anorexia nervosa. It was based on a theory of family interaction surrounding the eating disorder and a treatment model in which the parents are engaged in therapy, separate from the patient and other family members, which they are instructed to keep secret from the family. The aim is to develop clear boundaries between family subsystems and to change the interactional patterns that are seen to maintain the symptoms. Vaz-Leal and Salcedo-Salcedo, while attempting to use this model, found that they needed to vary their approach in order to take account of the different context in which they worked.

Clinical observations can also be used to guide and modify our treatment, such as the observation of differences in family patterns in anorexia nervosa and bulimia nervosa (Evans and Street, 1995: 115).

This study of three families, one containing a girl with anorexia and the other two containing bulimia sufferers, led the authors to speculate that a different form of treatment for each type of family is needed. Setting limits in families of bulimics is contrasted with creating flexibility in families of anorexic sufferers. Of course, generalizing from three clinical cases is risky. A study of 49 families with an anorexia nervosa patient (Wallin et al., 1996: 397) is an investigative approach to categorizing families, which then leads to speculation about changes in clinical treatment approaches. These authors found that families could be categorized as centripetal, centrifugal and balanced. They speculate that the chaotic, centrifugal families might benefit from lowering the general stress level and reducing guilt feelings.

There is a dialectic between those whose practice is based on theoretical beliefs and those who rely exclusively on research data. For example, clinical observations can lead to testable hypotheses such as the 'rule of appearances', which states that families which include an anorexic person are more than normally concerned with appearances; social acceptability is the measure of each family member's self-esteem (Lieberman, 1995: 133). This important dialectic has been explored (Dare et al., 1995: 31) in relation to family therapy for anorexia nervosa. This team explored the theoretical constructs of Selvini Palazzoli (Selvini Palazzoli et al., 1989) and Minuchin (Minuchin et al., 1978), comparing and contrasting their respective theories of intergenerational rigidity versus problem-solving rigidity with the empirical findings from their own Maudsley-based studies on the use of psychotherapies for anorexia nervosa. Colahan (1995: 79) wrote about the experience of being a therapist and a researcher in the Maudsley trials and the effect that curtailed clinical freedom, due to protocol constraints, paradoxically taught her to be more flexible by showing new ways of understanding her patients. The Maudsley researchers also reported on a preliminary study (Dodge et al., 1995: 59) of the use of family therapy in eight female adolescent bulimia nervosa sufferers, which contained 60 references and a good description of the particular type of family therapy employed. This team learned to favour a more respectful, less confrontational and less blaming approach to working with families as a result of their research.

A major aspect of eating disorders is their effect on the family system after the disorder has been discovered. In a study of 16 families (Levine, 1996: 463), an attempt was made to describe the perpetual motion, or circularity, of the family system, in which family dynamics and reactions perpetuate the eating disorder at the same time as the eating disorder upsets the family and keeps members overly focused on the individual. Levine found 12 criteria that helped establish a relational diagnosis, including changes in support patterns, changes in patterns of intimacy, the eating disorder assuming control of the household, and the use of denial, secrecy and suspicion in patient and family members. She recommends that family therapy is flexible in its emphasis and is not used as an exclusive treatment approach.

Note

[1]Although eating disorders affect both males and females, the large majority of patients are female. For the purposes of this chapter the feminine gender will be used for both patient and therapist.

Chapter 8
Group-analytic psychotherapy in the treatment of eating disorders

BONNIE GOLD

Psychotherapy groups for people with eating disorders are often resisted. The patient fears that as an individual in the group she will not receive sufficient attention from the psychotherapist and the therapist fears that the need and greed of the patients will overwhelm her. Group analysis can break through these prejudices as a group process develops from which everyone in the group gains at the same time. Interaction between group members becomes the focus of treatment, as past patterns of relationships and behaviour evolve, and understanding and analysis open the way for change and growth. Patients come to see themselves through the eyes of others and the sharing of experience between patients creates an atmosphere of exploration, support and reflection. A group-analytic approach that allows these developments to occur, at the patients' own pace, can lead to deep, lasting changes in their understanding of the underlying issues which have led to the symptoms of the eating disorder, and the effects of traumatic life experiences associated with the disorder can be worked through.

Eating disorders are complex conditions and a full understanding of them must take account of psychological, developmental, cultural and biological factors. It is recognized that the eating disorder provides a common pathway through which a variety of problems can be expressed. These range from the multi-impulsive bulimic exhibiting borderline pathology, to subclinical eating disorders, to the stage best described by Dr Bridget Dolan, where female over-concern with weight, shape and dieting is so common that being obsessed with food can be regarded as normal female behaviour (Dolan and Gitzinger, 1991). There are insights on, and explanations for, bulimia and eating disorders based on virtually all schools of learning theory, but group analysts are particularly well placed to offer an understanding of the contradictory, opposing currents to which women are subjected at the individual, interpersonal and institutional/social/cultural level. Many women engage in the symptoms without entering a pathological state. Women face enormous problems in freeing themselves from internalized and externalized culturally defined notions of 'woman' and in responding to the challenges of a new female identity in a world previously dominated by male attitudes. Despite some progress in the opportunities open to women, it is worth reminding ourselves that true social transformation is still fairly limited.

Research shows that interpersonal groups are helpful in dealing with the problems underlying eating disorders and many forms of group therapy have been recommended treatment models for bulimia. There are now a number of group analysts working specifically with patients with eating disorders, combining a social and dynamic perspective to offer an understanding of the interplay of the internal and external worlds which we inhabit and the way the various personal, familial, cultural and social networks interpenetrate. A special edition of *Group Analysis, the Journal of Group Analytic Psychotherapy* (Gold, 1999) describes the work of these practitioners.

Group-analytic psychotherapy

Group-analytic therapy is 'therapy in the group, by the group, including the group conductor', and the emphasis is on communication and translation of the autistic symptom that murmurs more and more loudly to be heard (Foulkes, 1964: 3). In the case of patients with eating disorders, the task is to help them understand why the symptoms, food, eating and body image are a preferable means of communication to language and feeling, helping them to find both the individual and cultural explanations.

Foulkes, the founder of group analysis, defines therapeutic factors which are group specific – that is, those not to be found in individual analytic therapy. All have extreme relevance for group-analytic therapy with patients with eating problems and I briefly outline these important. concepts in the following few paragraphs.

Matrix

Communication occurs across the group within a network of communicative relationships, always with the possibility of operating on any one or all of four levels – current, transference, projective and primordial. The exchange that occurs leads to a widening and deepening of personal and group understanding and the development of a sort of 'group mind' operating in the *Gestalt* of foreground/background, individual and society.

Mirroring

Aspects of the self are seen in other group members, with the help of the other group members, and thus outsight leads to insight as the recognition and reintegration of projected parts is made possible. Group-analytic therapy is sometimes likened to a 'Hall of Mirrors'.

Resonance

Themes and feelings are expressed and resonate through the group at the intrapersonal and interpersonal levels, creating identifications that lead to bonding, shared experience and understanding – a group culture and history.

Group as a forum

In the free-floating discussion, group members, on a conscious level, contribute in their own time and at their own pace while sparking off one another and enacting the group-specific factors of mirroring and resonance. The group forum allows the social realities of the external world and the personal realities of the internal world to be re-examined and challenged, so that an 'ego training in action' facilitates socialization and a revision of the boundaries of the self.

Translation

Making the unconscious conscious is the work of the group and is what is meant by 'therapy by the group, in the group, including the group conductor'. In the eating disorder group, the language of the symptom is given a social and individual meaning. This translation encompasses all the group factors: 'The conductor strives to broaden and deepen the expressive range of all members, while at the same time increasing their understanding of the deeper, unconscious levels' (Foulkes, 1964: 112).

The group conductor

Foulkes' view of the democratic group encompasses a therapist who conducts as in an orchestra and he distinguishes between leadership, analysis and interpretation. The conductor is both part of the group and apart from the group, which requires extreme sensitivity and skill but is essential for the success of therapy with these patients. The conductor must be able to immerse herself emotionally in the group matrix while retaining an analytic attitude.

Leadership

The conductor's leadership is not of the inspirational variey; overactivity on the part of the conductor is seen as encouraging a wish for the leader to develop an authoritarian fixation in the group. Minimal interference activates that which is latent. In the case of eating disorder patients, where developmental issues rooted in the mother/daughter relationship and concerning separation/individuation are central, such a therapeutic attitude is essential. The conductor uses herself by following the group and working with the consequences of what is generated and omitted through repression and regression.

Analysis

The fundamental attitude of the conductor has been termed the 'analytic attitude'. This enables the conductor to deal with the transference and her counter-transference and with all other events that happen within the group forum in the same spirit, moving from the manifest to the latent, a translation to the correct and underlying meaning. The process of moving from symptom to underlying conflict or problem contains many steps – confronting, exploring, facilitating, clarifying, interpreting – all of which fall within the concept of translation. The conductor places herself at the service of the group, tracking the group, and as part of the group, is there to facilitate the broadening and deepening of the communicative range of the group and its members.

Interpretation

A block in communication – when there is resistance to the process that impedes the free and spontaneous work of the group – calls for interpretation. These are the only times this is appropriate. For its location and timing, the conductor responds to the emotions of the individuals and the 'temperature' of the group, making particular use of her counter-transference. Generally the interpretation encompasses the group as a whole.

Psychodynamic approaches

This chapter concentrates on both the individual roots and the social and cultural roots of the explosion in food obsessions and eating disorders and on the larger questions of the relationship between culture and psychopathology. It is not my intention to focus on the large body of literature concerning practical treatment issues, including group treatments; Garner and Garfinkel (1985) offer an extensive review of current treatment models in the *Handbook of Psychotherapy for Anorexia Nervosa and Bulimia*. However, in this section I wish to look briefly at psychodynamic understandings relevant to group analysts working in this field, defining bulimia as a disorder of development that revolves around the core issue of shape and body weight and in which the person

– 90% are women – obsessively focuses on this as a defensive substitute. Most bulimics have suffered significant emotional deprivation at some point in their early childhood experiences. Whatever the exact cause, the child's emotional needs remain unfulfilled as the parents are preoccupied with their personal problems. The void left by parental remoteness – the child's feelings of loss and abandonment – is filled by food as an alternative comfort. The child's positive appearance conceals feelings of neediness, isolation, dependency, unhappiness and hurt, yet at no point can she risk directly revealing these feelings, which are revealed instead as periods of bingeing and purging. The adult patient continues this facade.

Most psychodynamic theories build on the work of the pioneer of eating disorders, Hilda Bruch. Bruch was the first to see a pattern in the families of women with eating disorders, where weak and emotionally absent fathers and mothers were either unavailable to their daughters or overinvolved with them. She related these experiences to specific symptoms and realized that they resulted in the child's failure to allow him/herself to emotionally connect with any experience and learn about themselves from it. Her therapy aimed at eliciting and respecting her patients' feelings and was directed at centring, cultivating and nurturing the self.

Object relations-based theories view bulimia as a faulty separation/individuation process in which the bulimic disavows the process in a comfortable, social compromise with the true/false self facade. The oral drive for nutrition, and the use of food as a transitional object, allow a compromise that prevents the bulimic from having to face more threatening, unconscious anxieties. These sorts of conflicts around identity and separation have been written about extensively, both in more popular styles such as Kim Chernin's (1983) *Womansize* and Geneen Roth's (1992) *When Food is Love* and in a body of object relations work by psychotherapists such as Susie Orbach and Louise Eichenbaum (1982) and Myra Dana and Marilyn Lawrence (1988).

Dana and Lawrence propose that the eating disorder is activated by the defensive split – the desire to incorporate the breast and a fear that the neediness will be so destructive as to destroy the source of love. A surpassing of mother would be damaging so that the mere idea of individuation/separation from mother causes and creates the symptoms. Kleinians view the mother–daughter relationship as central to eating disorders:

> The shame and agony involved in vomiting up the nourishment is a compensation, a suitable punishment for having greedily swallowed it in the first place. It's not just that too much food has been consumed and the fear of fat makes vomiting inevitable ... it is that needs have been perceived that are so

terrifying that they must simultaneously be denied ... it is about having a clean, neat, good, un-needy appearance which conceals behind it a messy, needy, bad part which must be hidden away (Dana and Lawrence, 1988: 42).

The difficulty mothers have in meeting the real needs of their baby daughters and, because of their shared gender, the mother's tendency to unconsciously project her own unmet needs on to her baby is described. Through the cycle of emotional deprivation and identification, mothers teach their baby daughters not to expect too much from others but rather to expect to look after others' needs. The suggestion is that the 'normal' mother–daughter relationship may contain within it certain elements which are destructive enough to lead to serious difficulties in the area of self-nurturing and the meeting of personal needs.

The bulimic's family presents a false self facade too, in the pretence that all is well, thereby providing no space for the growing child to allow bad or negative feelings (as is the case with child sexual abuse). It's quite common to hear bulimic women in therapy talk about family mottoes such as 'Keep it in the family'/'Don't talk to strangers'/'Let's keep it to ourselves', rules that are incorporated into the woman's way of viewing the world, binding her pathologically to her mother and family.

Not only are feelings not allowed but they are not recognized so that the child grows up full of anxiety and anger about her mother's approach. It can be seen from this perspective how women – with their close connection with food and their tendency to regard the body as a source of confirmation and self-esteem (as I shall explore later) – turn to bulimia and other eating disorders as a way of expressing distress and unhappiness, thereby protecting their mothers from their aggression by attacking their own bodies.

Bulimia also reflects and expresses the daughter's wavering feelings of panic and guilt. Guilt is stimulated and provoked by the idea of doing better than mother and leaving her behind. Panic is provoked by the idea of having to stay with her and becoming frustrated and unfulfilled like her. The binge/purge syndrome represents the fluctuations between the idea of the possibility of individuation in the introjection and the rejection of this possibility in the expulsion.

Janine Chasseguet-Smirgel (1985) explains a specific form of feminine guilt that becomes fixed at the moment of Oedipal crisis when bad is projected on to mother and good on to father. If the father does not offer the attributes necessary to sustain projection of good aspects, there can be a fusion of aggressive and erotic instincts which affect a woman's adult sexuality and potential for achievement. The counter-identification with the bad aspects of the mother is maintained, while a trusting identification with father is damaged and the bulimic response may be one way of expressing this conflict.

If they accept these views as fundamental to the origins of the eating disorder, psychotherapists must validate and articulate their women patients' repressed yearning for the mothering that they have been denied. This is an important aspect in the initial stages of therapy, particularly when sharing experiences with other women, as is offered in slow-open group-analytic psychotherapy. The approach taken by the group-analytic conductor will be not only to validate and articulate female patients' repressed yearnings but also to acknowledge the self-sacrifices bulimics have been asked to make as daughters, wives and mothers. Women will be encouraged to identify character traits which develop from female socialization and may have become identified as negative, destructive or manipulative by those treating these patients. Much emphasis is placed on working with this in the transference and counter-transference, emphasizing the maternal values of holding, supporting, nourishing and promoting growth. In involving the entire group group-analytic psychotherapy offers the group body as a containing mother which at these times frees the conductor to offer herself as a consistent and potent father.

For whom a group-analytic approach?

Dana describes the bulimic obsession with taking in and forcing out as a rejection of nurturing, an effect of the mother's failure to validate her daughter's needs appropriately (Dana and Lawrence, 1988). This is reflected in the therapeutic relationship, in which the patient will be continually testing, stopping and starting, suffering extremes of love and hate, depression and aggression, inhibition and impulsivity, vacillating between a longing for isolation and yearning for attachment, leaving the therapist feeling pushed and pulled.

Many eating disorder patients cannot endure the dyadic relationship, experiencing the situation as such a terrifying re-enactment of the early parental relationship that a safe container cannot develop. The perception of a group as a looser organization, in which shifts of attention occur, allows a varying and tolerable individual focus and enables the gradual establishment of a safe container. This environment and culture supports an ongoing examination of the eating disorder patient's early developmental issues without the patient feeling scrutinized and claustrophobic as in her childhood. The group member finds allies, and is provided with a sense of safety in numbers which helps to mediate the fear of retaliation from mother with which such patients continually exist.

The therapist working with eating disorder patients in both individual and group therapy assumes, in the extreme, the projected character of an unconsciously hated and/or beloved parent who attracts resistance, transference and other intolerable intrapsychic pathology. The working through ambivalence in depth is a central task in understanding the eating problems, and is central to the work of the group. The conductor will be projected as superior, contemptuous, arrogant, controlling or benevolently patronizing. The intensity of these projections experienced by the group conductor may go some way towards explaining the aversion many psychotherapists express to working with eating disorder patients. A patient who has felt severely rejected or traumatized may find accepting help from any one individual terrifying and humiliating. While on the conscious level she may know that she is in need of help, she will defend against the knowledge that there are great unattended wells of need and dependency within her – the 'thought unknown'. She will find the horizontal associations of the initial stages of the group process a bearable way to introduce these ideas to herself as she gradually comes to see that she has spent her life conforming or rebelling and has left no space for her own ego, judgements, reality or creativity. The re-examination within the mutuality of the group forum alleviates the shame, humiliation and isolation in which such patients are mired.

In assessing a patient's suitability for group-analytic psychotherapy, patients need to exhibit interest in understanding the psychological and interpersonal underlay to their problems. The assessor will want to test the patient's motivation to engage in the painful process of uncovering long-repressed feelings and the ability to stay with the group when the going gets tough. Generally, the group conductor will take one or two assessment sessions to get a feel for the patient's current outlook on the eating problems and patterns and her personal and family history to decide whether a patient is suitable for the specific group. It is important to hold in mind that some patients specifically will not be helped by a group, for example, those with recent or active psychosis, those who are actively misusing multi-substances and may be diagnosed as multi-impulsive, and those with an antisocial personality disorder. At the same time, considerations about the level of intimacy and closeness which the patient can tolerate at this time will inform a decision about individual or group treatment. Liaison with any other professionals involved with the patient is essential to establish continuity and containment and to minimize the potential for splitting.

Personality disorders, most commonly narcissistic and borderline disorders, are prevalent in eating disorder patients. The group conductor will therefore need to make a careful and skilled assessment of any one particular patient's ability to work with any one particular group, in that behaviour and attitudes will vary widely in the diagnostic category, as will a group's ability to cope with different behaviour and attitudes. It is unlikely that a group will manage to sustain cohesion and stability with more than one or two personality disorders.

A homogeneous outpatient group for bulimics

The unstructured, free-floating discussion allows the emergence of familiar patterns of relationships so that it will seem as though the group is working well, somewhat cosily, with women talking about their anxieties and fears in the language of food and body image. The group conductor initiates a culture of enquiry, musing about fat as a feeling and so on, so that slowly the group comes to recognize that these symptoms mask other concerns. For long periods, conflict and competition will be held at bay as the members reassure and support one another and ignore or idealize the conductor.

The following vignette illustrates some of these situations.

Clinical vignette

The group, which has been meeting for almost two years, began the session with niceties but quickly led into a theme of putting oneself on the line. A had managed to disagree with her boss and had disputed the length of a garment with him; K, having rehearsed her grievance, had told her business partner how she felt; P had been more open with her boyfriend. All were surprised that it had been easier than they thought; in fact, they mused, this seemed to happen so often – the worry and build-up being far more troubling than the event.

K went on to tell the group about the 10-page letter she had sent to her mother, the culmination of many months of anguish and understanding that she had gone through in the group. She had told her mother that she loved her but could not be her surrogate for life. She had expressed strong feelings concerning the past and the present and the group were both delighted and apprehensive.

The group suddenly found itself discussing food and, while I was wondering silently about this, a long-term member, J, challenged what was happening – 'We haven't done this for ages, why now?'

P arrived in her usual dramatic way and sat down, exclaiming that she had had a really hard week and that she was all over the place. Her eating was bad, she was behind with her college work, she was arguing with her mother, her friends were not helping her. No one responded to either her or J directly, but S began to talk of her difficulties with her father.

She had been to a local event with her brother and met someone she fancied. She wanted to stay with him overnight but felt that the comments from her father would not be worth the effort of defying him. She said this was ridiculous; despite being 27 years old, she still worried

(contd)

---

about his reaction. She talked in a matter-of-fact way of her father's conservative, repressive approach to her, and her mother's unavailability, both now and when she was a child. C and K sat listening to her with tears streaming down their faces.

This was the first time I felt I needed to say something to the group and I said: 'It seems as if C and K are feeling what you are unable to feel'. S was somewhat dismissive. I felt clumsy.

The session ended with my feeling that something important had happened in this session, that K had come a long way, that the group was beginning to work more independently, but ... I was left feeling that I was somewhat straitjacketed and with a sense of not having understood something.

The following week, having organized the group room, I went to collect my messages and found a number of notes. Each group member had dutifully notified me that she was unable to come – mirroring the way K had communicated to her mother. I sat in the circle alone (one of many fearful fantasies entertained by group therapists of all persuasions!) and the line from Elijah, 'Call him louder he hearest not', floated into my mind. Unable to confront me directly, carrying a sense that they are bad and destructive, fearing that I would be like their mothers, unable to withstand their own feelings or enjoy their progress, the group had unconsciously arranged to let me know en masse how difficult it was to talk directly to me. I did not, of course, know precisely what it was that needed to be said, but both this and the feeling that these women could not allow themselves to hold on to anything good were in my mind.

The following week, all were there and gradually the group realized that I had sat alone waiting for them the previous week. There were exclamations of embarrassment, amazement that this had happened and then one member asked me how I had felt. I replied honestly, saying that initially I had felt annoyed and had felt emotionally abandoned by the group, but I came to see that this was an important communication. I told them that I had sat in the room alone and wondered about this happening in the week following K's letter to her mother and a group theme of beginning to show dislikes and disagreements. Perhaps we could think what this might mean?

The group went on to think about this together, one of many sessions in which they came to see that what is felt to be so dangerous and terrifying is, in reality, ordinary human feelings, and that communicating directly is not disastrous. All of this had been mooted in the first session described, but bulimically evacuated. These rhythms of taking in and getting rid of self-knowledge, of taking a risk and then retracting, are key notes in such bulimic groups and are essential to translate.

Refocusing female identity

> Male-female competitiveness ... concerns itself with the basic human situation of sex difference and the interplay of feeling between the 'haves' and 'have nots'. The neurotically exaggerated pride of the male provokes the neurotically exaggerated envy of the female, and the ensuing conflict tends to focus on the rivalry between the sexes, at first on a manifest level, but eventually deepening to the unconscious level (Foulkes and Anthony, 1990: 173–4).

There is a basic disagreement about whether women's mental health 'problems' are an expression of neurotic conflict or whether:

> it is our very definitions of femininity and the feminine role that are a pathogenic cause of female symptomatology. This is not just a matter of theoretical interest, for a therapist's position regarding this controversy (whether conscious and explicit or unexamined and unconsciously held) determines the very course and process of treatment (Lerner, 1993: 197).

Gilligan (1990) emphasizes that the different voice does not and must not solely relate to women; that there is an interplay of these voices within each sex that converges at times of crisis and change; and thus that there is a need for these ideas to be incorporated into the group-analytic body of work. Foulkes' basic law of group dynamics is that members of a 'therapeutic group collectively constitute the very norm from which individually they deviate' (Foulkes, 1964: 297). Identity conflicts and role confusions based in changing social attitudes are being played out continually in our groups, and the group therapist needs to be informed by modern psychodynamic theory, cultural norms and with a clearer view of the different developmental pathways pursued by men and women.

There is ongoing debate about whether women therapists should have exclusive involvement in dealing with women patients with eating disorders – about whether eating disorders should be seen solely as a women's issue (the psychoanalytic versus the feminist) or as a social issue (individual versus cultural). A group-analytic approach emphasizes how the functioning of the early mother–daughter dyad is embedded in the family group, which is influenced by its particular community group, which is again defined by the particular culture to which this community and family belong. In other words, group analysts will always be working with the internal and external realities of the patient's overlapping worlds. The eating disorder and treatment process cannot be bracketed off from daily life.

By focusing only on the analytic idea of irrational displacement, we may fail to acknowledge the 'rational' messages about food/sex/women bombarding us daily. A group-analytic approach has the potential to tackle these cultural messages, to understand the colossal forces that permeate the individual to the core.

An ethnic disorder

George Devereux's concept of an 'ethnic disorder' describes a pattern that, because of its own dynamics, comes to express crucial contradictions and core anxieties in a society (Devereux, 1980). Like hysteria in the 19th century, eating disorders express core cultural dilemmas and social contradictions of the 20th century, resonating to the increased desire and movement among women for greater freedom.

Devereux describes a continuity of symptoms and an underlying dynamic of any ethnic disorder, where the normal elements of the culture are expressed in the disorder in degrees of intensity and in a spectrum from borderline to subclinical forms, just as we are now seeing with eating disorders. The recent literature defines subclinical eating disorders as an area between eating carefully and full-blown anorexia and bulimia. Professor Haber of the UCLA Eating Disorders Clinic estimates that 80–85% of women in the United States have a problematic relationship with food.

Eating disorders draw on the common cultural vocabulary latching on to the mania about dieting, thinness and food control. Women use these cultural preoccupations as defences that allow them to escape from, and achieve some control over, unmanageable personal distress, much of which revolves around personal female identity, rooted both in early mother–daughter disturbances and women's place in the cultural symbolic order. Like hysteria, these disorders generate fascination and repugnance simply because they are so closely tied to the social conflicts and contradictions experienced by us all. They are also closely allied to sexual politics as eating disorders tie in to control of the female body, commonly accepted standards of beauty and appropriate female expressions of distress, generated within a patriarchal society. Group-analytic psychotherapy can provide a setting in which these latent disturbances can emerge and be understood in both the personal and social domains.

Full-blown eating disorders with severe mental and accompanying physical problems are merely a point on a continuum that includes most women's experiences. Society is seeing an exaggerated response that is common to literally millions of women, representing a social phenomenon where many women do not feel entitled to eat without guilt. The move towards defining new female identities has left many young women at risk of developing eating disorders. The previously unexperienced emphasis on women's achievement and accomplishment is in sharp contrast to previous emphases, which focused on conformity, humility and docility. The new sexual ethos has also given rise to additional problems, including greater exposure to manipulation and fears among those from more traditional backgrounds. At a time of rapid change in Western society, young women are trapped by the ambiguities inherent in a radically altering set of expectations. It is important to understand how women have come to internalize the view that eating is for others and not themselves – why women are afraid of their appetites.

The striving for a new female identity in these situations is made more complex by a complete lack of clarity as to what exactly is expected of women in a new social role. A multiplicity of conflicting role demands – combining the aggression and expectations for achievement of the new with the demureness of more traditional femininity – makes life extremely difficult for young women, even those who do not experience eating disorders per se. African-American women with a strong racial/ethnic identification have been found not to have internalized restrictive ideals and are less prone to eating disorders. Young women from families, such as in the Asian or Jewish communities, where there is a clash between the traditional values transmitted in the home and the transitional values communicated at school and in the wider cultural milieu, report an increase in eating problems as they struggle to retain an acceptable and accepted role in their family and community while finding a place in the wider society.

Clinical vignette

S has been in the group for some weeks and is beginning to talk of her conflicts and loyalties to her Italian mother. Her father died when she was an infant and her mother struggled to provide for her and her brother, settling in England and establishing a family-run restaurant business. She is crying about her mother's claustrophobic expectations, her rejection of her English friends' lifestyle and her guilt when she argues with her.

K, who has struggled to free herself from her Eastern European mother's hold on her in two years in the group, exclaims 'Oh God, S, it's like listening to how I used to feel. P, from a Greek family [who has now left the group], used to sound the same – it's something about foreign mothers which is so hard to explain. They leave you feeling like you don't know where you begin or end.'

This resonance offers S a transforming experience and she proceeds in this and subsequent sessions to explore with K and other group members how she has felt when required to act as a mirror to her own mother; to contain her mother's feelings and to feel guilty if she wants something different for herself. Her mother's difficulties in adapting to a different culture, which become S's difficulties, are understood through the experience of other women in the group. She is no longer isolated and ashamed of her feelings.

It would seem that femininity and being female are continually devalued, both in spite of and because of feminist gains. Female attributes and abilities are rarely respected and are frequently seen as a threat to male authority and control. In many areas, female intelligence is overlooked or derided as unfeminine or pushy. At the same time, Western society degrades traditional female roles such as caring and nurturing. Higher-functioning women are particularly drawn into this battle as it is increasingly difficult to balance career and family aspirations. Many women have dealt with this conflict by becoming more 'male' – tough and controlling – but managing only at the expense of repressing their nurturing qualities. This simply reinforces the bulimic's predicament in reconciling her aspirations and ambitions with her femaleness. The false solution of bingeing and purging can be interpreted as the internalization of society's covert misogyny.

These ideas are central to the work of Carol Gilligan, whose research showed that superego development is different for men and women because they absorb societal influences in different ways (Gilligan, 1990). Her ideas are important because they relate to sex-role identity, self-definition and future expectations and the real process of decision-making – all highly charged areas which are approached from very different bases by men and women. Group analysis, with its understanding of social process, social context and the social unconscious, has the potential to allow an exploration of these issues.

The symbolic order

> The most important point ... remains that group constructive tendencies are of necessity conducive to the norm because being compatible with a particular group in hand, they must be compatible with social life in general and even more specifically with the mode of life of the particular community to which this group belongs. Therefore adjustment in a therapeutic group means social adjustment (Foulkes, 1964: 90).

No one can grow from earliest childhood without an awareness of messages about gender and sexuality, not only in personal and familial terms, but shaped through fairy tales, myths, films, books, magazines, television and advertising, all culturally mediated through language. Stories of sexual violence scream at society every day, both personal and reported through mass media. For example, during the war in Bosnia, rape has been a common tool of war; sadism towards women is a leitmotif of pornography; advertising uses women as sexual objects. Films such as *Rising Sun* and *Fatal Attraction* equate the idea of sexiness with death and destruction – modern woman as deadly predator, promoting the idea that a sexual woman is bad and dangerous. Alternatively, the media portray women as wives and mothers, endlessly feeding and caring for men and children, putting their own needs in second place.

The message that beauty, success, personal happiness and self-worth are based on a thin figure assaults women from every quarter. Bruch has speculated that the fashion industry, films, magazines and television are all responsible for promoting the view that one can be loved and respected only when slender. The pressures on women to maintain a thinner shape have become more and more unrealistic and destructive.

For women struggling to develop an identity in a changing culture, society's messages are mixed and often obtuse. Psychoanalysts since Freud have repeatedly documented the defensiveness and fear of women and things feminine that characterize the most normal of men in our society. Kernberg has noted the intense envy and hatred of women in many male patients, and Horney, Klein and Jones, among others, reflect similar findings. Stoller, in his early work, demonstrates how hatred and the desire to humiliate the other, taking revenge and triumphing over childhood trauma, form the basic script of perversion and pornography, which are traditionally masculine. The sort of responses women now endure in trying to form a new role are partly about unconscious male needs to repress, subjugate and master their own losses. Group therapists should be informed of the different arguments and approaches to assess for themselves their own position when offering therapy.

Clinical vignette

A, a designer, tells the group she wants to change jobs and has her first interview for several years. She is anxious, talks to the group and wonders what to wear for such an interview.

B, who works as a stockbroker, responds indignantly: 'Dress conservatively if you want to be taken seriously, that sort of short skirt is fatal. I got called into my senior partner this week to be told that my skirt was too distracting for my male colleagues – I know you'll all say I should be furious and I am, but what can I do?'

A: 'What did you do?'

B: 'Cried in the loo, went back to work and at home that night had a supreme bulimic binge' (said with a glance at me and beginning to cry). 'If I'm going to succeed there, I have to play by their rules and the only other woman in the office is such a prude.'

C, a nurse who has managerial responsibilities: 'You won't believe what I'm doing next week – I'm going to a one-day workshop on Corporate Imaging for Women, you ought to come.'

K, an actress, retorts: 'I really do object to that idea; although I know it's a reality, it feels such a bind that we're all in.'

(contd)

Other group members join in with their own stories of workplace pressures to maintain a facade of perfection and competence. It begins to feel as if, having held on to these conflicts for so long, a competitive purge is taking place and I reflect and say that, as in the privacy of the bathroom, their facades of perfection and competence can be dropped here and they are beginning to express the 'unacceptable' feelings of anger and powerlessness which up until now have been expressible only in their eating preoccupations.

After a short silence, S responds to my comment with a story about a conflict with her mother which ends with her talking of her mother's ability to always state the obvious, which she finds 'so bloody patronizing'.

K grins and looks at me: 'I sometimes feel, Bonnie, that you think this group revolves around you and our reactions to you.'

There could be a variety of responses and interpretations to the above but it can be seen that a group-analytic approach enables the group to work on many layers of personal and social issues and to begin to address the childhood and cultural adaptations which have been split off and hidden for so long.

So far, disorders among higher-functioning women have been poorly documented but are discussed in both Squire's *The Slender Balance* (1983) and in Gamman and Makinen's *Female Fetishism – A New Look* (1994). We know that the bulimic syndrome may appear in the context of any diagnostic category, as discussed by Schwartz (1988) in *Bulimia – a Psychoanalytic Perspective*, in which he states that, in higher-functioning women, bulimia can emanate from a fragment of the ego which still operates on the earliest level of ego organization, loose enough to allow ongoing structures that seem relatively isolated from the rest of the personality. Thus it is that bulimics are sometimes able to switch to primary-level ego states in private while operating successfully, without the knowledge of those around them, as if they were well-integrated adults. Overall, while it seems that they may have achieved a high level of interpersonal maturity, these women are still struggling internally with issues of independence and self-assertion and, since the bulimic maintains a normal weight, she can be trapped in this pattern for many years, unknown and undetected behind a facade of normality. This is an important concept – that part of the self has reached a greater level of integration and therefore contact with the real world – which needs to be held firmly in mind by the group therapist during treatment to prevent a cosy collusion.

Group experiences

If women along the bulimic continuum are expressing an inability to find an identity acceptable to themselves and society, I hope I have clarified that focusing solely on the mother–daughter relationship is not enough. The nature and intensity of this dyad is potentially problematic but, in order to fully understand the problem, we must also understand that women are caught between conflicting cultural demands which require integration of contradictory values of achievement and mastery with an underlying self-concept that is defined in terms of nurturance and physical attractiveness. It is therefore crucial to have a therapeutic milieu such as that present in group analysis, in which the interaction of the foundation and cultural matrix are understood, together with the personal and interpersonal.

Group-analytic theory has the potential to expose and thereby shed light on transpersonal processes involved in social practices, institutions, gender and power relations in the context of the cultural and foundation matrix. However, by exclusively adopting the mother-centred object relations theories of Bion, Klein, Winnicott, Balint, Fairbairn, Mahler and so on, and emphasizing the safe maternal aspects of the group, the importance and impact of the male element is denied, both positively – the phallus as a powerful source of energy, targeting, pushing and competing – and negatively – prohibiting and denying.

Hearst writes:

> The mother image is almost ubiquitous in present-day therapies, and one must ask oneself the question whether there are in our society features which produce this intensification of pathogenic relationships in early childhood with the other. The group analyst, possibly more clearly than the psychoanalyst, may well be presented with a socially conditioned or at least intensified psychic phenomenon, since the therapy group represents the wider social environment of its members. What we encounter in the groups is the vague, blurred image of the absent father ... we experience parents who, in a fast-changing society are out of touch with their children's experience (Hearst 1980: 29).

Foulkes did not elaborate on the idea of the group as mother and parts of mother, but Prodgers (1990) and subsequent group analysts take this further. They focus on the dual aspects of mother so that, while the emphasis on the feminine caring and nurturing can be empowering and validating for women in the group, there are other aspects to consider. The maternal space may enable an exploration of the woman patient's inner world and hold her in the early stages, but paternal power and external culture may be underrepresented, both because of the way in which men experience the group and the regressive pull on them, and 'the analyst's fear of going where it's hottest' (Hopper, 1982: 136). It would seem that men and women hold images of the archaic mother – the good, omnipotent mother (generous breast, fruitful womb, softness, warmth, wholeness, abundance, harvest, the Earth) versus the bad, omnipotent mother (engulfment, intrusion, frustration, invasion, death and sickness). In the group, in contrast to the 'real world', men are brought face to face with aspects of women that emphasize fears and losses which are possible to defend against outside the group environment. Men can often be rendered passive and speechless by these encounters while the women in the group may experience their passivity as withholding and withdrawing, thus confirming to them that their female appetites are too much. And so the cycle continues.

Going where it's hottest

Group analysts work with transpersonal processes involved in social practices, institutions, gender and power relations in the context of the cultural and foundation matrix. These contentious issues will often bring with them destructive and self-destructive forces that the group conductor ignores at her peril. Foulkes may have underestimated the negative forces that may be at work in a group with his injunction to trust the group, and these primitive forces will always be lurking in some form in eating disorder groups. These groups can unleash powerful forces of aggression and conflict which, if not recognized, may have a painfully disruptive effect on the individual and the group as a whole. The group may acquire a negative or destructive connotation in the minds of the patients.

Nitsun (1996) has termed these forces the Anti-Group – a set of attitudes and impulses, conscious and unconscious, which can become the destructive aspect of groups and which can threaten the integrity of the group and its therapeutic development. This may help to understand the resistance to analytic groups that can occur in some settings – an underlying scepticism about whether groups can be therapeutic or are in reality quite damaging. When conducting an eating disorder group, it is essential to be aware of the potential for the anti-group to take hold. Selection, the regulation of the setting, the conductor's role and counter-transference are issues for consideration. Ambivalence among this patient group is intense and this can lead to conflict between creative and destructive tendencies, which in turn can produce a crisis. The therapist will feel that the group is tottering as questions about the group's survival are raised, but if the group can be sufficiently contained and understood, the group will be strengthened and able to move to a new level of awareness. The working through of aggression and ambivalence, even at its most intense, usually leads to reparation and renewed creativity. It requires strength from the therapist to withstand these tempestuous times with a broad view of the group process. An understanding of the importance of confronting these darker aspects with patients, to work through ambivalence in depth, is essential for the conductor of a group for eating disorder patients. The group then becomes a container for both the positive and negative forces, which leads to a transforming therapeutic experience for the eating disorder patients.

An appreciation of these dilemmas within the framework of the anti-group enables the conductor to recognize the primitive forces and feelings that will emerge in the group. These forces, which are expressed in the symptoms of the eating disorder, can be terrifying and powerful when translated into the language of feelings unless they are properly understood by the conductor. The contemporary woman looking for a new sense of identity is often caught between two interacting and modifying forces. Women struggle on the border of the imaginary (maternal) and the symbolic (paternal) which, if castrating and prohibiting, is experienced as destructive and can leave them feeling potentially psychotic and certainly out of control. The destructive energy can be contained by channelling it into the binge/purge cycle so that it can be viewed either as a creative compromise or as a gradual slide into illness. In fact, Lacan, writing on psychosis, says that what is ejected out into the world is the Name of the Father, a failure of the paternal metaphor.

An emerging change, according to Melissa Benn's current research, is that the masculine ethic of paid work which morally rewards those who earn well, manage others and possess impressive-sounding titles, is no longer challenged as the height of achievement by women (Benn, 1998). The paternal metaphor is neither ejected nor rejected but incorporated. Women are attempting to combine the masculine work ethic with the feminine nurturing model. Even feminism, once the politics of wider personal and social transformation, has narrowed to become a language of worldly power. The historian Theodore Zeldin claims that emotional achievement is now valued as highly as public action, but reaching the goal of true intimacy is quite different from deciding who does the dishes (Zeldin, 1994). Every survey reflects women trying to do it all and not enough of a shift in real gender infrastructures.

Homogeneous or heterogeneous groups

Group therapy for women with eating disorders (medically or self-referred) is often undertaken in a homogeneous group. It is felt that identification with other women can spring patients from the trap of isolation, secrecy and alienation by enabling them to explore their personal and social positions without the pressure of taking on familiar stereotypical roles, as might be the case in a mixed group.

In the first stages, there is less resistance to talking about the secret, whereas in later stages members resonate to the resistances and defences employed by fellow members and can more effectively challenge one another. In a slow-open group where members are at different stages of self-understanding, the risk of group collusion is far less. Despite the homogeneity of the group, there will be considerable heterogeneity and essential work will be accomplished as members acknowledge their differences.

However, my feeling is that support for the emerging self can be given to women in a mixed group and that, by putting women automatically in a single-sex group, they are denied the opportunity to reveal and articulate the unconscious social constructs. Patients are denied the opportunity to work with men and in a 'real' way to transform themselves. Mixed-sex groups are able to explore parental and marital conflict and other relationship issues which underlie the eating disorder, more fully and in an appropriate social context.

This is not to deny the very real benefits some women get from women-only groups, but the ego training in action that can occur in a mixed group has a greater potential than any other medium to rearrange a consciousness about male/female interactions. In the lived group experience, low self-esteem, shame, anxiety and rage – all aspects at the core of identity struggles – emerge in context.

Foulkes' view that group constructive tendencies work constructively in the group and foster adjustment to social norms is problematic and limited. If there is a cultural distortion or an ethnic disorder within the community at large, the group, by implication, could become an agency of accommodation. The group analyst, in the free-floating communication, can help develop a culture in which unacceptable areas of normal social interaction are possible so that patterns of eating, and feelings about food and body image can be discussed. Considering the evidence that women are preoccupied with these issues, it is interesting and significant how often they are left outside the analytic group.

However, if there is a cultural distortion or an ethnic disorder in the community at large, the group, by implication, could become an agency of accommodation. The group analyst, in the free-floating communication, can help develop a culture in which unacceptable areas of normal social interaction are possible so that patterns of eating, and feelings about food and body image can be discussed. Considering the evidence that women are preoccupied with these issues, it is interesting and significant how often they are left outside the analytic group.

Patients without a language for their distress feel ashamed about admitting a preoccupation with looks, appearance and food, and will be very cautious about bringing this into the group. They often fear being experienced as superficial and trivial and can sometimes be used by other patients as a vehicle on which to displace their narcissism or to defend against primitive experiences which food, shape and weight concerns invoke – 'fantastic representations of malignant mothering, of the engulfing, depriving mother' (Prodgers, 1990: 29). At the deepest level, primeval fears about sustenance and existence, and life and death, may be stirred. Discussing these issues inevitably means looking at the visual evidence, a truly double-sided, multi-faceted mirror which challenges both therapist and patients. Lacan sees the body as a 'lived anatomy' regulated by the symbolic order (Benevenuto and Kennedy, 1986), so in taking up these areas in the group, strong moral overtones and cultural taboos can surface. Women fear that talking openly with men about these appetites will expose them as the archetypal woman, all needing and all wanting, an image which shapes and permeates women's internal and external world.

It is not good enough to suggest that patients do not fare well in mixed groups because the group cannot come to grips with the hidden eating disorder pathology. Careful preparation of the patient for the group and the cultivation of a culture in which both conductor and group are able to work in these areas are essential.

In locating where the resistance to these issues entering the group forum may lie, we need to recall Foulkes' words concerning the need for a group analyst to be intimate with:

> The individual's attitude towards his own self, particularly in its unconscious aspect (instinctive impulses and reactions against them, defence mechanisms) and towards his own body. I consider the understanding of P. Schilder's work on the 'Image and Appearance of the Human Body' as of fundamental importance. A Group-Analyst without this as part of his equipment would be comparable to a Psycho-Analyst without knowledge of the interpretation of dreams (Foulkes, 1948a: 135).

Conclusion

The location of resistance to working with eating disordered patients in groups of mixed gender and pathology is not only to be found at the level of the individual conductor's self-understanding and prejudice but also at the level of the setting in which the group is situated. The system needs to be as open to the issues as is the individual group conductor. The conductor, particularly in a hospital or clinic setting, will be part of a team reflecting societal behaviour and attitudes which may prefer the eating disorder patient to be seen in a certain way. The challenge to these teams is to allow space for reflection and an openness to new ideas and perspectives such as I have suggested, not always easily achievable in overworked and stressful situations.

In working with the patient with an eating problem, group analysis bears witness to dynamic problems of the mother–daughter dyad and the prevalence of an ethnic disorder – the regressive result of so far insoluble conflicts within women and between women and men and their changing world. If the group, as a representative of society/public opinion, is to facilitate change, we must enable women to express their symptoms more freely and to consider carefully whether specialized eating disorders/women's groups or mixed groups, to use Foulkes' words, enable us to view 'the group as a forum symbolising the community as a whole' (Foulkes, 1948: 168).

Note

This is an expanded version of an article that first appeared in *Group Analysis, The Journal of Group Analytic Psychotherapy* 32(1), March 1999 (Gold, 1999).

Chapter 9
Eating disorders: A psychodrama approach

JINNIE JEFFERIES

Much has been written about the subject of eating disorders. It is impossible in the scope of this chapter to give an extensive account of the pathology, but it is nevertheless useful to try to summarize the main features of this condition in order to assess the extent to which psychodrama psychotherapy may be conceived as useful in its treatment.

The term eating disorders refers to a collection of symptoms and feelings which relate to eating behaviour, weight and feelings about one's own body and food itself. There has been much debate as to whether anorexia nervosa and bulimia constitute two separate conditions or whether they are interrelated. They do, however, have specific features that are particular to whichever condition predominates. In both conditions there is repeated restriction of food intake, whether by restriction or repeated vomiting. Patients with eating disorders usually have a great resistance to treatment, especially treatment that is not directed specifically towards symptomatology.

It is perhaps understandable that those called on to treat the condition get caught up in a tortuous battle around food, pushing for adjustments in eating patterns by rewarding improvements or punishing when there is a deterioration in body weight. However, although on one level the condition is all about food intake, those of us who have been involved with these clients know when such a restricted approach becomes unhelpful and how such an approach can overlook other important dimensions of the condition, such as the patient's whole body experience and the relationship with self and other. It is therefore more helpful in the treatment process to come to a better understanding of the patient's 'inner world experience', paying particular attention to such issues concerning separateness, autonomy, individual identity and relatedness.

It is my intention in this chapter to briefly explain the theoretical position of psychodrama, which may provide a clearer understanding of how psychodrama as a method of group psychotherapy may assist patient and clinician. I will from time to time draw on clinical material to clarify certain theoretical points and use two psychodrama sessions to illustrate how the method can be useful in treating the patient presenting with an eating disorder.

Psychodrama group psychotherapy and sociometry was developed by Dr JL Moreno. As a therapeutic method it employs action methods to encourage the expression of repressed emotions and to introduce the possibility of change by correcting the maladaptive learning that has taken place. In the context of the group the patient is helped to find new ways of perceiving and reacting to past and present life experiences, and to develop a more cohesive sense of self.

A classical psychodrama consists of three stages: the warm-up, the enactment and the sharing.

The warm-up

This increases a sense of trust and group membership through techniques that encourage interactions between the group. It stimulates the creativity and spontaneity of group members and helps them to focus on personal issues. The client, whose work will be the focus of the enactment, is selected by other group members who feel sympathetic to the issue presented. In this way, s/he works for the group, carrying the group concern, as well as for herself or himself.

The enactment

In the enactment, the protagonist explores the issues heightened by the warm-up process with the support of group members and the therapist. In psychodrama there is no script; the drama is spontaneous, created in the moment by the protagonist, group members and the director (therapist).

The sharing

The final stage of the psychodrama process is where the protagonist and group members come together to share ways in which they identify with the protagonist's psychodrama. It is not a time for interpretation or comment about what has taken place, for the protagonist will need time to fully internalize and integrate the process. The sharing phase allows the protagonist to feel once again integrated within the group and allows other group members to share their own powerful feelings and thoughts which will have emerged from either participating in the psychodrama or observing the action. Sharing serves the purpose of focusing on future psychodramatic work.

Because psychodrama is intrinsically an action method, the protagonist is encouraged to move quickly into the drama, creating the space in which events took place and to have an opportunity to re-experience rather than retell events. The physical setting of scenes and their portrayal evoke memories and emotions associated with the space.

Central to the understanding of psychodrama as a method of treatment is the theory of 'role'. Moreno defined role as 'the functioning form the individual assumes in a specific moment s/he reacts to a specific situation in which other persons or objects are involved. The form is created by past experiences and the cultural patterns of society in which the individual lives. Every role, therefore, is a fusion of private and collective elements' (Moreno, 1962, in Fox, 1987: 62). The concept of 'role' is usually employed to describe complexes of behaviour limited to a social dimension, but psychodramatic role theory carries the concept through all dimensions of life to include the somatic, psychological and social dimensions. The total of all the roles in which a person interacts is referred to as his/her role repertoire. Each role may contain other subsidiary roles or 'role clusters'; for example, the role of mother includes subsidiary roles or role clusters such as carer, teacher, disciplinarian, nurturer and so on. It follows, therefore, that an individual may experience difficulties within a particular role cluster. Like other role theorists, Moreno believed that the self arises out of social interactions with others.

Moreno's role theory has been expanded by Dalmiro Bustos, a Brazilian analyst and psychodramatist, to help us understand how development difficulties may occur. In defining the role of the individual he identifies three main role clusters an individual is required to incorporate. It will no doubt be noted by the reader that these 'role clusters' have similarities with Freud's oral, anal and phallic stages and Erickson's psychosocial stages.

Cluster one

At various stages of our life we move along a continuum ranging from a state of isolation to one of fusion. We strive to balance our conflicting needs for separation and relatedness, but when dominated by either extreme we are precluded from establishing a sense of self. In our present society, the term dependency has negative associations and the individual is encouraged to be autonomous and self-sufficient, but there are various times in our life when we need to be able to depend on another and for others to depend on us. Paradoxically, individuation demands that we allow ourselves to be able to depend spontaneously and maturely on others. In the earliest stages of development the infant finds him/herself completely dependent on another for his or her physical survival and emotional wellbeing. This dependency is total and is linked very much in the early stages with bodily functions and the ingestion of food. Bustos states that if these early experiences occur with more spontaneity than anxiety, then the capacity to fulfil adult acceptance of necessary dependency will be positive. However, if these early experiences have generated anxiety and are linked with fears of abandonment and annihilation by the other, the individual will avoid close intimate relationships (Bustos, 1994: 70).

Levens argues that the anorexic's need to control bodily functions is a need not only to avoid the need for dependency but to avoid the risk of such needs not being met by the other: 'The enormous hunger for care and for relationships is denied through the fear of being abused, deceived or made utterly dependent' (Levens, 1996: 26). She argues that patients with eating disorders wish to satisfy their own hungers. The roles in cluster one are dynamically passive and dependent.

Cluster two

In the normal stage of development the infant passes from total dependency to a more autonomous awareness and begins to have control over bodily functions. During this stage the conditions are laid down for the future taking of active roles which involve self-confidence, the capacity to achieve what one wants, to exercise power, to be autonomous and to involve oneself in the world of work. The roles in cluster two are: to be able to look for what we want, to achieve and to be autonomous.

We know that many clients with eating disorders feel quite unable to affect things around them by any means other than having control over body weight. A client in a psychodrama session working on her eating disorder stated: 'There was nothing I could do about what was happening to me but I could do something about the food I ate. It was the only way I could stop myself from falling apart'. This statement clearly illustrates the anorexic's belief that she has no voice in the world in which she lives and that by gaining some control over a body which is experienced as weak and fragile in relation to others she is living out a desire to control both her internal and external worlds. By maintaining control over bodily functions the anorexic maintains the illusion that by doing so she avoids the ultimate catastrophe of having no control.

Cluster three

In this cluster the individual has to learn to compete, to be rivalrous and to share with others. The prototype of the roles in this cluster is the fraternal relationships that one forms with siblings and friends. The interaction is a shared responsibility so no party is officially responsible for it.

In order to respond to our needs and the needs of others, we must have experienced permission to initiate relationships. If the mother is motivated by her own need for control, with no basic acknowledgement or respect for the child, then the interactions with mother and therefore with others will be seen as invasive, and consequently the individual will have difficulty in more than one of the above role clusters.

Bustos argues that understanding the concept of role and role clusters helps us to understand and identify the internal dynamics of our patients and the dysfunctional role clusters. Application of psychodrama role theory requires two sets of skills: identification of the dysfunctional role response and intervention.

Session one

Ellen came to the psychodrama session wanting to work on her eating problem. She told the group: 'I cannot control my diet. I binge on food until I am sick and then I feel ashamed and guilty. I want to understand why I cannot have a good relationship with food'. Because psychodrama is an action method based on the existential belief that our 'here and now' experiences are shot through with anxieties relating to the past, present and the future, Ellen was asked to show us a present scene in which she faces her problems with food.

The protagonist, having stated her problem, was encouraged to move quickly into the action, creating the space in which events take place. Ellen immediately takes us to an early morning scene in which she opens her family fridge filled with delights. In psychodrama the protagonist is often asked to embody inanimate objects. Ellen is therefore asked to reverse roles with the contents of the fridge so that we can witness the temptations our protagonist is facing and to explore her perception of the situation and the function food has in her emotional life. In the reverse-role position Ellen shows us how tempting the contents of the fridge are. As the contents of the fridge she states: 'I am calling her to eat, look at my delights, cheeses, juices, cookies, milk, cream cake, pie, home cookies. I can relieve her anxieties'. In response to the fridge's enticing messages, on this occasion, she takes only the milk, returning to the group stating: 'If it's a good day I will not be tempted'. The therapist is naturally inquisitive as to what constitutes a good day: 'If I do not feel anxious, if I feel in control.'

Most of us like to control our lives, but for women with bulimia and anorexia this is of particular importance. They have frequently been the recipient of someone else's need to enforce control and therefore the therapeutic relationship is of vital importance. It is a very different experience for them to learn that in the therapy setting the therapist is not trying to control every wish and thought. In psychodrama the therapist works, with the support of group members, alongside the client unfolding the appropriate material. The client therefore experiences himself or herself as being co-director of their work, and as such is helped to become autonomous in the psychodrama action and life itself.

Ellen is therefore asked if it is important to show the group a bad day. For her such a day is one in which she feels angry, has little control over the day's events and wishes that there was someone there for her. She begins by showing us a scene in which she experiences her boss controlling and dominating and herself helpless without any power or control. She returns home tired, exhausted, having to face the family's demands: a dependent, invasive and possessive mother; an unsupportive, aggressive sister. Ellen feels controlled by their behaviour. She feels she can do nothing about their demands, and cannot express her own need for support; instead she walks into the kitchen, removes the contents of the fridge and in the secrecy of her room eats until she reaches a stage of vomiting.

In psychodrama, identifying the dysfunctional role (in this case Ellen's disordered eating pattern) means making a role analysis by paying attention to all aspects of her role response: her beliefs, her emotions, her behaviour and finally the consequences of her response. Role, the functioning form, is defined by context.

From the action of the first two scenes we observe that Ellen is in a situation in which her emotional needs are not met by others and in which she has no control over life events (context of role).

She feels:	Angry, rejected, disappointed, alone and controlled by others.
She believes:	That she cannot allow herself to depend on others, that she must be in control or others will control her. She must not show her feelings, for to do so would make her vulnerable. She believes that food will at least relieve her immediate problems, either by providing emotional comfort or providing herself with the (illusionary) belief that she does have some control over her inner and outer world.
Her behavioural response:	She says nothing about how she feels but either binges, throwing up later, or fails to feed herself.

Consequences: She maintains a poor relationship with food and does not resolve her real problems.

These observations are fed back to our protagonist, for it is important for her to understand her own role response to the practical and emotional situation she finds herself facing.

To check our role analysis, Ellen is asked whether there has been another time in her life when she felt that her emotional needs were not met and that she had little control over what was happening to her. Ellen takes us back to age 23 and creates a scene in which she is sitting at home all day in front of the television. She feeds herself constantly on junk food until she vomits. We learn from the action and from interviewing Ellen in role that she is depressed. She has recently broken up with her boyfriend, having learned that he is married. During this scene she becomes very upset and is encouraged to speak her thoughts out loud: 'A great piece of me feels as if it has died; how can I trust? It was difficult to let myself dare to love. I am never going to allow anyone to get close to me or get hurt again.' It is apparent during the enactment that she is very angry, but rather than state her angry feelings she becomes destructive towards herself, abusing herself with food as a way of taking control over her emotional life and seeking emotional comfort. She believes she can do nothing about the relationship and the feelings of abandonment and betrayal. She can do something about what she eats, but is finally left feeling self-disgust and guilt about her bingeing behaviour.

When Ellen broke down in front of the group, sharing both the out-of-control emotions and the shame surrounding the bingeing behaviour, it was therapeutic in itself. The self-disgust that is often associated with bulimia perpetuates the secrecy that leads to isolation; the individual hides behind a 'false self'. Such group disclosures break through this socially isolating condition and are usually met with support and a willingness to understand. They also lead to identification of similar problems by other group members.

Having made a role analysis in psychodrama, we are interested in tracing the role response back to its earliest origin – that is, the earliest time the protagonist can remember when the dysfunctional way of responding first occurred. In Ellen's case, this was when she used food as a way of coping with her feelings of betrayal and abandonment.

Moreno believed that we have choices in the way we respond to situations, but that our role repertoire becomes undeveloped or restricted through early experiences, distorted belief patterns and a lack of spontaneity and creativity. For the client with an eating disorder, the only way of responding to situations that remain beyond the realm of control is to have control over bodily functions.

Ellen moves further back in her life cycle to an earlier age when she experienced herself as controlled and betrayed by other loved persons. From as early as she could remember, her parents were constantly arguing. Her father was seeing another woman; her mother was emotionally dependent on her: 'It felt that everything that was happening to my mother was happening to me.' Set against this backdrop her grandfather became a substitute good parent. She would accompany him on his bread rounds (he was a baker) and regarded herself as his favourite person.

In the scene Ellen presents we see grandfather telling her he no longer wants her with him now that she is no longer 'his little girl'. Ellen experiences his actions as a betrayal of her love, of her emotional needs. Left behind in grandfather's bakery she eats the cookies he has baked until she vomits. When questioned by the therapist about her behaviour, she replies 'It's all I can think of doing'.

The therapist is reminded here of the writing of Klein (1961). According to Klein, during the feeding process the baby feels that he or she takes into herself the nourishing function of the mother, which is then capable of living inside him or her, fulfilling his or her needs. When the baby is angry or frustrated, however, this experience is transferred to having something bad pushed inside and it provokes an anxiety lest the object should attack from within. The infant's response is to push or project the bad object out of his or her own body. At this point of the psychodrama, the therapist conjectures but does not share that Ellen's bingeing on grandfather's cookies can be likened to taking in the nourishing aspects of the idealized figure of grandfather which is later experienced as bad and attacking and has to be vomited out. What is shared is the observation that she does not tell anyone of her feelings of abandonment and betrayal. When asked why not, Ellen echoes the statement of our earlier protagonist: 'This way I stay in control of my feelings.' In her dysfunctional way she has some control over events that feel beyond her control.

Having helped Ellen to understand her own process – the origins of her role response – it is now time to intervene and challenge the distorted belief system that motivates the dysfunctional behaviour and to help her find new ways of dealing with what she feels she cannot deal with. She needs to express her anger at the betrayal by those she dared to become dependent on, and towards her mother whom she describes as 'invasive'. In the psychodrama she learns that there are other ways in which she can have some control over her internal and external worlds, by asserting herself and expressing her needs. By using the psychodramatic technique of 'surplus reality', a technique Moreno described as embracing that which happens beyond life itself, Ellen confronts her internalized grandfather, the parents of her early childhood, her past lover, her boss and her present-day family. She is encouraged to confront them in ways she was unable to do in life itself.

Finally, the group shares how they resonate with Ellen's psychodrama experience.

As already discussed, many patients with eating disorders, particularly those with anorexia nervosa, fear being taken over or, worse still, overwhelming others by their possessive and devouring need. They have failed to establish the dynamic process of developing boundaries, a process by which the other is perceived as being different and separate from self. Ellen said, 'Everything that happens to mother feels as if it is happening to me.' We know that an important factor in considering boundary development concerns the experience of the body. Rose (1963) describes the body image as being symbolized in a magical, archaic way so that all objects, relationships and feelings come to be experienced in actual physical changes in an image of one's body. At a very early age of body image symbolism, actual body feelings and sensations come to signify the gratification and frustrations that were experienced in relation to mother. The power struggle between mother and self is very apparent with these clients, as is often shown in the role reversals that take place between mother and daughter within a psychodrama.

Session two

Clare was referred to the psychodrama programme as part of her hospitalization for anorexia nervosa. Beginning with a warm-up in which patients were asked not to talk specifically about their eating but the feelings often experienced, Clare reported that she often felt angry in the presence of her mother. She was invited to bring her mother on to the psychodrama stage (the place reserved for the action). In reversing roles with her mother, we learn that mother felt burdened by her own life experiences. She had struggled to keep the family together after Clare's father had left and had suffered several bouts of ill health. Her need for her daughter to be there for her was very apparent. Another member of the group was asked to hold the role of Clare's mother while Clare, back in her own role, was encouraged to express her anger towards her mother. She was unable to do so: 'Compared with my mother's burdens my feelings seem so insignificant.' Clare was reminded of the angry feelings she was in touch with during the warm-up phase of the session and was asked to give shape and form to them by using other group members to sculpt her anger. Then, in the role of anger, she began telling mother how she felt about being used by her, about her own sense of insignificance in the light of mother's problems, of not being noticed by her .... and then she began to sob for the loss of her childhood, for all that she had missed. The anger and unexpressed sadness concerning the unmet needs of Clare's 'inner child' had formerly found its expression through restricting her food intake, for she knew this upset mother. Her refusal to eat and subsequent weight loss also made her the centre of everyone's attention. As in Ellen's work, the psychodrama offered a new and more direct way of Clare feeling and expressing her emotion.

The advantages of working with a psychodramatic approach, as opposed to a purely verbal approach, are as follows:

1. Psychodrama awakens repressed emotions both in the protagonist and in other group members.
2. It offers the possibility of insight into behavioural patterns.
3. It explores the intrapsychic relationships within the family and perceived invasive others without increasing the intensity of the real relationships.
4. It allows concretization of the internal struggle and brings some understanding of the consequences of the client's behaviour.
5. Rationalization as a defence mechanism is not a feature in emotional psychodramas.
6. The psychodramatic double is empathetic and supportive in counterbalancing the protagonist's self-destructive feelings.

Like other psychotherapies, psychodrama (through dramatic representation of self) is based on the knowledge that a person has the ability to be self-correcting when given accurate information about behaviour, and an area for repressed emotions.

Chapter 10
Making a mark: An exploration of an art therapy group for clients with eating disorders

MICHELE J.M. WOOD

Introduction

In this chapter I wish to present my work as an art therapist with a group of clients attending an eating disorders unit in a London psychiatric hospital. Art therapy is a recent addition to the treatment offered by the unit, and I was the first art therapist to join the multidisciplinary team (MDT). This chapter is intended to convey something of art therapy's unique contribution to the treatment of those who suffer with an eating disorder and some of the factors that influence any clinical work in an MDT setting. In order to maintain the confidentiality of those individuals with whom I worked I have removed identifying features and all names used are pseudonyms.

The current thinking about the treatment of those who suffer with eating disorders emphasizes a combination of interventions. Garfinkel (1995) describes this approach to treatment as addressing weight changes by behavioural means in a therapeutic environment that provides psychological therapies. This approach was initiated at the Maudsley Hospital in London and seems to have become the accepted model of care throughout the UK and North America. It certainly informed the model used in the unit in which I worked.

Art therapy is a form of psychotherapy in which the client's spontaneous art making occurs in the presence of an art therapist and is the focus of their interaction. The substance of art therapy comprises several elements: a consideration of the client's choice and use of materials, the relationship between client and therapist, the process of making the artwork and the product that is eventually made. Training for art therapists is at postgraduate level and the full-time course takes two years. There are currently five accredited diploma courses in art therapy in the

UK. Approval for the state registration of arts therapies (where art therapy, music therapy and drama therapy have been considered together) was granted as an extension to the Act of Professions Supplementary to Medicine 1960 in March 1997. Consequently, anyone now practising as an art therapist in the statutory sector must be state registered.

The literature

Art therapists have worked with men, women, children and adolescents suffering with the full spectrum of eating disorders: anorexia, bulimia and compulsive eating. The literature describing this area of work has been growing steadily since the early 1980s and several key principles have emerged. Many writers have noted the physical use of art materials as beneficial. The resonance between the physicality of art making and bodily sensations and movements is particularly relevant to eating-disordered clients who experience a disconnection from their own bodies. As MacLeod (1981) writes:

> It is important to recognise that the split between body and self is a fundamental tenet of anorexic thinking, and that recovery must necessarily entail a closing of the gap, a healing of the split between the two, however imperfect the reconciliation may be (MacLeod, 1981: 111).

The work undertaken by art therapists with this client group has been focused on healing that split. The use of art materials is seen as providing a bridge between the self (where the impetus and ideas for art originate) and the body (which makes the marks). Through the processes of art therapy these separated spheres are brought together. The literature documents this in several ways: Murphy (1984) describes art therapy as partly aimed at increasing the sufferer's awareness of his or her actual body size with a view to gaining a more realistic self-image. Fleming (1989) highlights the sensory quality of the art materials as a mechanism for soothing and states that the permanence of the artist's trace with materials offers a mirroring function. She points out that both soothing and mirroring are important developmental needs which are more usually met by an empathic, responsive mother in relation to her growing baby. The absence or disturbance of this in the early lives of individuals who go on to develop an eating disorder is often remarked on in the literature on the aetiology of eating disorders. This developmental explanation has informed the work of many art therapists who suggest a role for art therapy in enabling the process of emotional or psychological maturation to take place.

Levens (1987, 1990, 1995a, b) suggests that the physical limitations inherent in art materials are ideally suited to an exploration of boundaries. Based on her extensive clinical experience she states that art materials provide clients with concrete boundaries in which they can explore and develop a sense of personal space. This can lead clients towards creating a corresponding mental space, where their previously disowned feelings can be recognized and worked through. The use of self-harming behaviours directed towards the body, which characterizes eating disorders, is, according to Levens (1995a), an indication that the individual is unable to conceptualize his or her difficulties, and so they are acted out instead. Likewise, Schaverien (1995a) sees the eating-disordered client's use of their body as the arena in which emotional issues are played out, and she describes this as a concretization of experience. If art materials (which are concrete and tangible) can be used as an alternative arena in which the client can communicate his or her distress, the capacity for symbolic thought can develop. Rust (1992, 1995) views the artwork as giving form to conflicts 'locked' in the client's body that he or she is not yet able to put into words. She suggests that once portrayed in the artwork, clients can begin to explore this material and thereby develop their self-image and identity. Inner states can be enacted through the pictures producing what has been termed 'embodied images', and feelings can become more conscious to the individual. In this way art can function as a link between the client's internal and external realities, a link that can aid recovery when used in the art therapeutic relationship.

However, this process of healing is not an inevitable consequence of employing art as therapy. Several writers (for example, Levens, 1987; Mann, 1990) acknowledge that using art is not automatically therapeutic but can be another form of defence or acting out. Warriner (1995), an art student with anorexia, describes this: 'It could be seen that, ironically, the art work had replaced anorexia as a numbing agent ...' (1995: 27).

The client's art making in art therapy occurs within the context of their relationship with the therapist, and often in the therapist's view. How the therapist responds to what has been made is a crucial part of the therapy. Although one eventual outcome might be that there is some discussion about the artwork, this is not the overall goal. Levens (1995a) points out that the client with an eating disorder conveys their inner disturbances on a concrete rather than a psychological level. This is true in their art making, and she warns that by too quickly giving a verbal interpretation the therapist is in danger of disregarding the client's concrete thinking, thereby preventing the client from having their real internal experience understood concretely. Both Levens (1995a) and Luzzatto (1995) suggest steps the therapist can use with the client to move from the state of making an image to looking at and discussing it. These steps involve viewing the image from a distance, and exploring the spatial relationships in the picture, as well as considering the experience of the activity involved in the picture's making.

Another aspect of the art therapy relationship is the client's responses to the therapist as these are manifest in the transference, by which I mean the process whereby feelings from his or her past are evoked and exposed in the here and now of the group. It is a well-observed fact that a good working therapeutic alliance is extremely difficult to form with clients who have eating disorders:

> The client will treat the therapist as she does all adults, as a figure of authority ... She will need to keep the therapist at a safe distance, in order to maintain her control of the situation.... Attempts on the part of the therapist to mobilise unconscious forces are likely to be frustrated. The anorexic is the expert at the relational game and she is terrified of letting go (Schaverien, 1995b: 136).

In this respect art therapy has an important advantage over single-modality therapies (such as verbal psychotherapy) in that it allows for a double transference. This is where aspects of the client are not only projected by the client on to the therapist, but also into their own artwork. The artwork also has another valuable function, for, as the focus of the relationship, it plays a very useful mediating role between therapist and client. It can function as a distance regulator between the two, and importantly it is in the client's control.

Control is a key issue for this client group. A profound sense of being out of control, and of not having any control over their lives, is manifest in an obsession about their food intake and often in other obsessive rituals.

As Lemma (1992) writes:

> My own experiences of working with anorectics has convinced me that they can only take in and use the therapeutic relationship if they have prepared it themselves, in the same way that they need to prepare their own food to ensure they will not be tricked into eating more than is planned (1992: 188).

It is also important to recognize that eating-disordered behaviours occur in a cultural context which determines different ways of mothering male and female children, and which also prescribes norms for body size and gender roles for developing young adults. The discrepancy between the number of female and male sufferers of eating disorders (with females outnumbering males) points to these cultural influences, as does the increased prevalence of eating disorders among Westernized nations. In this Chapter I briefly refer to two male clients who attended the art therapy group.

The art therapy group

The art therapy work described here took place nine years ago, when I was a recently qualified therapist. In setting up a new art therapy service in the eating disorder unit I had few guidelines for the most appropriate model (I did not have the benefit of the literature on art therapy and eating disorders that has emerged during the past five years). The model that I describe below developed from my understanding of various clinical considerations and in relation to my experience with the clients. Like all creative endeavours it involved taking risks and making 'mistakes'.

The art therapy group was of the slow-open kind, with the occasional change in membership when one patient left and was replaced by another. It met once a week over a period of 15 months. For the first four months sessions were one hour in length, after which they increased to an hour and a half. The group was open to both inpatients and day patients. Although there were some changes in the membership of the group during its life, there was always a core of six patients, with five patients staying the entire time. In this chapter I will refer to members of the group as Audrey, Branka, Carolyn, Daniel, Estelle, Frances, Gerald, Harriet and Imogen. They all had a chronic history of anorexia often in combination with substance misuse, self-harm and bulimia, and were between the ages of 20 and 30. The purpose of this chapter is not to discuss individual cases but to describe the model of art therapy with this client group, and so I will not describe the group members in any more detail.

The aims of the art therapy group were to facilitate freedom of expression, to facilitate imagination and to facilitate the development of the clients' autonomy. The overall objective was to assist in the development of the individuals' sense of self. My primary task with clients in the initial stages of the art therapy group was to establish a willingness to be active with the art materials. The available materials offered a range of possibilities, from making a 'mess' (soft pastels, finger paint, clay, runny paints) through to more controllable media such as charcoal, pencils, felt pens, crayons and oil pastels, and those which allowed layering and quick coverage such as collage materials (tissue paper and magazines). By inviting patients to use the art materials and to think about the sensations involved in their use, my aim was to develop and increase a consciousness about body movements and sensations through art making. My concern was to create a familiarity with the art materials that would give rise to each person spontaneously making their own images, and to thereby strengthen their own choices and expressive capabilities. In contrast to the projective art groups run by the occupational therapists, I did not require members to respond to set themes.

In the early groups, which lasted for one hour, my emphasis was that members should spend most of that time experimenting with the art materials. I explained that time for talking about what had been done was a minimal 10 minutes, but that this might well change as the group developed. This initial brief was the starting point for a group of clients unfamiliar with art therapy, and it was designed to make the best use of the very short session time we had been allocated. Apart from directions in the first two groups, and an implied expectation that the art making was more about the process than the product, I gave little else in the way of direction. My approach was to empower the members to work spontaneously and to take some responsibility for how they used the session time.

The explicit task in the first session was for everyone to experiment and find out which materials they liked using and which they did not. Everyone looked through the materials, although only a few attempted to use more than two different media. Everyone managed to make some marks. In the second session I invited them all to carry on with this process of experimentation but, this time, to work together on one large sheet of paper. My reason (although I did not state this) was that I was curious about the cohesion and dynamic among this group of people, who also met for several of the other groups provided by the unit. My request, however, was met with stony silence. Eventually, I was able to establish with them that sharing a sheet of paper was a terrifying prospect. Branka said that she was unsure how much space to take up on the paper, and Carolyn commented that it was difficult with one sheet of paper, adding that individual pieces would be better. This suggestion of mine immediately highlighted the tension between my direction of the group and the members' autonomy within it; how much did the group have to follow my suggestions and how much could they challenge me? This suggestion was also a diversion, as I was using the concept of a shared piece of work to get a picture of the group for my own purposes, rather than facilitating my original aims for these clients. This 'mistake' threatened to undermine the self-directed playfulness I hoped to develop and I had to find a way of resolving it. I used the situation as an opportunity to encourage personal choice by suggesting several options for the art making and raised the possibility that my instructions could be questioned. Eventually, everyone except Branka and Audrey helped themselves to new sheets of paper. Branka and Audrey chose to work on the large sheet in separate corners.

The first nine sessions of the group were characterized by a developing freedom in the use of the art materials and a tentative willingness to talk and reflect on the experience of their use. The artwork was often abstract and patterned. There was an open acknowledgement in the group of the constraints of our working environment, with members commenting that an hour was not enough time to make sense of their artwork.

By the ninth session a distinct change was seen to occur in members' artwork, where patterns gave way to images with a more personal quality.

> Carolyn used wax crayons and worked differently today. She titled her picture 'ovary', and talked about having an ultrasound scan. She spoke of wanting her own children but of being worried that she would have to be too fat to get her ovaries working again. There was much sympathy among the other women, who nodded as she spoke (session notes – session 9).

The initial brief of the group was not altered by me in any way as time moved on. I still focused on members' experience of using the materials, directly reinforcing an awareness of bodily sensations, with an emphasis on affirming their choices and perceptions. A new member joined in session 8. Fairly quickly, group cohesion developed, with imagery appearing in the pictures which clearly expressed personal struggles and issues to do with illness.

> Audrey had drawn several shapes on her sheet with soft pastels, at the centre of which was a diamond. She talked of this shape as being the illness; it was overpowering and much stronger than she had thought. She felt engulfed by it, as though she was drowning in it. She wanted to move to the outer shapes which she considered were warmer and comforting (session 11).
>
> Daniel's pictures always contained similar shapes, two halves with a central zig-zag. These gave the appearance of a split. Daniel talked about one of his pictures: 'It seems as though I'm balancing between the past and the future. Something is pulling me back although I want to go forward' (session 13).
>
> Gerald first joined the group in session 19, in which he worked quietly in charcoal and then paint. He was the last to return for the discussion time and cleared up before doing so. Although I had distinctly observed Gerald working on two pictures he returned to the group with only one. This comprised words and angular shapes. I discovered in the bin after the session a more sensitively drawn image of a boat and a house which contrasted with the diagrammatic image he chose to show. His sleight of hand at disposing of this image bore the quality of anorexic deceit, and left me wondering what feelings were stirred within him by his picture for him to choose to do this (session 19).

The location of the group and its structure changed over time and had a significant influence on the group members. After 14 sessions we changed rooms, moving from the cramped dining room in which the patients ate their meals to a larger room which was also used to teach typing. We were there for only two weeks, when, because of shifts in the clients' programme, I was able to introduce two further changes. The group moved again to an even more suitable room, which had a sink and in which arts and crafts materials were stored. The length of the sessions was also extended – to one and a half hours (a more usual length for an art therapy group). The increase in time was welcomed by the patients, and both changes brought to light a different view of art therapy as being more integrated with the rest of the treatment programme. It was clear that up until this time art therapy had been seen as separate from the rest of the package.

With the increased time for the group I also instituted a change of style by giving the decision for structuring the use of time over to the group. It was now up to group members to decide how much time was spent using the art materials and how much was spent talking. My role was to maintain the boundaries, comment on what occurred and help facilitate the clients' thinking about their responses to the art and other aspects of the group process. By now the group had developed its own culture: sessions began with everyone sitting in a circle, the art making always took place outside the circle on various surfaces around the room and there was now a degree of ease in using the art materials. The group resumed the circle of chairs for the final viewing of work made, and images would sometimes be displayed in the centre.

In the early part of the group's life, members used the materials with increasing confidence. The art making had a private quality, with everyone withdrawing for a while to get absorbed in their work. Sometimes materials were used by the quieter members with a great deal of noise, with scratching and tearing taking place. This contrasted with the presentation of the images, when little, if anything, would be said about them. There were two members, Frances and Harriet, who were allowed by the rest to dominate the sessions. Both of these women were different from the other members – Frances' presenting problem was bulimia rather than anorexia and Harriet was a day patient rather than an inpatient. These women were more prepared to take centre stage in the group, particularly Frances, who would monopolize the brief discussion time. In some senses, other members seemed to encourage this as a way of diverting attention away from themselves and their work. The only man in the group at that time took up a silent position, with his pictures 'speaking' more than he seemed able to. Overall there was a feeling of commitment to the group by its members and a genuine sense of engagement in the art making. Through the art work members were able to reflect on different aspects of their experiences, with their pictures clearly communicating feelings. Here are examples taken from my notes on session 23:

Audrey showed her picture. She had used oil pastels to draw herself clinging on to the edge of a cliff by her teeth. There was a sense in the picture that at any moment she might drop off – by opening her mouth she would fall. Audrey found it hard to articulate the consequences of falling, eventually saying that she was afraid of disappearing, of ceasing to exist.

Estelle spoke of using a smaller sheet of paper on which she had drawn butterflies. She had filled the space between the butterflies with words because she 'did not like the emptiness of too much paper'. It made her panic, and feel sad and alone.

In the following examples I wish to demonstrate the differing communications that can be made through the artwork. In the first example, the group is using the art activity as a way of dealing with anxiety provoked by changes to the structure and location of the sessions as well as the addition of new members. In the second example, the clients have chosen to describe similar experiences concerning the discrepancies they perceive within themselves.

Example one: words as pictures

Collages made up of words cut from magazines started to appear in the 18th session. After one person created their picture in this way, within a few weeks everybody had had a turn at making a word collage. Generally, these word pictures appeared in sessions in which very little discussion took place, almost as though the words had been translated into pictures of words. The art making was a slow and painstaking business, with magazines being read carefully before words were selected. Little time was left for reflection or discussion of what had been made. These collages appeared at times of change (of time, location, or the admission of new members) when people may have felt little control over the circumstances. Rather than being another form of self-expression, the collages seemed to provide a means of resisting the therapeutic process while staying within the terms of the original brief of the group. In making their word collages members had found a way of complying with my 'demands' to engage in art making, of going through the motions, but firmly keeping me at bay. Each new change had threatened the safety and trust that was being built between members and myself. I do not believe that the use of word collages was a conscious act but rather an expression of what has been termed the 'anorexic defence', where clients withdraw and hide behind other people's words: 'As she feels powerless and ineffective she tries to avoid the conflict inherent in human relationships by withdrawing from the world of public and intimate relationships' (Lemma, 1992: 187).

The loss of their own marks in favour of other people's words underscores this sense of a powerless and diminished self.

Example two: splits

The thinking of people with an eating disorder, particularly anorexia, has been described by many workers in the field as 'all or nothing', 'black or white', indicating the difficulties sufferers have with tolerating ambiguity, or the dynamic tension between extremes of feelings. This gives rise to splits within the individual, and these were clearly seen in the artwork of those in the group.

The following is an extract from my notes on session 38:

> Although at first glance all the pictures looked quite different a similar underlying theme emerged as each person chose to speak about their image. There was a greater sense of openness between people in this session, perhaps because two members were away.
>
> In the centre of Audrey's picture she had drawn a circle which was dissected by a line running through its middle. On one side there was a tree with deep roots, a sun, clouds and rain. On the other side was a red sun which was drying everything, hardening it and scorching it. This illustrated the battle inside herself, she said. It indicated the pain of leaving the past behind. However, the central circle was hopeful – it was an acorn from which a strong tree could grow, and she pointed to its deep roots. Audrey sobbed as she spoke, but unlike previous groups she did not attempt to leave the room, being able now to tolerate this experience of emotion.
>
> Estelle's picture showed a face in the centre which was crying. The face was surrounded by many other faces which, by contrast, were all smiling. The faces were encircled with question marks – the demands that other people placed on her. Estelle initially talked of her isolation and the discrepancy between these two facets of herself. However, it was clear that she favoured the 'smiling' position and found it hard to accept that crying was not a weakness. She felt it was wrong to show inside feelings and talked of the shame and guilt at doing so.
>
> Imogen talked of having to wear a mask. Her picture showed a woman cut in half and the dialogue she was having with herself. Imogen had placed the words in two categories – positive and negative. Her image conveyed an intense pain at the variance between the outside appearance and the inside thoughts, and also her attempt to deal with contrary feelings by splitting them off.
>
> Daniel's images were always characterised by a split. In time a chasm between the two halves appeared, which became a form in its own right. It seemed to me that there was no way of linking these two halves. In one picture Daniel had portrayed a man being pursued along a road by an enormous rectangle of black. He said that however fast the man went, the black rectangle remained in pursuit, always at the same distance. The blackness was what Daniel was trying to leave behind. I asked Daniel what might happen if the man turned and faced the black shape. He replied: 'The man will be sucked into it and will never be able to escape.'

In thinking subsequently about these two examples (word pictures and 'splits'), I have found the concept of the 'group image' described by

Skaife and Huet (1998) to be helpful. In discussing the reasons why art psychotherapy groups work, they identify 'enabling solutions' which can contain group members when anxiety and frustration are raised and can ultimately promote their psychological growth. One of these enabling solutions is the 'group image'. This is where an image or many images form the focus of the group's attention because it, or they, exemplifies some shared unconscious theme. This group image provides a solution to group conflicts and, as it mirrors something of the group's feelings, it enables an exploration of issues which resonate with all its members. The word collages brought to light the members' struggles with the ambiguous nature of images and their sense of exposure through them. Their solution was to use something 'clear cut' and unambiguous, particularly when the safety of the group was undermined by changes. A recognition of this process was a vital part of the group's work. The issue of 'splits' seen resonating between members' images indicated another facet of the 'group image', with different aspects of the individual's personality being brought together in a single representative image.

Ending

Three months before what was to be its eventual end I announced that the group was changing to a closed one. No new members would be admitted, and those currently attending would be required to give four weeks' notice if they wanted to leave before our end date. This was so we could have time to reflect together on the work that had been done, and also to give enough time to consider issues around endings. I was five months' pregnant with my second child and decided that the slow-open format would not be containing enough to allow this group to conclude the good work that we had begun. However, I did not initially give the reason for this change, but invited the members to speculate. Consciously, I wanted to establish how much the members had perceived my changing shape and perhaps unconsciously I found it hard to admit to news that would be difficult for many in the group to hear. Members made several suggestions for my reasons for ending the group before Estelle wondered if I was expecting a baby. At this point everyone smiled and it was clear that this 'knowledge' had been around in the group for some time. Although my colleagues had not noticed my changing shape, this group had evidently been monitoring my physical size closely. In fact, Daniel said: 'I usually go round with my eyes closed, but even I was beginning to wonder!'

The fact of my pregnancy introduced a new dynamic to the group, one that brought the notion of 'the body' even more clearly into conscious view. The onset of eating disorders at around the age of puberty has been used to explain the condition in terms of a withdrawal from sexuality and reproductivity. It has been postulated that this represents (for female sufferers) a view of womanhood which is weak and debilitating. For my eating disordered group, responses to my news were complex and multi-layered. Audrey was pleased, but also envious: 'Why do good things happen to other people?', she said. Branka focused her concern on the ending. She had been worried about how she was going to leave the group because it had become so important to her. Now that the ending had been announced she felt like a baby bird pushed out of the nest and made to fly. Carolyn, the only member of the group who had spoken openly about wanting children, never referred to my pregnancy and dropped out of the group before it ended. For many weeks references were made to painful things that could not be directly seen. There were comments and images that conveyed a sense that although everything seemed to be fine on the surface, underneath there were difficult feelings and memories. However, there was a reluctance in the group to link these feelings to either my pregnancy or the group's ending. Something of this was reflected in my feelings of discomfort about the physical effects of pregnancy, for it was hard for me not to feel self-conscious either about my size or the vigorous movements of the baby inside, which were sometimes clearly visible through my clothes. My conscious intention was that my pregnancy, although being clearly acknowledged by me in the group, should not dominate. Perhaps this paralleled or even instigated a process whereby the detrimental effects of my pregnancy (causing the group to end, and a break in the provision of art therapy until a new appointment was made) were referred to obliquely but never directly explored.

The group had been talking about making a group painting together as a possible way of ending, but it was not until the penultimate session that they decided to act. Interestingly, Daniel, the only man in the group at the time, was absent.

All the women worked together to assemble the paper. Imogen and Branka found a corner each and began working in them. Estelle started splashing paint, and Audrey began to make large brush strokes across the join between two sheets of the paper. She then moved in a provocative manner across to the side of the sheet where Branka and Imogen were working. She openly acknowledged that she was invading their space and Branka and Imogen moved. Estelle's splashes and brush strokes were getting bolder and, like Audrey, she too moved. Branka began to use the finger paints and made marks reminiscent of her 'mess' in previous artwork. She scraped and scratched the paint with her fingers, which was one of her usual working styles, and blended the colours as she worked. Branka continued to move until she was in the middle of the sheet. Imogen moved again and repeated her earlier image of a spinning top. This time it was more definite and she separated it from the marks made by the other women with a strong black line. At this point Imogen stopped working. Branka followed suit, and Estelle and Audrey paused. They all agreed to end. Audrey's immediate response was to recognise their efforts as messy and to suggest they do another neater picture. Estelle quickly intervened and said that she felt pleased with their work. The group resisted Audrey's suggestion and the ensuing discussion explored the process of making the picture, including the various provocations. Imogen admitted that she did not like mess, and said that she had been afraid that she might get paint on her. Branka talked of enjoying the mess. While the group worked, I sat watching and felt excluded, an outsider. It occurred to me that the group had created with their large sheet of paper a symbolic womb into which they retreated away from me. The picture was evidence to me of their creativity and their capacity to survive without me when I was gone (taken from notes on session 56).

This session shows the group working together in a way that would not have been possible when it first began, and contrasts dramatically with the difficulties those in the second session had with the suggestion of a shared painting. The negotiations, confrontations, mess-making and movement within the painting, and then to some extent the discussion afterwards, demonstrated how far each member had developed and gives some indication of how the aims of the group had been realized.

Discussion

The experience of using art therapy in a group context with eating-disordered clients shows several things. First, that clients' spontaneous use of the art materials can convey their conflicts and inner struggles in a very direct and often powerful manner. Second, that the permanence of the image and the concrete and tangible nature of the materials used to make it provide a sensory experience that can be satisfying and can reflect the relationship the sufferer has with his or her body. Branka often applied finger paint with a characteristic stroking and scratching motion at times of anxiety in the group. This seems to confirm Fleming's (1989) notion of the self-soothing function of art therapy. Initially the client's choice of art materials seemed to reflect something of their presenting problems: for example, Estelle always used half a sheet of paper, because she could not bear the emptiness of too large a sheet, and Gerald's disposed-of pictures. Parallels can be made here with the clients' self-harming behaviour in relation to their body and a similar destructive use of art materials. In describing the importance of art therapy Schaverien (1995b) suggests that pictures provide a medium through which the client can relate to themselves and then to other people. This sequence could be recognized in my group as it developed from the initial exploration of the materials to covert conflicts with the therapist, and then in the non-verbal play of the group painting. The art making raised many strong feelings in the group, such as anger and sadness, which members initially found impossible to tolerate in the group context. However, as the group evolved, these feelings were more easily expressed both in the artwork and in discussion.

The self-directed nature of art therapy, which depends on clients' initiative and active participation, can provide a highly suitable way of overcoming the difficulties of developing a positive working therapeutic alliance with eating-disordered clients.

The model of art therapy used for this group was informed by the group analytical art therapy model favoured by many British art therapists and described by Skaife (1990). This model requires the group members, rather than the therapist, to determine how the session's time is spent (how much time is used for art making and how much for talking). The process involved in decision making is then explored, along with other aspects that emerge in the group. However, my initial brief for this group differed crucially from this model in that I structured the time, with 50 minutes for art making and the remaining 10 for talking briefly about the experience. I decided on this as a way of addressing the difficulties these clients might have in a totally undirected setting. The difficulty with instigating things for themselves is often expressed in a lack of motivation and depression, which are characteristic of those with eating disorders. In the first few groups I emphasized only the process of using the materials, encouraging members to explore their different qualities, and I placed no emphasis on the content of pictures. In this way I wanted to develop a body-felt relationship with the materials. For those members who attended from the start, this was achieved and was demonstrated in their artwork. Unfortunately, of the three members who joined the group after the early months, only one continued in the group. Although there were reasons why the two members passed through, it was evident that for the time they were in the group they felt at a disadvantage in their use of the materials. These clients lacked a confidence with the art materials in comparison with those who started from the beginning. This leads me to conclude that a period of time to become familiar with the materials might be an important first step for clients new to art therapy. The change in the group from slow-open to closed made a difference to the clients. The closed group structure provided a greater sense of continuity and consistency than when people could come and go, and there seemed to be value in having a sense of working towards a definite ending.

In addition to theoretical and clinical considerations, the model used to run the group developed in relation to specific practical and personal constraints. I was initially given an unsuitable working space – the dining room – and only one hour in which to run the group. The reason for this was timetabling problems and indicates something of the dilemmas of multidisciplinary working caused by sharing limited time and space. I was faced with the practical problem of creating an adequate therapeutic environment in which to see clients. The room was cramped and had no running water; it was also not the ideal neutral therapy space. Although there are links between food and art materials it was important for the aims of this group that the art therapy was not perceived by the clients as trying to tackle their eating behaviours directly. I made the shift from 'dining' room to 'art therapy' room by discouraging artwork being made on the tables. I moved the tables to the side, taped sheets of paper on the walls and invited members to use the floor if they wanted. This allowed for an increased range of movements, as well as the opportunity for some privacy away from the gaze of the group, and it worked reasonably well.

It is interesting to consider the allocation of rooms and time for the art therapy group from another angle. As the art therapy group progressed, there seemed to be a growing recognition among the staff team of its value and correspondingly more suitable spaces and times were made available. In other words, once art therapy demonstrated its worth then more resources were provided and it became more accepted into the multidisciplinary team. This in turn informed the clients' view of art therapy, as demonstrated in their questions about its position within the team.

My position in the MDT as a newcomer also influenced the parameters of this group. I was aware that art therapy was viewed with a degree of scepticism by some colleagues, who felt that at best it would be ineffectual and at worst it might replicate the group work already being offered by the unit. On account of this I was keen that art therapy should be viewed as an opportunity to extend current good practice rather than threaten it, and so accepted the somewhat unsatisfactory space and time given. The fact that I established a culture for my group which limited the chance for talking and discussion was, on some level, an attempt to differentiate it from the verbal psychotherapy group that these clients also attended, and to ensure that I was not treading on my colleagues' toes. This sensitivity highlights the fact that the dynamics in the MDT have a bearing on the clinical decisions of the professionals within it. Any consideration or evaluation of the model must take into account the interactions between the different interventions and practitioners which comprise the whole MDT.

Moving from the professional influences on the work, I want now to explore something more personal by recognizing the influence of my pregnancy on the therapy. Although there have been female therapists writing about their work since the pioneers of psychoanalysis such as Anna Freud and Melanie Klein, it was not until the 1970s that the impact of the therapist's pregnancy on her clients was beginning to be discussed in the literature. It is an important factor to consider, especially for clients whose difficulties are focused on the body. Maat and Vandersyde (1995) recognize pregnancy as a profound experience which becomes the focus for a woman in her relationships with others, regardless of whether she herself speaks about the pregnancy. In discussing the impact of the art therapist's pregnancy on her clients, they emphasize the interplay between the clients' transferences (which they consider to be exacerbated by the therapist's changing shape) and those of the therapist. They point out that the pregnant therapist experiences both physical and emotional changes which will influence her responses to her clients. My response to my group was to endeavour to become as consistent and as 'unchanging' as possible. I tried to minimize any external influences that might alter the group in any way – hence my decision to make it a closed group. However, I also had to acknowledge that I was changing week by week, getting larger as each session went by. I experienced what seemed like a correlation between my increasing body size and a decrease in body size of the group members (an observation that I never confirmed). However, the changes in me were never discussed by the group, although they were acknowledged obliquely by clients offering to help move the tables in the art room, and to carry any heavy materials. There might well have been a correlation on an emotional level too, initiated by my reluctance to be explicit about my pregnancy when informing the members of the group's ending; thereby giving the cue that this was a difficult topic for discussion. My reticence may have been due to a desire to protect the growing baby from potential 'attack' or 'aggression' from members who, because of it, were losing something they valued. Skaife (1997), in an exposition of her countertransference as a pregnant art therapist, says something similar, recognizing that she suppressed her feelings as a way of coping with the many internal changes she was undergoing in order to attempt to present herself as a consistent and solid figure. She wonders whether, as a consequence of this, her group members responded likewise. Despite this limit that the pregnant therapist may unwittingly place on her group, Skaife (1997) also points out some benefits of using art in art therapy groups where the therapist is pregnant. She describes how it gives group members the opportunity to engage with feelings that may not safely be directed straight to the therapist, for fear of damaging her and her baby in some way. This is reminiscent of the notion of the double transference mentioned earlier, where the negative and more dangerous feelings can be kept out of the relationship with the therapist and contained in the artwork. Skaife also notes that the art making gives the members a means of identifying with the creativity of the pregnant therapist. The example of the group painting in the penultimate session of my group illustrates this. In it I felt that the members were demonstrating their creativity and their capacity to develop a new container to replace me as containing therapist – the therapist who was evidently already full up. I found it interesting that the joint painting happened when the only male in the group was absent. This particular session began with a tirade of anger focused on Daniel. In some respects I felt that he was being used by the group to represent the male who was responsible for my pregnancy and hence for the group coming to an end. Despite having both men and women in this group, sexuality or gender was never acknowledged either verbally or non-verbally. It seemed to me that Daniel's absence also enabled the women to enjoy a certain kind of intimacy as they worked together, an intimacy that did not have the threat of a sexual encounter. The joint group painting also indicated a degree of independence which has parallels with the sudden maturation seen in older siblings as a new baby arrives. For this group of women we were coming to the end of what had been an intense and on the whole positive relationship. Their ability to create a space for themselves through their art, and to take a step away from me, while remaining in my presence, was also a testament to the increased autonomy, imagination and freedom of expression that had been aims of this art therapy group. As a symbolic act of separation the group painting could be regarded as an appropriate and creative response to our ending. A more direct response to the ending occurred in the final session, when I was presented with a goodbye card they had bought for me.

In art therapy the person with eating disorders has the opportunity to experience and acknowledge his or her body in a creative way that develops a sense of autonomy and identity. She or he can engage in a relationship with a concrete object of their own making, and with a non-intrusive therapist. Both forms of relationship offer the possibility of their feelings being recognized, contained and reflected on and eventually owned as the client begins to be able to tolerate and possess their own body. The therapist's task is to provide the optimum conditions in which the client can use art therapy. These conditions comprise an understanding of models of clinical practice and the realities of the resources available at any one time. I hope that I have been able to indicate in this chapter something of the inevitability of the constraints that real life puts on clinical work. The therapist's response to such constraints is first to recognize them, and then to mould his or her therapeutic practice within these in order to achieve a good enough fit with best clinical practice. She can also, however, use the creativity inherent in art therapy and in clients' responses to it to challenge some of the constraints, to push them back and even to use them as springboards from which to develop good clinical practice.

Note

For more information about art therapy, contact the British Association of Art Therapy (BAAT), Mary Ward House, 5 Tavistock Place, London WC1H 9SN, UK.

Chapter 11
Consumerism and being consumed: Putting eating problems into the context of modern society

Mary-Jayne Rust

Introduction

My step-daughter, who is seven years old, loves Barbie. At the most recent count she was the proud owner of seven Barbie dolls, each of a different colour and dress. She is besotted with Barbie, whether I like it or not, and I have to admit that I do not like it! It seems to me that Barbie is the epitome of the Hollywood facade, the perfect female figure, who even has feet made to fit high-heeled shoes. There is no sign of mess, no sense of a real person living inside this facade. What's more, if Barbie were blown up to life-size proportions, her waist would be 14 inches. This gives an unreal image of a woman's figure to girls at a vulnerable age.

It would be pointless to deny her the things that she loves, for this would simply make her feel bad about her desires. At the same time, I cannot remain silent on the matter. She has been worried about the size and shape of her body for at least two years, despite having the most delightful little body. She is obsessed with eating sweet things and thinks that to be thin is wonderful.

In my attempts to address this with her, I make comments on Barbie's body: 'Doesn't Barbie look thin? I bet she's very, very hungry. I would be if I were that thin. Perhaps we could make nice big meal for her, then she might feel better...'

These comments feel like a drop in the ocean. It is hard to go against the grain of society when we are surrounded by media images that portray thin as glamorous, successful and the key to gaining everything a woman could ever want. I feel angry as I see the seeds of an eating problem take root in this girl of seven years old, knowing there are many other girls out there starting on this treadmill so very early in life.

How do we begin to make sense of what is happening here? I suspect that there is a combination of causative factors at work; family difficulties and the pressures of modern, Western society are at least two of them. When eating problems[1] and a disturbed relationship with one's body start from such an early age, how do we help those coming to us, several decades on, to get out of the mess in which they find themselves?

I believe that one of my functions as a psychotherapist working with this client group is to put their symptoms into a context. Contexts help us to see how something began and the journey it has taken since, how it has changed on its way, and how it is enmeshed in the whole spectrum of our emotional, physical and sociocultural beings. When we put an apparently nonsensical symptom into the context of our lives, it can turn into an understandable response to a difficult situation. When we begin to understand, we start the journey towards forgiveness, and forgiveness brings flexibility and change.

In this chapter I will be looking at the different ways we can employ personal, familial, social, cultural and archetypal contexts to make sense of the symptoms of eating problems. In Part One, I will use the case history of a bulimic woman, named Stella,[2] to illustrate how the perspective on her symptoms changes as the context expands. In Part Two, I will explore the links between eating problems, gender and society. In Part Three, I will show how making these links has influenced the way in which I work as a psychotherapist.

Part One

The case history of Stella

Stella as an individual

Stella is a teenager who is eating and vomiting huge amounts of food at least once a day. She appears helplessly out of control and is getting into debt with this habit, sometimes stealing from her mother's purse. Much of the time she is in such a frenzy, she often does not even like the food she eats. She is unable to stop behaving in a way that might seem rather crazy to someone who has no understanding of the issue. Seen in isolation, we pathologize her.

Stella's family

If we widen the lens and bring Stella's family into view, the scene begins to change. Her parents have recently separated but are acting as if everything is fine and under control. Her familiar world feels suddenly shattered; she feels frightened, angry and out of control. Stella's family has difficulty in working through conflict, and anger is an emotion that they all shy away from. Seen in this context we can understand Stella's bingeing as a means of finding comfort in this painful situation; her vomiting is an expression of her anger about her world changing. Her secret bingeing and vomiting is a reflection of her family's attempts to hide their mess beneath a glossy veneer of normality. She is also acting as the family's outlet for difficult feelings that no one wants to own.

Who does the symptom belong to now? An individual's response can seem more understandable when viewed in the context of his/her family. The symptom is still Stella's responsibility, but we are less inclined to pathologize her. We pathologize her family instead.

The family within society

If we widen the lens again, we can look at the society surrounding the nuclear family: the family of the family. At first glance, our society tends to be rather disparaging towards couples who cannot stay together, especially when they have children. Yet, given the pressures that many families are under, it is little wonder that this breakdown occurs. Let us look further into the lives of Stella's family.

Stella's parents have moved many times over recent years, because of her father's job. They have no stable base of friends or family as a result and, as a consequence of the unsafe inner-city area in which they live, most of their leisure time has been taken up with looking after their children as an isolated nuclear family. Stella's mother feels more and more lonely. Her own mother dies; she is desperately upset and begins to eat compulsively in the search for some inner nourishment. Eventually Stella's father is made redundant, but her mother finds work. They have never been good communicators and they cannot cope with this role reversal. Their fraught situation leads to the breakdown of their marriage.

Seen in this light, we begin to understand how the breakdown of Stella's family has occurred. The pressures of modern living undermine communities, taking away the support that families have had in the past, leaving them as isolated units. Redundancy and gender role reversal, together with personal loss and isolation, is a situation that many couples would find hard to steer their way through. Yet this scenario is not so uncommon today. Stella's parents have a responsibility to try to stay together, but with this perspective we are less inclined to patholo-gize the family. We pathologize society.

Modern Western society and its symptoms

We could widen the lens further still, to look more broadly at Western society as it spreads across the world. We can see all kinds of apparently crazy 'symptoms' emerging. Violence, debilitating illnesses and break-down of community are increasing, despite the myth that technology is making our lives easier. Murderers get younger; pornography, sexual abuse and paedophilia are widespread; crimes become more perverse and inhumane. One half of the world has too much to eat, too much of many things, while the other half starves. Our financial markets become more and more volatile. We are bombarded, daily, with all kinds of gruesome items on the news, the most worrying of which is perhaps our current ecological crisis. We have no guarantee that our species will even survive this catastrophe. We are told that we must change our way of life drastically, *now*, if we are to arrest this situation. Yet we go on consuming at an increasing rate, regardless. We are also very unclear as to how or when this crisis will take effect; whether the climate will turn hot or cold; which resource will run out first. Those in power seem powerless to agree on satisfactory strategies to put in place to reverse the damage being done. We face a very uncertain future, if we, *Homo sapiens*, have a future at all.

When we take a surface view at these 'symptoms' we shake our heads, unable to make sense of what is happening. Has the world gone mad? When we begin to connect things up, however, people's responses on a mass scale become more understandable. Let us return to Stella, as there are many parallels between her responses and those of modern society.

Parallel symptoms

Stella feels shattered by her parents' separation and the consequent move from the family home. Her familiar world feels as though it has fallen apart. We find a similar position in today's society. Our familiar world is changing extremely rapidly. There is much evidence to suggest that it will deteriorate irretrievably, unless we radically change our ways.

Stella's initial response is to try to mend the conflict. Her attempts fail and she is left feeling out of control of the situation, alternating between anger and despair. Society has a variety of responses to the situation: some people try to mend it; others comment on it; many people are so overwhelmed by the scale of the difficulties, and confused by the conflicting information that they receive, that they cannot bear to think about it; and many people lack the energy to look beyond the struggle of their own lives. We are left feeling impotent, out of control, alternating between anger and despair.

Stella's eating problem fulfils several functions: it is a need for a comforting experience in the face of such painful feelings; it is an attempt to blot out her feelings of impotence and rage; it is a means of expressing her anger through her body; it is a form of self-attack. In a similar way, society attempts to blot out pain by turning to mass consumerism, pornography and other addictions of various kinds. If we cannot find the appropriate routes to channel our outrage, we start to fight each other and/or attack ourselves for what is going wrong. Hence the rise in violence to self (illness) and others (crime). The moment we stop this repetitive behaviour, we are faced with stored-up feelings of anger, grief, pain and so on. Like Stella's cycle of bingeing and starving, our society continues in a vicious circle of despair, depression, violence and manic consumerism.

Seen in this light, the distressing symptoms of bulimia nervosa and the 'symptoms' of modern society mirror one another. We cannot see Stella as separate from her wider environment. The influences on her development must surely come from the society in which we live, as well as her nuclear family. In other words, Stella's development is a result of an interaction between herself and her whole environment.

The need for questions

It is tempting to use a narrow lens to look at Stella's symptoms; it is less complicated to focus on her individual distress and to leave aside the problems of her wider environment. Is there not a danger, here, of making the individual fit into society, of making Stella a Barbie Girl in a Barbie World? Or might we see an eating problem as an understandable, but self-destructive, response to a sick family in a sick culture? In this case, we are encouraging the transformation of an individual's suffering into a constructive, creative response to an environment in distress.

If female fashion models, our role models for today's young women, are so dangerously thin, and our ideal way of life is seen as going further in the direction we are already headed, perhaps it is our Western cultural notions of health and livelihood that need to be questioned. Is there not something very wrong indeed when we glorify women who are thin to the point of starvation?

Few writers or therapists have examined the complexities of the links between eating problems and the wider social context in which we live (see Orbach, 1986). We are familiar with thinking that media images are responsible, in part, for the rise in eating problems, but we need to go further and ask:

Are eating problems specific to modern Western society, and if so, why?
Has the incidence of eating problems increased rapidly over the past few decades, and if so, why?

Why are the large majority of sufferers women?
Why has extreme thinness become so fashionable?

In Part Two of this chapter I will respond to each of these questions, exploring the links between eating problems, gender and society.

Part Two

Are eating problems specific to Western society, and if so, why?

Since the Second World War, the Western economy has boomed. We live with the myth that we have struggled through a Stone Age darkness to reach this magnificent pinnacle of the Technological Age. According to this myth, we have more wealth, more leisure time, remarkable medical facilities and we are no longer at the mercy of extreme weather conditions for the supply of plentiful food, to name but a few of the major achievements claimed. Few people question that we have progressed, or count the cost of these achievements.

Despite our apparently better way of life, millions of people, 90–95% of whom are women (Wolf, 1990: 182), suffer from debilitating eating problems which seriously affect their ability to cope with everyday life. Most of the rest of the female population are troubled by their body image and relationship to food. It is hard to find a woman who has never been on a diet or who has not, at some point in her life, wanted to change some part of her body or looks. In fact, this painful issue has become so endemic to our culture that we think it is normal to be on a diet. Recently, the psychiatrist general of the USA declared: 'It is dangerous for a woman not to be on a diet.'[3]

One needs only to scratch the surface of this symptom to discover that the sufferers have an appalling sense of self-esteem. Years of clinical experience with this client group have taught me that they are emotionally starving. They feel empty inside, while expending more and more energy attempting to make their outside image look beautiful.

The wish to emulate Western culture is so strong that very few places left in the world remain untouched by its influence. Developing countries see our achievements, along with the Hollywood glitz, and they desire to have not just what we have, but to emulate our way of life, our very way of being. This desire is spreading like wildfire, and alarming stories emerge about the extent to which some women will go in order to 'be Western'. Ten years ago I met a woman who had been teaching in an isolated region of southern China. The nearest English-speaking person was several hours' travel away. Yet even in this remote region, the young girls would spend their first savings on having their oriental eyes surgically changed to look Western.

There are no records to inform us of the history of the incidence of eating problems throughout the world. However, we know that these symptoms are absent in non-Western cultures. As developing countries become more Western in their lifestyles, the next generation of women starts to suffer from eating problems, where their mothers had not. We also know that the incidence of eating problems has increased in Western cultures in the past century. It is hard to know exactly what the causative factors are in our society, but clearly there is a direct link between our way of life and these symptoms (Dana and Lawrence, 1988: 26–7).

Ladakhi society

One method of trying to unravel the complexities of the link between eating problems and society is to look at traditional societies which are rapidly adopting Western lifestyles. One such example is Ladakh, a small Buddhist region situated on the Tibetan plateau, east of Tibet. It is part of India, but because of its proximity to China, its borders had been closed to the West until the late 1970s. Over the past 20 years this small region has been flooded with tourists bringing their Western goods, money and ideas. As Ladakhi society is rapidly infused by Western society and its values, it provides a rare opportunity to compare our socioeconomic system with another. Western influence is so recent that we have documented evidence as to what life was like in a traditional, sustainable society, which has existed untouched for centuries.

Some years ago, I had the fortunate experience of travelling to Ladakh. One of the first things that struck me when I arrived was the sense of deep joy and pride in the Ladakhi people. It was not an arrogant pride, but a dignity that comes from integrity and humility. Eating problems have not been known to exist. Some might argue that they are simply hidden in silence, and would come to light when dug out. But this cannot be the case. We would see the evidence of anorexia and obesity on women's bodies. We would also hear the familiar gossip about diets, figures and food that is incessant in the West. There is none of this.

In the space of one generation, people who were so contented and joyful now believe that they are among the poorest people in the world. They are desperate to exchange their beautiful, spacious house in the countryside for a concrete town house. Where once there was virtually no incidence of violence or crime, theft is beginning to take place.

The role of women is changing dramatically. Traditionally, work was farming the land around the home so the women were very much part of decision making. Now there is a monetary system and the men go out to work, the children go to school and the women are left to manage the farm and home. They are left 'holding the baby', without access to the new and exciting culture coming in. As a result, they are rapidly turning into lonely, second-class citizens, viewed as poor peasants through the eyes of Westerners; and it is shocking to see their corresponding decline in self-esteem. Men, on the other hand, are familiar with the new goods, the language and the people (Norberg-Hodge, 1992). There is a direct link here between the change in economy and culture, gender power balance and the resulting psychological impact on both women and men.

Another big change is their diet and amount of exercise they take, which is in evidence only in the main town of Leh. Chocolate and other Western sweets are now available, and the women in town spend endless time on their own, indoors, watching television. Having contact with other Western cultures through television reinforces Hollywood stereotypes, and the notion that Western ways of life are better.

The change that is occurring in Ladakh shows how susceptible we are to wanting what seems to be an 'easy way of life'. We all want to move away from farming the land to having labour-saving devices in the belief that this will free us from a life of hard labour and drudgery. But rather than having more leisure time, our lives are speeding up. We live in a lottery society where vast numbers of people have work that is repetitive and unfulfilling, while the 'winners' reap the rewards of modern culture. I would suggest that the rise in eating problems is just one symptom among many which speak of the immense dissatisfaction, emptiness, isolation and insecurity that many people are experiencing in our society.

Has the incidence of eating problems increased rapidly over the past few decades, and if so, why?

It is clear that in the records of the incidence of eating problems, there has been a dramatic increase in the symptoms of eating problems since the 1960s. Some people argue that these difficulties have been present for much longer but, as with sexual abuse, they have not been talked about openly. However, obesity and anorexia are easily recognizable on women's bodies. We know, at least, that the incidence of these two symptoms, at the opposite ends of the spectrum, has increased (Wolf, 1990: 181–3).

What accounts for the increase in incidence of these symptoms? I have already made some references to the recent and rapid changes in Western society. Consumerism has boomed since the Second World War. Technology has developed so fast that our society is barely recognizable, compared with how it was a century ago. One of the assumptions we make about technology, and other major developments of the 20th century, is that it gives us more time, more wealth and more control over our lives.

However, our lives are rapidly speeding up and I would suggest that the experience of most people is that we have less time, not more. We seem to have more control over production of certain types of food, and perhaps of providing shelter, but in other areas, such as chronic illness and environmental damage, things are escalating out of our control. Our lives are more wealthy in terms of Gross National Product, but if we were to measure Gross National Contentment, we might find a different picture (Goldsmith, 1994: 9–11). Evidence cited by Oliver James in his book *Britain on the Couch* shows that, as a nation, we have become more depressed over the past 50 years, despite being materially richer. James argues that one of the reasons for the increase in clinical depression is that we are bombarded by media images of people who seem to be extremely successful, in a variety of ways. This leaves many people feeling that their lives are not as exciting as those 'out there', and increasingly dissatisfied with what they have (James, 1997: Chapter 3).

The more our economy and culture become globalized, the less diversity there is. There is a great deal of pressure on women to conform to a certain image. We are presented with glamorous, young, Barbie-like women in the media who seem to 'have it all'. It is easy for a young woman to feel herself lacking in comparison with these 'supermodels'. If a mother, and father, are affected by these images, this will filter through to the children in the family; thus self-confidence is eroded from generation to generation.

There have been huge changes for women in the twentieth century. Contraception methods are almost foolproof and, as a result, women are able to make choices about when, and whether, to have children. Many women are choosing to start a career in their 20s, leaving families to their 30s and 40s. This has enormous implications for relationships between men and women, who are having to adapt to changing roles very rapidly.

Mother–daughter relationships are also affected. Daughters long, and fear, to go beyond mother. Mothers feel excited, and envious, about daughters having more choices. For many of the women that I see in my practice, their binge–starve patterns express the ambivalence of their new-found situations. A woman can long to stay with mother, in a merged sense, but fears being engulfed. She can also wish, but fear, to tread on new ground, away from mother's experience. If the tensions within these conflicting drives become too great, repression takes place, but the unconscious drive re-emerges through bingeing, starving or vomiting.

I would suggest that the more rapidly our society changes, the wider the gap is between generations, and the more scope there is for inter-generational tensions. It is interesting to note that, as traditional gender roles change, there has been a concurrent rise in eating problems among men (Maine, 1993: 15–16).

Why are the majority of sufferers women?

Bottom of the pile

It is an almost universal phenomenon that men have more power in the world of decision making and politics. In any hierarchical system, the people with most power attack those underneath them, while those at the bottom of the pile attack themselves. If we regard our society as patriarchal, and we acknowledge that men have more power in governing society, women are in the majority at the bottom of the pile, and are more likely to attack themselves than others. One could say that men tend to put their aggression out into the world, while women turn it in on themselves.

Even in traditional societies there is still division of labour between men and women. Women look after the children more than men and this has always left men free to be more active in the external world of politics and work outside of the home. Now, with reliable contraception, there is more opportunity for women to be part of central government: one-third of all MPs in the UK are now women. There is change, but women are by no means on an equal footing with men in this respect, yet.

If women are brought up to feel they have no power in the world, one of the responses they might have is to search for a place where they can gain it. If they see that having the right image will get them the things that they want, then their body becomes the seat of their power, the place where they struggle with control.

Women as objects of beauty

Another reason that women are concerned with their image is that in our society they are valued as objects of beauty, whereas men pride themselves on their success in the world. Historically speaking, a woman's traditional role has been to have a family. She needs to be attractive enough to 'catch a man' who is successful enough to support her in doing this.

It is interesting to note that in a traditional society such as Ladakh, a woman's beauty is judged in terms of who she is as a person, not on her appearance. In the West, our society has become obsessed with how a woman looks. The definition of a woman's external beauty has become narrower. Barbie epitomizes this definition: young, thin, Caucasian, with long, preferably blonde or chestnut hair. It seems that the more our culture 'progresses', the tighter these definitions of beauty become.

Women are objects, not subjects, of desire in our consumer culture. They are trained to be wanted, not to be wanting. This pattern can start in the very earliest experience. Susie Orbach and Louise Eichenbaum (1982) describe how mothers unconsciously teach their daughters not to expect too much. This can take the form of curbing their appetites at a very early age. A mother may chide her daughter for being greedy while relishing the appetite of her baby boy. Research shows that boys spend longer at the breast than girls (Orbach, 1986: 46).

Christianity

The theme of asceticism exists in many religions throughout the world. Indulging in the realm of the senses is seen as being tempted by the Devil in Christianity, which has shaped Western culture for the past two millennia. Ideally, one should attempt to transcend one's material and bodily desires in the search for God. Indeed, fasting for periods of time has been used by many spiritual seekers to rid the body of its impurities, in an attempt to gain spiritual purity.

In the original Myth of Creation of the Bible, Eve is the one to have fallen from grace by eating the apple from the Garden of Eden. She is the one who tempts poor Adam astray, and both are cast out of Paradise. Struggling with, and attempting to repress, sensual desires is surely a human condition. But to denigrate sensual desire, and to place it in the body of the woman, is to see her as the way to the Devil.

Alternatively, there is the image of the Virgin Mary – a woman who has not indulged in sex and still remains pure. These polarized images of women, the virgin and the whore, face us every day: the untouchable fashion queen, thin and demure, versus the full-bodied, pornographic temptress. Such myths are powerful; they lie at the core of our culture and our psyches. It is no wonder that women still confuse matter with spirit, and attempt to purge their bad feelings by eating as little as possible. They seek unconditional mother love, a sense of 'being at one with another', in their binges.

Why has extreme thinness become so fashionable?

It is fascinating to look at the history of Western culture, and the many other cultures of our world, to see how the definition of attractiveness for a woman has changed, and what meanings have been ascribed to 'fat' and 'thin'. For example, in an Arab culture, and many African tribes, a woman is highly prized at the size we would term morbidly obese. In India, to be thin and dark-skinned implies that you are a poor peasant working out in the fields. To be fat and pale skinned is conversely seen as a sign of wealth. The same was true in the West until the end of the last century. This shows a direct correlation between the distribution of prosperity in a culture and the desired weight of its women.

However, as Western culture has become materially overabundant, so concern has arisen about obesity. Western medicine attributes many diseases to obesity and high-fat diets. Fat is no longer a sign of opulence, but of greed and illness. In fact, in the West I would suggest that fat people are one of the most oppressed minorities. Kim Chernin, from her book *Womansize*, states:

> 'In an era, when inflation has assumed alarming proportions and the threat of nuclear war has become a serious danger, when violent crime is on the increase and unemployment a persistent social fact, 500 people are asked by the pollsters what they fear most in the world and 190 of them answer that their greatest fear is getting fat. Indeed in our land today, 20,000,000 people are on a diet at any one moment. Between them they are spending $10 billion each year in an effort to take weight off and keep it away' (Chernin, 1981: 37).

In recent decades, fat and pale skin have become signs of greed and having to work indoors all day. Thin and tanned skin, ironically, are now signs of being in control of one's body and having leisure and money to spend time in the sun. Thin and tanned equals power and wealth.

The picture is more complicated than this, however. Although thin is equal to being in control, when taken to an extreme it can also express vulnerability and the wish to remain prepubescent. Some people argue that today's glamorization of very thin, young women is the fear of the power of a fully mature, sexual woman. There is a virgin/whore split in the portrayed images of women: fashion magazines present thin, untouchable, androgynous supermodels, while pornographic magazines portray women with outsize breasts, hips and thighs, displaying their sexual wares. Thin in this context becomes not just a denial of physical hunger but of other bodily desires as well. Anorexic thinness can represent a more religious/Christian notion of saintliness, a model of living on air, above earthly desires. It becomes a paragon of virtue in this overabundant society.

Advertising methods constantly use semi-naked images of women to sell anything and everything. So women become equated with any desirable product in this culture: they are there to be consumed and cast off when aged and worn. This leaves women in a highly ambivalent state about thinness: they want to be desired, but not consumed and then discarded.

In her ground-breaking book *Fat is a Feminist Issue*, Susie Orbach suggests that for a woman to become fat is a statement, be it conscious or not, about her position in today's society. It can be a protection against being the desirable object and a statement of her own desire. On the contrary, thin becomes a statement of joining the masses, of losing one's identity, of selling out to the Barbie image, with the threat of being desired and devoured (Orbach, 1978).

Part three

Implications for the process of psychotherapy

I have argued, here, that our way of life in modern Western society plays a large role in causing eating problems. When I work with individuals it is the total environment I am looking at. The strands of individual, family, culture and society all weave together to form the matrix out of which we grow. It would be impossible to separate one influence from another, in order to single out any one particular cause. The way in which we understand and explore the origins of eating problems, or any illness, has a bearing on how we might work with any given individual.

What is fruitful, in my experience, is to seek the patterns running through the layers of individual, family, society and beyond, to the arche-typal. The images that clients bring, in the form of dreams, fantasy, or the stories of their lives, reveal patterns which resonate through these different layers, and can be linked to any one of them. I will try to illus-trate what I mean by way of the following case study of a woman whom I shall call Jan.

Jan: A case study

Jan came to see me for psychotherapy on a once-weekly basis. She had suffered from an eating problem for many years. This took the form of bingeing on large quantities of sweet foods, which she would then throw up and flush away. She would do this, on average, once or twice daily, although there were periods of time when her symptoms would suddenly disappear. At other times she would give up vomiting and attempt to lose weight through rigid dieting. She was also troubled by obsessive sexual fantasies about women. She longed for a woman and yet, every time she grew close to allowing herself what she thought she wanted, she became adamant she was heterosexual.

Jan was a successful young woman in her late 30s, who had set up her own business. She worked extremely hard and allowed herself little time off. In her leisure time she felt empty, rudderless, unable to know who she was or what she wanted. It was during this time that she would binge. When she began therapy, she told me she would need only a few sessions to 'lick the problem'.

Like most women in this client group, Jan suffered a difficult relationship with her mother. Her father was eminent in his profession and went away for periods of time to work. Mother would then rely on Jan, her only child, as his replacement, even taking her into bed with her at night. By day, Jan's mother would have periodic alcohol binges. When her father returned, Jan felt displaced, as her mother's attention was devoted to her father. Neither position gave Jan what she needed from her mother. Either she and her mother were merged in an unhealthy way, or they were too separate. At age 11, Jan decided to go to boarding school, in her words, 'to escape this stifling environment'.

Jan felt that her needs were always too great to be met. As an adult, she had compensated for this by becoming like her successful father. In this role, she was fearless, unstoppable and quite omnipotent. This gave her the adulation she craved, but left her feeling empty. It was the competent, logical, efficient side of her that was being admired, while the needy, vulnerable, messy, hungry little child inside was still hidden. She hated this needy, vulnerable part of herself. If only she could just get rid of this neediness, she would say, her life would be fine. But the more she tried to deny it, the more insatiable her hunger became. This was evident both in her eating patterns and her desire for a woman's body.

As a heterosexual woman, she said that she felt passive, that the man had the appetite and would initiate sex. In her fantasies of longing for a woman, she owned her hunger and lust, but this was absolutely terrifying to her. She would quickly restore the situation by persuading herself she really was heterosexual, thereby placing her neediness back into the man. Inevitably, she felt overwhelmed by such a needy, hungry man. It seemed that she chose men who actually matched her projection. She would end the relationship after a few months, feeling drained, as if she were the one who had to give all the time. In a similar way, she would move from bingeing to evacuating the food, first having the hunger, and then denying it by getting rid of the food.

It was clear to me that Jan had not received enough nurturance from her mother and that she was unable to find the maternal side of herself. She suffered from recurring nightmares. Either she was submerged by rising seas, or drawn into a circling vortex, like a black hole. This seemed to represent the nightmare of being drawn into mother, whom she experienced as constantly needy with nothing to give. She would look forward to seeing mother, in the hope that she would at last get the food that she longed for. Invariably, she experienced mother as a demanding child whom she, herself, had to mother. She could not devour, but felt devoured by her.

My experience of Jan in the sessions was double-edged. I found myself both captivated and drained by her, lurching from one drama to the next. I liked her enormously and she seemed to have a way of eliciting my attention in every second of the session. Afterwards, I felt overwhelmed and realized I had once again been gripped by the immediacy of her latest storm, and need for crisis intervention, as if this were a matter of life and death. 'Tell me how to fix it *now*,' she would implore, relentlessly. She was letting me know the level of her need and panic, her fear of being drawn in by the black hole of her dreams and of being swamped by tidal waves. She was fighting for her life to hold on to her tenuous sense of self, and yet the adulation she received in the external world meant that she could deny how very small she felt inside.

Another recurring fantasy was that she had an 'alien'-like creature living in her stomach. This image, from the film *Alien*, has emerged in the fantasies of other women with eating problems. *Alien* is a science fiction film, in which the crew of a spaceship land on a strange planet. While they are carrying out explorations, a creature from an egg leaps on to one of the crew members and clings around his face. They are taken back to the mother ship and an operation successfully removes this creature. However, several hours later, this same crew member complains of feeling ill at supper and, in a horrifying moment, a creature bursts out of his stomach and hides somewhere on the ship. The rest of the film is a gripping story of how the crew members are, one by one, killed by this monster, which grows larger and larger. One of its most frightening features is its multi-layered mouth with row upon row of teeth.

Jan describes her attempts to starve as a means of stopping this creature from growing any bigger. If it did, she feared it would not only devour and destroy her, but others too. As we explored what this image might mean, there emerged rich layers of meaning.

It became clear that this alien creature represented a split-off part of herself which was too frightening for her to own. It encapsulated all her needy bits. Jan feared that if she were to give way to her hungry, needy side, she would consume everything and everyone in sight. The more she tried to hide this hunger and longing, the more it grew, and the uglier and more uncomfortable it felt inside. Outside was the fearless woman, but inside was the alien monster to be hidden at all cost. It was so ugly, it had to be disowned.

We can also understand this image as an introject of Jan's mother's needy self which had never been met. Her mother was still too tied up with her own unmet needs to be able to adequately meet the needs of her daughter. Mother would look to her daughter to meet these longings for love and holding. Consequently, Jan experienced being intruded upon by an 'alien mother', a mother who was trying to get inside of her daughter, to be mothered. Her mother was a needy baby herself.

It is easy to see how Jan's binge and starve pattern has arisen in the context of her immediate family. Her dreams and fantasies relate directly to her early relationships, particularly to her mother. In the course of therapy, Jan has begun to listen to this very needy part of herself, realizing that it may be of value to her, instead of silencing it with food. If she can manage to stop bingeing when she is emotionally rather than physically hungry, she can begin to differentiate between the wide variety of needs and longings she might have during the course of a day. Some of them can be met, whereas, at other times, she has to tolerate the frustrations of living with a sense of unfulfilled yearning.

Widening the lens: Jan in the context of modern society

We can look beyond this, to see how Jan's dreams, fantasies and patterns of behaviour connect to modern society.

Jan's fast and pressured lifestyle is not uncommon among her peer group. She is not just proving herself to be competent in her family, but also in a society where women are fighting to become equals with men. Many women feel that in order to achieve this, they must become like men. In such a highly competitive workplace, where efficiency, logic and speed are prized, there is little room for mess, emotion, softness or any of the traits traditionally associated with femininity. It is little wonder that this unbalanced way of being leaves Jan craving for a breast, longing to find the softer, more nurturing side of herself. Jan's experience is not isolated within a society that devalues women's work. Her parents' dynamics (that is, the 'great man' and the childlike, adoring woman) merely echo the values in a patriarchal society.

Alien is not only a symbol of Jan's hunger. We live in a consumer society where many people are anxious about the way our species is draining and damaging the Earth's resources. Although Jan's anxieties are clearly related to the fear of draining and damaging her mother, perhaps they also relate to what modern society, of which she is part, is doing to Mother Earth. Like many of my clients, she is well aware of current affairs and the political world around her. She reports feeling anxious after watching news and documentary programmes. If we see Jan's images only in the context of her early experience, are we not in danger of denying the reality of the wider context in which we live? Information we receive through the media about situations that could potentially threaten our lives, be it the state of the planet, or a third World War in the Gulf, is very overwhelming. Jan's dreams are about her intrapsychic life and a potential future threat.

Perhaps these images are particularly relevant at this point in the history of humankind. Never before has a whole society been faced with such material abundance. In the past, people have always had limits imposed on them by external conditions. Now, in this era of consumerism and free trade, it is left to the individual to take responsibility for how much to take. Indeed, we are taught that the more we consume, the more our economy will thrive. The consequences of taking too much are not easy to see, immediately. But if we believe in the existence of the unconscious and the notion of repression, surely we are all feeling some kind of guilt as a result of our overconsumption, even if most people are not fully aware of the consequences of their actions. Is our society not in a state of denial, using consumerism as a means of blotting out the overwhelming fear, rage and impotence in the face of such massive threats to our species? I suggest that it is our job, as therapists, to link the individual's guilt and anxiety to the wider context, when appropriate.

Helping Jan to relinquish the comfort of bingeing is enabling her to live with the fear of not being in control, both in terms of her primary object, mother, and in terms of the chaotic and unstable modern world.

Universal themes

Jan's dreams and fantasies could further be described as archetypal images. It was C.G. Jung who first coined this term in a psychological context. Jung describes an archetypal image as one that emerges across race, culture and class as a result of common, human experience (Jung, 1959). For example, all children are conceived in, and born out of, a woman's body. A child's first feeding experience is almost always from a woman's body. As a result, the associations we have to a woman's body have elements in common throughout the world. The ways in which these associations emerge, in dreams, fantasies or stories, vary according to culture and individual, as do the ways we deal with them.

Jan's wish to consume more of mother, and her consequent fears of devouring and destroying her, could be said to be archetypal in nature. We all struggle with a sense of 'having enough' as opposed to 'wanting it all'. *Alien*, or similar kinds of greedy monsters, appear in an individual's nightmares, as well as society's myths or stories throughout the world, representative of the all-consuming side of human nature.

Likewise, the fear of the suffocating, smothering mother could be said to be universal. Jan's nightmares of being swamped by tidal waves is an archetypal image, symbolic of both the overprotective mother, and the capacity of Mother Earth, to engulf and destroy.

Jan's fear of being sucked into a vortex is another archetypal expression of the fear of returning to our origins. Rather than being a nourishing and fertile womb, the place of Jan's beginnings is experienced as an empty, needy, dark place from which she will never return.

The fear of the dark, more sinister side of the Mother archetype is a collective one. We imagine that the further we advance through our technological achievements, the better our lives become, away from the dark, hard past. Alternatively, our beginnings become the lost paradise of the Good Life, the golden time which we ever yearn to return to.

Mother's body becomes the symbol of our place of origin and, as such, embodies a double-sided nature. It represents the golden paradise and the Stone Age primitivism. It engenders ambivalent feelings of both yearning to return home as well as longing to get away, for fear of being sucked back, unable to escape. As individuals, this multi-sided aspect of the archetypal Mother is shaped by our individual experiences of our personal mothers as well as the age and culture in which we live.

Some final thoughts

Jan's eating problem is an expression of all these layers of experience. It speaks of her ambivalence towards her own mother, whom she both longs to be nourished by but fears devouring and destroying. She wants to be close to her, but fears being engulfed by her. Her emotional hunger is translated into physical hunger and she plays out these patterns using food; eating it, vomiting it, being frightened of having too much around.

Jan's eating problem also speaks of living in a consumer culture, where our collective appetites are out of control, threatening to devour and destroy the resources of Mother Earth, damaging the environment on which we rely.

Lastly, Jan's eating problem speaks of an age-old struggle with appetite, power and control; the wish to merge with the archetypal Mother and the need to separate from her. Perhaps, in another era, these fundamental drives, present in all human beings and their societies, might be expressed through other forms and/or other illnesses.

Seen in this light, a plague of eating problems is individually determined in how it manifests, but culturally determined by where we are in history and universally conditioned by our age-old struggles with power and greed.

Notes

[1]Throughout the chapter, I will be using the term 'eating problems' to cover the following conditions: obesity, anorexia nervosa, bulimia nervosa, compulsive eating and obesity, and their accompanying psychological disturbances.

[2]This case history is fictitious, but represents a typical situation in which someone might suffer from the symptoms of bulimia nervosa.

[3]Orbach, S. Personal communication.

Chapter 12
The multidisciplinary team: Bringing together all the pieces of the jigsaw

DOROTHEA HINDMARCH

Each of the previous chapters describes the perspectives of the professionals involved in the treatment of eating disorders, with the exception of Chapter 3 which is written from the patient's point of view. The chapters have been set out in order, starting with the medical-biological position of the psychiatrists and concluding the clinical aspects of the book with Chapter 11, which considers the wider sociocultural aspects of the disorder.

In this the final chapter, I want briefly to consider the multidisciplinary team as a whole, and to look at the concept of a team, its management structure, the basis of the use of theory as a means of achieving understanding – and, from this, enabling the individual sufferer to emerge from the illness into health.

Is there such a thing as a multidisciplinary team or is it a myth?

The establishment of the multidisciplinary team (MDT) began in the 1950s, when the health services had to recognize the need for a wider range of skills to meet the demands of the task of delivering health care. Originally, the professions concerned were limited to doctors and nurses. The increase in technology called for skills and personnel able to perform a range of complex tasks, which could not be adequately performed by a single profession. Radiography, physiotherapy, the medical specialities, and so on, were developed to meet the demand. The diversification of staff into skilled groups continued with more recent formal recognition and registration of the art and drama therapies. The current trend for generic workers has occurred because of the high costs of health care and the scarcity of resources. The competition resulting from economic pressures between specialities is in danger of triggering a move away from diversity towards a single model of care – the medical model. In order to try to solve problems of managing the diversity created by the different professions, the concept of the MDT was formed.

Each professional group formed its own management structure in the organization. The development of these institutional structures ensured the survival of the strongest professional groups and the professional bodies took on a political role in lobbying parliament and influencing the way forward for the National Health Service. The risk of exploitation of the client/patient required professional bodies to perform duties of discipline and set professional standards of clinical practice. In the late 1980s, the government under Margaret Thatcher set out to challenge the power of professionals in all spheres. This led to a decline in the social status of the professional classes and a change in the attitude of those who work in the NHS. The idea of 'vocation' and 'calling', which was once attached to these roles, is now less apparent, and being a doctor or nurse has taken on the value of any other work. This change in culture has resulted in health care competing in the general work marketplace and leaves it vulnerable to market forces. In times of unemployment it can recruit to its unskilled workforce without difficulty, but when there is an international demand for skilled and professional staff it is in danger of losing out or paying a high price for the skills it needs.

In this cultural context the MDT has survived. Why has it and what are its strengths and weaknesses? The incidence of mental illness is on the increase as we develop better methods of treatment for our physical ills and our life expectancy increases. There seems to be a relationship between increased wealth and the prevalence of mental illness in the population. Mental illness is rarely the result of biological mechanisms alone or the ageing process. It is deeply embedded in the individual psyche, the family and society at large. Understanding and treating mental illness is a complex matter, even in the simplest cases. Our mental illness services can cope with only a small percentage of the mental distress that is referred to them by general practitioners. Diagnostics and risk assessment filter out many problems because priorities in treatment have to compete for the available resources. The multi-skilled team is currently the most effective and efficient way of meeting the multiple and varied needs of the patient. The multidisciplinary team has survived because it has proved its value over time, validated its effectiveness and proved relatively efficient in its use of resources. Hopper and Weyman seem to capture in the following passage why the MDT is so successful, particularly in dealing with the complex problems of eating disorders.

The study of any problem requires choices of its boundaries. The resources available and the kinds of solutions sought set these out. However, if all elements of the system are not taken into account, then, by definition, the solution to the problem will be partial (Hopper and Weyman, 1987: 162).

The problems that arise from the group of conditions called eating disorders are highly complex. A single professional is unable success-fully to cope with the difficulties of these illnesses. The multiprofes-sional team forms a containing matrix which is able to analyse, diagnose, treat and promote change in the individual and the containing founda-tion matrix.

Chaos theory – the application of theory in clinical practice

The previous chapters describe the role of the team members and, more importantly, how they view the patient and how the patient can use the treatment medium. This many-faceted mirror is capable of reflecting a single image through the collective work of the team. In describing the role of psychiatrists in one of two round-table discussions held between all the contributors to the book, the consultant psychiatrist used chaos theory to demonstrate the complexity of this role. He said that, viewed separately, each part of the problem is clear and manageable; viewed together, the whole merges into itself and loses definition. Hopper and Weyman (1987: 162) again illustrate this by stating: 'It is impossible to consider everything at once but it is essential to realise that every study involves a choice to concentrate on certain aspects and not others'

In the development of theoretical models we can afford to separate out what we choose to focus on. In the clinical setting, where the patient's life may be in danger and the traumatic effects of illness on a young person's life can potentially have a profound effect on the rest of their lives, there is no time for the luxury of reflection. Decisions have to be taken about management and action taken to alleviate suffering. The team approach provides the potential for seeing the patient in a holistic and as near to total context as possible.

Survival of the fittest or what fits?

If there are reasons why the team has survived, what, then, are its weaknesses and can these be minimized? The demand for services in the West has outstripped the ability of the economies on these conti-nents to meet it. This has resulted in governments introducing methods of rationing or prioritizing services. How does this impact on the MDT?

> The combination of economic scarcity, the recession of the late 80s and 90s,
> the widening gap between demand and resources in public services such as
> health and education, the rampant influence of technological change has
> produced a deeply uncertain organisational world which affects not just
> organisations in their entirety but groups and individuals at all levels in the
> organisation matrix (Nitsun, 1996: 253).

In times of scarcity, individuals, groups and organizations are set
against one another in a competitive battle for survival. This can have a
damaging effect on services; communications between groups become
distorted and may break down altogether; staff morale is low; and the
focus of concern moves away from the task towards the individual's
preoccupation with survival. Common symptoms in teams are high
sickness and absence rates, poor recruitment and retention, high
accident rates, poor productivity, conflict and ineffectual leadership.
Because the driving force behind the change is occurring at a political
and organizational level, members of the team will often be bewildered
at their own actions, so splitting occurs and projection of bad feelings
are placed outside the group. Fearful of their own survival, the team may
develop a false sense of cohesion where day-to-day conflicts cannot be
resolved and important tasks are forgotten or neglected. The staff
support group can help to provide a means of understanding how
outside forces may be responsible for internal difficulties in the team
and help them to take responsibility for managing the problems successfully.

Internally, the team comprises individuals with both a professional
and a personal dimension. The dynamic between the therapist and the
patient is the pathway to understanding the illness or presenting
problems. In the team, its success is dependent on the maturity and
stability of its members. If stressful life events weaken a member of the
team then the strength of the containing wider organizational matrix will
be called on to support the MDT. This is where human resource departments and occupational health are important in maintaining the team's
ability to function effectively.

If, as described above, the team is vulnerable to organizational
change and individual team members' strengths and weaknesses, what is
it about the current structure that seems to be robust, and what, if any,
are its weaknesses?

The matrix

The use of word 'matrix' is common to group analysts, sociologists and
anthropologists, who describe how individuals are influenced by what
occurs in the internal world of the person and the external influences of

the family, organizations and society. To others, the term may be less familiar. Foulkes, the founder of group analysis, described four levels of group process (cited in Brown and Zinkin, 1994: 14–18):

1. The world of physical and social reality.
2. Whole-object transference relationships (the working of the dynamics of the family of origin – father, mother, sibling transferences).
3. The projected aspects of the self, for defensive reasons, into other group members – the level of part-object relationships.
4. Transformation – the deepest level. Similar to Jung's 'collective unconscious' and termed 'foundation matrix'.

The foundation matrix is equal to the cultural and collective existence we all have in common or which separates us from one group or another. This view of man's existence as both part of the whole and separate can be demonstrated in physics. The new science of quantum physics seems to suggest that no physical entity can be separated from the environment in which it exists. The observer cannot escape participation and reality cannot be divorced from experience.

In organizational management theory, the matrix structure in the workplace is often the method of choice for carrying out the task. In a matrix structure, specialities are brought together by the 'project leader or manager'. All members of the project team have the same status. The project manager is responsible for ensuring the task is carried out. His or her leadership role is one of coaxing and motivating the team members to ensure that the work is carried out in the time and resource constraints of the contract. The person chosen to take on this role usually has a good grasp of all the disciplines in the MDT but is not an expert in any one area. He or she understands what has to be achieved and holds on to a view of the task as a whole. The model is used in engineering, film making and so on. It is effective and efficient.

How does the multidisciplinary team work in comparison with the project team?

Members of the project team are directly accountable not to the project manager but to the divisional head of department. The members of the MDT, apart from medical staff, will be accountable not to the co-ordinator or consultant but to a professional departmental head. In the MDT, the consultant, who often takes on the clincal lead role, has a medical and statutory role as RMO (responsible medical officer) and senior medical practitioner/consultant. The project team leader is responsible only for the project. In a project team each member is of equal status. In a multiprofessional team the hierarchy is part of the underlying culture. Traditionally, the medical profession has been conferred with higher status than other professionals on the team. Nursing has power and status because of its size and political strength in the organization.

The NHS as an institution has reflected the cultural values of society at large. The sketch by Peter Cook and Dudley Moore in the 1960s described the class system in the UK. It features a line of men – with the largest and best dressed at one end and the smallest and most poorly dressed at the other. The businessman in the City suit looks down on the middle-class man and the middle-class man looks down on the working-class man. The joke on the class system is equally applicable in the MDT, where status is conferred by team members according to an internal and institutional value system. It may be the team's success at maintaining this hierarchy that has resulted in its survival. The low morale of teams in trouble is often caused by tensions between staff groups in the wider culture being acted out in the small NHS group.

MDT

Clinical lead/primarily medical
Medical staff/registrar/senior registrar
Nursing staff
Occupational therapists
Art therapist
Drama therapist
Family therapist
Administrators/secretaries

Role of clinical lead

This person will be a medical specialist or clinician and the coordinator of the team

Accountability

Direct to speciality heads of departments with the exception of the medical staff

Status/hierarchy

Hierarchy

Durability

Ongoing, with individuals being replaced as and when they leave the team

Project team

Project manager

Deputy project manager/coordinator

Speciality experts:
Mechanical engineer,
Chemical engineer and so on

Administrative support

Conclusion

An MDT has the advantage of being able to handle complex problems. Each discipline has a unique contribution to make to the process of understanding the clinical picture as a whole. However, the management structure of the team can militate against effectiveness because it harbours traditional structures that inhibit creativity and openness. The MDT may be reflecting gender bias and institutionalized values from the past, which is particularly important in a disorder which mainly affects women – this may unwittingly militate against successful outcomes in treatment. The success of the MDT may be because it mirrors established hierarchies rather than challenging them.

Lessons could be learned from other organizations which have similar structures, and the consideration of a true matrix structure for the team may help to minimize unhealthy aspects of the current multidisciplinary approach. The project team leader model requires dedication of resources to this role.

The series of chapters in the book include those written by the professional groups of psychiatry, family therapy, group analysis, psychotherapy, nursing, art therapy, drama therapy, dietetics and occupational therapy, which comprise most of the groups represented in the MDT. Psychology is not represented, and nor is physiotherapy or speech therapy. This is because they are well represented in other texts or because they are not often seen as core members of the team in eating disorders. Each profession represents a theoretical framework for understanding the complex problem presented by the patient with an eating disorder. This group of professionals comes together to form a mosaic which potentially enlightens the patient during the course of the illness and illustrates how they can manage difficulties in the future with greater effectiveness. Bringing about change in human behaviour is difficult, especially if it is part of the individual defence mechanism against anxiety and chaos and has familial and social reinforcements.

References

Barker DJP (1991). Programming of cardiovascular disease in fetal life and infancy, early diet, later consequences. British Nutrition Foundation, Nutrition Bulletin 16 (supplement): 29–37.

Benevenuto B, Kennedy R (1986). The Works of Jacques Lacan – An Introduction. London: Free Association Books.

Benn M (1998). Madonna and Child: Towards a New Politics of Motherhood. London: Jonathan Cape.

Bray J (1998). Psychiatric nursing and the myth of altruism. In P Barker, B Davidson (eds) Psychiatric Nursing: Ethical Strife. London: Arnold, pp. 95–114.

Breines E (1995). Understanding 'occupation' as the founders did. British Journal of Occupational Therapy 58(11): 458–64.

Brown D, Zinkin L (1994). The Psyche and the Social World. London: Routledge.

Brownwell KD (1995). Effects of Weight Cycling on Metabolism, Health and Psychological Factors in Eating Disorders and Obesity. New York: Guilford Press.

Bryant-Waugh R, Lask B (1995). Eating disorders – An overview. Journal of Family Therapy 17: 13–30.

Bustos D (ed.) (1994). Locus matrix status nascendi and the concepts of clusters: Wings and roots. In P Holmes, M Karp, M Watson (eds) Psychodrama Since Moreno. London: Routledge, pp. 61–76.

Chasseguet-Smirgel J (ed.) (1985). Feminine Guilt and the Oedipus Complex in Female Sexuality. London: Maresfield Library.

Chernin K (1981). Womansize. London: Women's Press.

Chernin K (1983). Womansize: The Tyranny of Slenderness. London: Women's Press.

Claude-Pierre P (1998). The Silent Language of Eating Disorders. London: Bantam Books.

Colahan M (1995). Being a therapist in eating disorder treatment trials: Constraints and creativity. Journal of Family Therapy 17: 79–96.

COMA Report, Department of Health (1991). Dietary Reference Values for Food Energy and Nutrients for the UK. Report on Health and Social Subjects No. 41, London: HMSO.

Cooper PJ (1995). Bulimia Nervosa and Binge Eating: A Guide to Recovery. London: Robinson.

Cox A (1995). Autumn Dawn: Triumph over Eating Disorders. Lewes: The Book Guild.

Crisp AH (1980). Anorexia Nervosa: 'Let Me Be'. London: Academic Press.

Crisp AH, Joughin N, Halek C, Bowyer C (1996). Anorexia Nervosa: The Wish to Change. Hove: Psychology Press.

Dana M, Lawrence M (1988). Women's Secret Disorder – A New Understanding of Bulimia. London: Grafton.

Dare C, Eisler I, Colahan M, Crowther C, Senior R, Asen A (1995). The listening heart and the chi square: Clinical and empirical perceptions in the family therapy of anorexia nervosa. Journal of Family Therapy 17: 31–58.

Davidson B (1992). What can be the relevance of the psychiatric nurse to the life of a person who is mentally ill? Journal of Clinical Nursing 1(4): 199–205.

De Silva P (1995). Cognitive-behavioural models of eating disorders. In G Szmukler, C Dare, J Treasure (eds) Handbook of Eating Disorders: Theory, Treatment and Research. Chichester: John Wiley & Sons, pp. 141–53.

Department of Health (1989). The Diets of British Schoolchildren. Report on Health and Social Subjects 36. London: HMSO.

Devereux G (1980). Basic Problems of Ethnopsychiatry. Chicago, IL: University of Chicago Press.

Dodge E, Hodes M, Eisler I, Dare C (1995) Family therapy for bulimia nervosa in adolescents: An exploratory study. Journal of Family Therapy 17: 59–78.

Dolan B, Gitzinger I (eds) (1991). Why Women? London: European Council on Eating Disorders.

Doyle W, Jenkins S, Crawford MA, Puvandendran K (1994). Nutritional status of school children in an inner city area. Archives of Diseases in Childhood 70: 376–81.

Duker M, Slade R (1988). Anorexia Nervosa and Bulimia: How to Help. Milton Keynes: Open University Press.

Evans C, Street E (1995). Possible differences in family patterns in anorexia nervosa and bulimia nervosa. Journal of Family Therapy 17: 115–32.

Fairburn CG (1995). Overcoming Binge Eating. New York: Guilford Press.

Fairburn CG, Jones R, Peveler RC, Hope RA (1993). Psychotherapy and bulimia nervosa. Longer term effects of interpersonal psychotherapy, behavior therapy and cognitive behavior therapy. Archives of General Psychiatry 50: 419–28.

Fleming M (1989). Art therapy and anorexia: Experiencing the authentic self. In L Hornyak, E Baker (eds) Experiential Therapies for Eating Disorders. New York: Guilford Press, pp. 279–304.

Foulkes SH (1948a). Introduction to Group Analytic Psychotherapy. London: William Heinemann Medical Books.

Foulkes SH (1948b). Introduction to Group Psychotherapy. London: George Allen & Unwin.

Foulkes SH (1964). Therapeutic Group Analysis. London: George Allen & Unwin.

Foulkes SH, Anthony EJ (1990). Group Psychotherapy – The Psychoanalytic Approach. London: Karnac Books.

Fox J (ed.) (1987). The Essential Moreno Writings on Psychodrama, Group Method and Spontaneity by J. L. Moreno. New York: Springer.

Gamman L, Makinen M (1994). Female Fetishism – A New Look. London: Lawrence & Wishart.

Garfinkel P (1995). Foreword. In G Szmukler, C Dare, J Treasure (eds) Handbook of Eating Disorders: Theory, Treatment and Research. Chichester: John Wiley & Sons, pp. xi–xviii.

Garner DM, Garfinkel PE (eds) (1985). Handbook of Psychotherapy for Anorexia Nervosa and Bulimia. New York, London: Guilford Press.

Giles GM (1985). Anorexia nervosa and bulimia: An activity-oriented approach. American Journal of Occupational Therapy 39(8): 510–17.

Gilligan C (1990). In a Different Voice. Cambridge, MA: Harvard University Press.

Gold B (ed.) (1999). Group Analysis, the Journal of Group Analytic Psychotherapy 32(1) (special issue).

Goldner V, Penn P, Sheinberg M, Walker G (1990). Love and violence: Gender paradoxes in volatile attachments. Family Process 29: 343–64.

Goldsmith J (1994). The Trap. London: Macmillan.

Graves R (1959). New Larousse Encyclopaedia of Mythology. Paris: Hamlyn.

Greer G (1999). The Whole Woman. London: Doubleday.

Harries P (1992). Facilitating change in anorexia nervosa: The role of occupational therapy. British Journal of Occupational Therapy 55(9): 334–9.

Hearst L (1980). The emergence of the mother in the group. Group Analysis 14(1): 25–31.

Heimann P (1950). On Countertransference. International Journal of Psycho-Analysis 31: 81–9.

Hill AJ, Robinson A (1991). Dieting concerns have a functional effect on the behaviour of nine year old girls. British Journal of Clinical Psychology 30: 265–67.

Hill AJ, Weaver C (1990). Dieting concerns of ten year old girls and their mothers. British Journal of Clinical Psychology 29: 346–8.

Hopper E (1982). The problem of context. Group Analysis 15(2): 136.

Hopper E, Weyman A (1987). A sociological view of large groups. In L Kreeger (ed.) The Large Group. London: Constable, pp.159–92.

Huxley A (1946). The Perennial Philosophy. London: Chatto & Windus.

Hytten FE (1980). Weight gain in pregnancy. In FE Hytten, G Chamberlain (eds) Clinical Psychology in Obstetrics. Oxford: Blackwell, pp. 193–233.

James O (1997). Britain on the Couch. London: Century.

Jones E (1993). Family Systems Therapy. Chichester: Wiley.

Jung CG (1959). Collected Works, Volume 9, Part 2. (Edited by H Read, M Fordham, G Adler, W McGuire; translated by R Hull.) London: Routledge & Kegan Paul.

Keys A, Brozeck J, Henschel A, Michelson O, Taylor H (1950). The Biology of Human Starvation. Minneapolis, MN: University of Minnesota Press.

Kielhofner G (1980). A model of human occupation, Part 1: Conceptual framework and content. American Journal of Occupational Therapy 34(9): 572–81.

Klein M (1961). Envy and Gratitude and Other Works 1946–63. London: Hogarth Press.

Kolb DA (1984). Experiential Learning: Experience as the Source of Learning and Development. Englewood Cliffs, NJ: Prentice-Hall.

Kreeger L (1987). Transference and Countertransference in Group Psychotherapy (unpublished, available from the Institute of Group Analysis, 1 Daleham Gardens, London NW3 5BY, tel: 020 7431 2949).

Lacey JH, Smith G (1987). Bulimia nervosa: The impact of pregnancy on mother and baby. British Journal of Psychiatry 150: 777–81.

Lawrence M (1989). The Anorexic Experience. London: Women's Press.

Lemma A (1992). Starving to live: An existential analysis of anorexia nervosa. Changes 10(3): 178–89.

Lerner HE (1993). Female dependency in context. In C New (ed.) The Power of Lies and the Project of Feminist Therapy in Free Associations, Volume IV, Part 2, No 30, pp. 191–209. London: Free Association Books.

Levens M (1987). Art therapy with eating disordered patients. Inscape (summer issue): 2–7.

Levens M (1990). Borderline aspects in eating disorders: art therapy's contribution. Group Analysis 23: 277–84.

Levens M (1995a). Art therapy and psychodrama with eating disordered patients. In D Dokter (ed.) Arts Therapies and Clients with Eating Disorders: Fragile Board. London: Jessica Kingsley, pp. 159–75.

Levens M (1995b). Eating Disorders and Magical Control of the Body. Treatment through Art Therapy. London: Routledge.

Levens M (1996). Eating Disorders and Magical Control of the Body. Treatment through Art Therapy. London: Routledge

Levine P (1996). Eating disorders and their impact on family systems. In F Kaslow (ed.) Handbook of Relational Diagnosis. New York: Wiley, pp. 463–76.

Lieberman S (1995). Anorexia nervosa: The tyranny of appearances. Journal of Family Therapy 17: 133–8.

Luzzatto P (1995). The mental double trap of the anorexic patient. In D Dokter (ed.) Arts Therapies and Clients with Eating Disorders: Fragile Board. London: Jessica Kingsley, pp.60–75.

Maat MB, Vandersyde AD (1995). The pregnant art therapist. American Journal of Art Therapy 33: 74–83.

MacLeod S (1981). The Art of Starvation. London: Virago.

Maine M (1993). Father Hunger. London: Simon & Schuster.

Maloney MJ, McGuire J, Daniels SR, Specker B (1989). Dieting behaviours and eating attitudes in children. Paediatrics 84: 482–9.

Mann D (1990). Art as a defence against creativity. British Journal of Psychotherapy 7(1): 5–14.

Marlatt GA, George WH (1984). Relapse prevention: Introduction and overview of the model. British Journal of Addiction 79: 261–75.

Martin JE (1990). Bulimia: A review of the medical, behavioural and psychodynamic models of treatment. British Journal of Occupational Therapy 53(12): 495–9.

Minuchin S, Rosman B, Baker L (1978). Psychosomatic Families: Anorexia Nervosa in Context. Cambridge, MA: Harvard University Press.

Moorey J (1991). Living with Anorexia and Bulimia. Manchester: Manchester University Press.

Murphy J (1984). The use of art therapy in the treatment of anorexia nervosa. In T Dalley (ed.) Art as Therapy. London: Routledge, pp. 96–110.

NHS Centre for Reviews and Dissemination (1997). The Prevention and Treatment of Obesity. Effective Health Care. NHS Centre for Reviews and Dissemination, University of York.

Nitsun M (1996). The Anti-Group: Destructive Forces in the Group and their Creative Potential. London: Routledge.

Norberg-Hodge H (1992). Ancient Futures. London: Rider.

O'Neill H (1995a). Anger: The assessment and treatment of problematic anger: Part 1. British Journal of Occupational Therapy 58(10): 427–34.

O'Neill H (1995b). Anger: The assessment and treatment of problematic anger: Part 2. British Journal of Occupational Therapy 58(11): 469–72.

Orbach S (1978). Fat is a Feminist Issue. London: Paddington Press.

Orbach S (1986). Hunger Strike. London: Faber & Faber.

Orbach S, Eichenbaum L (1982). Inside Out, Outside In. London: Penguin.

Palazolli MS (1974). Self-starvation: From Intrapsychic to the Transpersonal Approach to Anorexia Nervosa. London: Human Context Books, Chaucer Publishing.

Palmer RL (1989). Anorexia Nervosa: A Guide for Sufferers and their Families. Harmondsworth: Penguin.

Prodgers A (1990). The dual nature of the group as mother: The Uroborice Container. Group Analysis 23(1): 17–30.

Ritter S (1989). Manual of Clinical Psychiatric Nursing Principles and Procedures. London: Harper & Row.

Rose GJ (1963). Body ego and creative imagination. Journal of the American Psychoanalytic Association 11: 775–89.

Roth G (1992). When Food is Love. London: Piatkus.

Rust M (1992). Art therapy in the treatment of women with eating disorders. In D Waller, A Gilroy (eds) Art Therapy: A Handbook. Buckingham: Open University Press, pp. 155–72.

Rust M (1995). Bringing 'the man' into the room.... In D Dokter (ed.) Arts Therapies and Clients with Eating Disorders: Fragile Board. London: Jessica Kingsley, pp. 48–59.

Schaverien J (1995a). The picture as transactional object in the treatment of anorexia. In D Dokter (ed.) Arts Therapies and Clients with Eating Disorders: Fragile Board. London: Jessica Kingsley, pp.31–47.

Schaverien J (1995b). Desire and the Female Therapist. London: Routledge.

Schmidt U, Treasure J (1993). Getting Better Bit(e) by Bit(e). Hove: Psychology Press.

Schwartz HJ (ed.) (1988). Bulimia: Psychoanalytic Treatment and Theory. New York: International Universities Press.

Selvini Palazzoli M, Prata G (1982). Snares in family therapy. Journal of Marital and Family Therapy 8: 443–50.

Selvini Palazzoli M, Cirillo S, Selvini M, Sorrentino AM (1989). Family Games: General Models of Psychotic Processes in the Family. London: Karnac.

Skaife S (1990). Self-determination in group analytic art therapy. Group Analysis 23: 237–44.

Skaife S (1997). The pregnant art therapist in an art therapy group. In S Hogan (ed.) Feminist Approaches to Art Therapy. London: Routledge, pp. 177–96.

Skaife S, Huet V (eds) (1998). Art Psychotherapy Groups: Between Pictures and Words. London: Routledge.

Smail D (1987). Taking Care – An Alternative to Therapy. London: Dent.

Speed B (1995). Perspectives on eating disorders [editorial]. Journal of Family Therapy 17: 1–12.

Squire S (1983). The Slender Balance. London: Puttnam.

Stewart D, Raskin J, Garfinkel P, MacDonald O, Robinson GE (1987). Anorexia nervosa, bulimia, and pregnancy. American Journal of Obstetrics and Gynecology 157: 1194–8.

Treasure J (1997). Anorexia Nervosa: A Survival Guide for Families, Friends and Sufferers. Hove: Psychology Press.

Vaz-Leal FJ, Salcedo-Salcedo MS (1995). Using the Milan approach in the inpatient management of anorexia nervosa (varying the 'invariant prescription'). Journal of Family Therapy 17: 97–114.

Wallin U, Roejin S, Hanson K (1996). Too close or too separate: Family function in families with an anorexia nervosa patient in two Nordic countries. Journal of Family Therapy 18: 397–414.

Warriner E (1995). Anger is red. In D Dokter (ed.) Arts Therapies and Clients with Eating Disorders: Fragile Board. London: Jessica Kingsley, pp. 123–8.

Wolf N (1990). The Beauty Myth. London: Vintage.

World Health Organization (1993). The ICD-10 Classification of Mental and Behavioral Disorders: Diagnostic Criteria for Research. Geneva: WHO.

Yalom I (1985). The Theory and Practice of Group Psychotherapy. New York: Basic Books.

Zeldin T (1994). An Intimate History of Humanity. London: Sinclair Stevenson.

Index